The Social Framework

An Introduction to Economics

J. R. HICKS

Formerly Drummond Professor of Political Economy in the University of Oxford

The Social Framework

An Introduction to Economics

FOURTH EDITION

OXFORD

AT THE CLARENDON PRESS

1971

Oxford University Press, Ely House, London W. 1

GLASGOW NEW YORK TORONTO MELBOURNE WELLINGTON
CAPE TOWN SALISBURY IBADAN NAIROBI DAR ES SALAAM LUSAKA ADDIS ABABA
BOMBAY CALCUTTA MADRAS KARACHI LAHORE DACCA
KUALA LUMPUR SINGAPORE HONG KONG TOKYO

First Edition 1942 *Second Edition* 1952
Third Edition 1960 *Fourth Edition* 1971

PRINTED IN GREAT BRITAIN

Preface

When *The Social Framework* was first published (in 1942) it was a new departure in the teaching of economics. This was explained, in the original preface, in the following way:

'Until lately the problem of how to begin the study of economics reduced itself to a dilemma: either one might begin with economic theory—which meant in practice the theory of supply and demand—or one might begin with descriptive economics, the practical problems of industry and labour. Now there were serious objections against each course. To begin with the theory of value meant starting off with problems whose significance it is difficult for the beginner to realize, and on a field where generalizations which will stand up to criticism are singularly difficult to attain. Descriptive economics, on the other hand, taken without a sufficient grounding in theory, is inevitably either a dull collection of facts or, alternatively, a discussion of practical policies which may be lively enough, but which it is hard to raise much above the intellectual level of political propaganda. In practice, whichever of these solutions was adopted, some of these difficulties were incurred. The student who pursued a long course of study would of course find his way round them in the end, though not without some waste of time. But those people whose acquaintance with economics was confined to a one-year course (and they are a large proportion of all students of the subject) were either sent away thoroughly bored—if their teachers had followed the austerer path—or, in the other event, they were left with nothing but ready-made opinions on a few topical issues.

'As a result of the developments in economic knowledge which have taken place during recent years, we are now (I believe) in a position to resolve this dilemma, and to do so by something better than a mere compromise between the existing alternatives. It is now possible to mark out a preliminary stage in economic study, which is wholly concerned with topics which are obviously interesting and important, and which is yet systematic enough to give some of the mental discipline necessary for study on a scientific level. At the same time, this stage involves very little of that process of *abstraction* which is such a snare in the elementary stages of the theory of value. The ideas involved are simple and obviously sensible; the discipline is provided by the considerable demands which are made for care and patience in putting them together.

'This change has come about because the chapters on definitions, which formed so indigestible a portion of the old textbooks, have been kindled into life by the work of economic statisticians, and also by some of the newer developments of economic theory. They have grown into a distinct branch of economics, a branch which is being pursued with very special success at the present time, and which is, nevertheless, particularly suited to serve as an introduction to the science in general. If we want a name for it, it might be described as Social Accounting, for it is nothing else but the accounting of the whole community or nation, just as Private Accounting is the accounting of the individual firm.

'The greater part of this book is taken up with the study of Social Accounting; but in suggesting that this is probably the best way to begin the study of economics, I am not of course claiming that it can replace the conventional elementary theory and elementary applied economics. I would indeed claim that, in these days of shortened courses, a student who begins with Social Accounting will learn something useful and something worth learning, even if his studies are broken off at an early stage. But my main contention is that the other topics should come afterwards, after the groundwork of Social Accounting has been mastered. I hope and believe that when a beginner has mastered the substance of this book, he will be able to turn to the theory of value with some idea of what he wants to get from it; and that seems to be an essential preliminary to getting anything worth having.'

In the thirty years which have passed since that was written, the method of teaching economics which is there described has been very generally adopted; and *The Social Framework* itself has been one of the books that have been used for that purpose. But (as was obvious from the start) it could not go on being used—being properly used—unless it was kept up to date. Though the principles set out could well be expected to be permanent, the facts that were used to illustrate the principles must be expected to become less interesting, as they receded in time. It was essential to the method that the facts should be interesting—that they should tell the student about things on which he wanted to be informed. So, for this reason alone, the book would need, every few years, to be revised.

A first revision, in fact, was required rather soon. For when I did the first edition, in the middle of the war, the best year that was available to me, to be used as an illustration of the national accounts of the United Kingdom, was 1938—the pre-war year which the early national income White Papers used as a standard of comparison. It was urgent to get on with the revision for the second edition in order to illustrate with something post-war. But at the time when I did that revision, only the early post-war years were at my disposal (the year I took was 1949); and it soon became apparent that these, in an economic sense, were still war years—they were still dominated by war-time shortages. The war did not end, in that sense, until 1952 or 1953. It was not until after that that we got clear of the war. There was then a strong case for another revision, which would be descriptive of an economy in more normal order. That is what was done in the third edition (which this replaces). For that edition I found a quite good 'normal' year—the year 1957.

It was in fact so good a year that I have been able to leave the edition that was based upon it running on, unrevised, for quite a long time. But it is getting too long a time; the modern student cannot now be expected to take much interest in 1957—and still less in the comparisons between 1938 and

1957 which quite properly bulked large in the third edition. It has for some time been evident that the book must be moved in its time-reference: that it must be brought into closer relation with what is now the present day. That is what, in this fourth edition, I have done.

The year for which I do the accounts is 1969—the latest year for which figures are fully available at the time of writing. It is far from being such a good year, for my purpose, as 1957; one can already see (in the winter of 1970–1) that it was a very peculiar year. The impression that I have got of it, as I have been working, is that it may be regarded as a late stage, perhaps a Fourth Act, in a drama that began in the early sixties and is not yet finished. Perhaps I should have waited for it to be finished; but I am no prophet—not even a forecaster—and I might have to wait a long time before the end of it comes.

The specific alterations that I have made are the following. To the 'structural' chapters (I–III, VII–IX, XI–XIII) hardly anything. The principles of social accounting, as set out in earlier editions, remain quite unchanged. The classification adopted is not quite the same as that which has become conventional in official publications; but I remain convinced that for my educational purpose the classification I adopt is right. I still think that it is better for the student to learn to think in terms of National Income than in terms of the (curiously defined) Gross National Product; nevertheless, whether or not that is accepted, the bridge is not difficult to build. I have spelt out the way in which it is to be done—in most detail in Chapter XXI.

Chapters IV–VI, on population and labour supply, have been rather substantially altered—to take account of the curious things that have happened in these fields (which one might have expected to be slow moving) since 1957. The facts, it will be found, are surprising; the situation which they reveal has called for some change in comment.

Chapter X (on national capital) and chapter XIV (the elementary breakdown of national income) have been modified no more than is necessary for rewriting with the more recent figures.

My most extensive alterations are to chapters XV–XVIII

Contents

Tables and Charts

TABLES

CHARTS

INTRODUCTORY CHAPTER

Economic Facts and Economic Theory

1. Economics, the subject which we are going to study in this book, is a science, one of the branches of that great systematic study of the world we live in which we call Science with a capital S. The division of Science into sciences—physics, chemistry, biology, physiology, and so on—is largely a matter of convenience; we group together in a science those particular special studies which are conveniently pursued together and pursued by the same people. This means that we cannot tell where the frontiers of a particular science will prove to be until we have developed that science; and we need not expect that these frontiers will always be found in the same place. Even between the two most highly developed of the natural sciences, physics and chemistry, the boundary is distinctly fluctuating. Chemistry deals with those aspects of the world which are conveniently studied by chemists; economics deals with those aspects which are conveniently studied by economists.

All the same, within the broad field of the sciences in general, economics belongs, without any doubt, to a particular sub-group; it belongs to the Human Sciences, the sciences which are concerned with human behaviour. These include some, like psychology, which are concerned with individual behaviour; and some which are concerned with the behaviour of groups, or with the behaviour of individuals in relation to other individuals—the Social Sciences. Among the Social Sciences are economics, politics (the science of government), and sociology, which is not the 'science of society', for that should properly include all the social sciences. What are studied by sociologists are those rather miscellaneous aspects of society which economics and politics have left out, or are supposed to have left out. The lines are in fact not easy to draw; the student of economics should be able to look across them, so that he needs to have some knowledge, at least, of the other social sciences. From his point of view politics is probably the most important; the close connection between economics and politics is illustrated in the older name for economics—Political Economy.

Provisionally, we may say that the particular aspect of human behaviour which is dealt with by economics is the behaviour of human beings in business. Economics is the science which deals with business affairs. But if we allow ourselves to say this, then we must be clear that business is to be understood in a wide sense. When a housewife goes into a shop to buy some bacon, the resulting transaction is undoubtedly a business transaction from the point of view of the shopkeeper, and so would fall within our definition of the subject-matter of economics. We should not so naturally regard it as a business transaction from the housewife's point of view. But once economics has undertaken the study of this piece of behaviour, the transaction has to be looked at scientifically, that is to say, in the round; economics has to pay just as much attention to the housewife's side of the bargain as to the shopkeeper's. Buying the bacon is an economic question just as much as selling it.

To take some other examples. When men or women are paid wages to work in a factory, their employment is obviously a business question from the point of view of the employer. Consequently it comes into economics, but economics has to consider the worker's point of view as well as the employer's. The payment of taxes on profits is again obviously a business question; economics has to consider the payment of taxes in the round, looking at it from the standpoint of the firms and private people who pay the taxes, from that of the government which receives revenue from the taxes, and from that of the people whose wages and other incomes are paid by the government out of this revenue. Once we make these extensions—and they are absolutely necessary extensions—the subject-matter of economics loses most of the narrowness it might appear to have at first sight. The problems of profit-making business have been much more important at some periods of history than at others. But economic problems have always been of the utmost importance, and it is safe to predict that they always will be. Although there are wide stretches of human experience (the whole fields of art and religion, for example) on which economics has nothing, or nothing fundamental, to say, economic activities do occupy a large part of the life of nearly everyone, and are bound to do so. Economic science endeavours to study these activities scientifically; it has in fact made better progress in the application of scientific methods to the study of human conduct than has been made by the other social sciences. The study of economics can therefore take us a considerable way towards a general understanding of human society, that is, of men's behaviour to one another.

2. The method of modern economic investigation is the same as the method of all science. Economics studies facts, and seeks to arrange the facts in such ways as make it possible to draw conclusions from them. As always, it is the arrangement which is the delicate operation. Facts, arranged in the right way, speak for themselves; unarranged, they are as dead as mutton. One of the main things we have to learn is how to arrange our facts properly.

Where does the economist get his facts from? It might be thought that, since the object of economics is to study human conduct in business affairs, the simplest way of proceeding would be to go to the people engaged in business affairs, and to ask them questions. But a moment's reflection will show that this is not as promising a line as it looks. Even if we are lucky, and the particular man we select is willing to tell us about the things which seem to him to be important (in practice even that is far from certain), he is unlikely to be able to tell us about other things, which may be more important from our point of view. If we ask him about something which he did six months ago, he is not very likely to be able to remember. Yet that may be just the question we want answered. It is very difficult to get systematic information in this sort of way.

An improvement upon the simple method of interviewing is the questionnaire. If a large number of people are asked the same set of questions, some will not reply, some will make guesses or answer at random, some will reply seriously. By looking over all the replies together, it may be possible to sort out the replies which are significant from those which are not. The method of questionnaires has in fact been most successful in those cases where it is possible to induce the people questioned to take some trouble over the answers; this is becoming easier than it used to be, but it still presents some difficulty to the private investigator. Early investigators into the problem of poverty used to pay people to fill in their forms; but in most cases this would be quite impossibly expensive. Now that people are becoming used to official questionnaires, which they have a duty to answer, they can more easily be persuaded to answer questionnaires from non-official sources, provided that their interest is awakened by appropriate publicity. But the organization of such inquiries, and the digestion of the material when it has been collected, remains an expensive matter. Thus it is only in a few particular fields that we get much help from direct inquiries organized for scientific purposes; such inquiry is mainly used by economists as a means of supplementing another source of information which is, on the whole, far more valuable.

This other source of information consists in facts which have been collected for other purposes than for use by economists, but which can be used by economists. Naturally, since these facts have been brought together for other purposes than ours, there are pages and pages in these collections which are, from our point of view, sheer rubbish. But it is a perfectly feasible (though laborious) task to separate out from the rubbish the information we want.

Large quantities of facts, potentially interesting to the economist, are collected nowadays by business organizations; but the most important collections are those made by governments. Modern governments collect stupendously large quantities of facts, occasionally from pure love of knowledge, but more often for the pedestrian reason that they need these facts for the ordinary running of public affairs. A government which employs many thousands of people has the greatest difficulty in keeping its left hand informed of what its right hand is doing; publicity makes for efficiency in administration. In 'democratic' countries there is a further reason for publicity. The ordinary way of making decisions about public policy is by a process of argument, in which the pros and cons of every measure are stated by either side. Facts are required in order that this argument should take place. It is a purely incidental advantage that it provides the economist with valuable material at the same time.

When using this administrative information, it is essential to remember how it is compiled, and why; otherwise one may easily go astray. For example, when the government publishes a statement that so many persons have been unemployed on a certain date, the precise figure which is given will depend upon the definition of unemployment used—whether people who have only been out of work for two or three days are counted as unemployed, and so on. It occasionally happens that the definition of *unemployed* is changed slightly; when this occurs, the figure given may change without there being any real change in unemployment. The definitions of unemployment which are used in the unemployment figures of different countries do in fact differ very considerably indeed; so that the international comparison of unemployment is a very ticklish matter. This sort of difficulty is one for which we have constantly to be on the watch.

3. The British Government collects and publishes material on all sorts of subjects; from the economic point of view the most useful parts of it are the series which give us economic information of a similar character for a number of different years, so that we can make comparisons.[1] Among the more important of such series are the following:

[1] The most convenient place to find this information is the *Annual Abstract of Statistics*, together with the monthly *Economic Trends*, which is less complete but still contains a remarkable amount of information. Some similar information is available for many countries in the statistical publications of the United Nations, of the Organization for Economic Co-operation and Development (O.E.C.D.) and of the International Monetary Fund (IMF). These works are as essential to the economist as the bottles of chemicals on his laboratory shelves are to the chemist.

A. *The Census of Population.* A Census of Population has been taken every ten years since 1801, with 1941 the only gap in the series. Modern censuses tell us not only the number of people living in the country at the date when the census was taken; we also get information about their ages, the sizes of the families in which they were living, where they were living, and what work they were doing. This detailed information only becomes available once in ten years, but some parts of it can be estimated for the intervening years in indirect ways. Thus the total population can be estimated fairly exactly by using the registrations of births and deaths, figures of which are published quarterly.[1]

B. *Imports and Exports.* Some information about goods imported into England, and goods exported from it, has been available since quite early times; a high standard of accuracy was reached after the middle of the nineteenth century. Modern 'Foreign Trade Accounts' give us both the quantities and the values of most of these goods, and also tell us where the imports come from and the exports go to.

C. *Government Revenue and Expenditure.* These are the accounts of the government, which are presented in outline when the Chancellor of the Exchequer makes his budget speech, and are published later in much greater detail. They are very important in themselves, but they also convey much valuable information indirectly. Thus the unemployment figures, to which we referred earlier, are linked up with government expenditure, because some of the government's expenditure assists in the relief of unemployment. On the tax side, our most valuable information about the level of incomes in the country, and about the inequality of incomes, is derived from the accounts of the income tax.

D. *Production.* During the twentieth century a number of Censuses of Production have been taken. These record such things as the numbers of workers employed in various businesses, the rates of wages paid, the new materials and new equipment purchased, and the amounts of goods turned out in a particular period. Information of this sort is extra-

[1] An attempt at a check on these estimates was made in 1966, by conducting a 'sample census'.

ordinarily useful to the economist; it tells him just the sorts of things he wants most to know. The first census of production in Great Britain was taken in 1907, but only the larger firms were included. Later censuses were taken in 1924, 1930, and 1935; it is now the practice for a full census to be taken every five years. It is only by a census of production that information of this sort is forthcoming for the whole of industry; but a great part of the field is now covered, by more or less direct methods, at much more frequent intervals. Far more is known about production today, even from month to month, than would have been thought possible before 1939.

This information, which comes from government sources, has indeed become so comprehensive that it scarcely needs (and certainly it does not get) much regular supplementation in other ways. The principal regular sources of information, from other than government institutions, are only two:

i. *Company accounts.* It has long been the legal duty of every business, which is organized as a 'public' company,[1] to publish accounts, primarily for the benefit of its shareholders. In the form which the law used to lay down, these accounts were rather uninformative, for the purpose of economic study; but by a new Companies Act (1967) a good deal more of the company's activities has to be revealed. This has made it possible for the economist to acquire information, about individual companies, of more or less the same kind as he has long been able to get, from Censuses of Production, about industries (the total of the firms working in the same line of business). But this has not been going on very long; and to make much use of such information is very laborious.

ii. *Market reports.* If you go into a shop to buy a bicycle, the shopkeeper will make a note of it for his own purposes, but no information about that particular transaction will be published. There are, on the other hand, certain kinds of purchases and sales which are carried on by professional dealers, who do find it convenient to publish a record of their

[1] What is meant by a 'public' company will be explained on p. 115.

transactions, so as to inform each other. These records are sometimes published in some of the daily papers (as in the case of the Stock Exchange), sometimes in specialized trade journals (as with the markets for raw materials—though the scope of these was very limited for a long time after the war). These market reports are very useful so far as they go, but only a small proportion of all business transactions is covered by them.

There are other special sources of economic information, but these are the main regular types, which give us similar information for a large number of different dates. In themselves they comprise an immense mass of material—when it is put together with similar material from other countries it is enough to fill a library of considerable size. Even so, there are many economic questions we might like to have answered whose answers cannot be found within this material; that is why some part of the time of some economists is properly spent in collecting additional information, by questionnaires and so on. But the questions which can be answered from the existing material, more or less satisfactorily, are numerous and important; however, we can only begin to answer them properly if we go about doing so in the right way.

4. There are four stages in the process of acquiring economic knowledge which can be distinguished from one another, so much so that they are often regarded as separate departments of the science. But we should be quite clear about the sense in which they are separate departments. It is not that the problems they deal with are different—the same problem is often handed on from one to another of them. It is merely that they do different parts of the work of solution.

First of all, there is the stage or department which is called *Economic Theory*. The basic function of economic theory is to prepare the questions which we want to ask of the facts. It is absolutely useless to study a mountain of facts without knowing first of all, and very precisely and clearly, what one is looking for. We start from common sense and the broad lines of obvious information which we derive from our daily experience; we set it in order, so as to get our questions into a useful form. It is only when we have done some preparation of this sort that we can approach the facts with any prospect of getting something significant out of them.

At the second stage we make our approach to the facts. After we have decided what questions we want to ask, we have to pick out from the whole mass of economic information described above those parts which have something to tell us about the question in hand. Then, when we have made that selection, we have to examine the information and find out exactly what it means. This last is a very important step, as can be seen from the example of the unemployment figures which was given earlier. We have to examine how the figures were collected, and what definitions were used; we have to ask whether these definitions are the same as those we found convenient in our economic theory; if not, what adjustments can be made, on one side or the other, to allow for the difference. What is chiefly involved in this second stage is a knowledge of the material out of which we are to get our results.[1]

In the organization of the subject, this second stage is reckoned as a part of *Economic Statistics*. The word 'statistics' is used in two senses: in the plural, to denote the numerical facts, the figures, which are the material we have been discussing; in the singular, to denote the method of handling that material. Here we are concerned with statistics in the singular.

The third stage is also a part of economic statistics. When we have got our information sorted out we shall nearly always find that is is not complete; there are matters about which we should desire to have information, but unfortunately it has not been collected in the way we want. To some extent it is possible to remedy these defects by making guesses or estimates; a good deal of progress has been made in answering the delicate question what sorts of guesses are reasonably safe and what are not. This same problem of how to make reasonable estimates arises in many other sciences; we can, to some extent, borrow the methods which they have developed for this purpose. But a good deal of care has to be exercised in doing so.

[1] Useful guides to the British material are Ely Devons, *An Introduction to British Economic Statistics* (Cambridge, 1956); Conrad Blyth, *Use of Economic Statistics* (Allen and Unwin, 1960).

Finally, in the fourth stage, we have to arrange the facts so as to bring out the answers to our questions as well as we can. This is the stage which is usually known as *Applied* or *Descriptive Economics*. Since, as we have seen, the most useful sorts of facts are those which give us similar information for different dates, it is inevitable that the study of applied economics should come very close to that of economic history. Indeed, it is nearly true to say that economic history is just the applied economics of earlier ages; applied economics is concerned with the economic history of the contemporary world.[1]

5. In this volume we shall be concerned entirely with the first and last of these four stages: *Theory* for the purpose of clearing our minds and sorting out the questions, *Applied Economics* to the extent that we shall give some illustrations of the sorts of answers we get to our questions when they are applied to recent history, particularly to the history of Britain between 1950 and 1970. Economic knowledge is discovered, as we have seen, by co-operation between all the four stages, each of them passing on its difficulties to the others. But for purposes of learning what has been discovered, the first and last of the stages—the ones we are going to deal with—are the ones to begin on. Our basic ideas need to be sorted out before we can begin to think clearly about economic problems; and we have to start as soon as possible to get practice in the application of our theory to actual experience, if only

[1] As in all human affairs, it is possible to get a fuller understanding of events if one is not in too much of a hurry; but information (and analysis) is of more practical use if it can be provided quickly. It is therefore important that there is much economic information which can be 'processed' by more or less routine methods, and which is such that a good judge can see the sense of it in time for his opinion to be of practical use. Work of this kind is nowadays one of the main jobs (other than teaching) which economists are paid to perform. Much of their work is published, in newspapers, in bank reviews, and in regular specialized publications, such as the *National Institute Economic Review* and *The London and Cambridge Economic Bulletin* (extracts from which appear, quarterly, in *The Times*). These reviews are recommended to the student as sources of statistics—he will often find that he can get his answers out of them more quickly than he can from government publications. He should, however, remember that the opinions expressed, though they are the opinions of most competent people, have been got out against time; with longer perspective, and with more work and reflection, it should often be possible to do better.

because in the absence of such practice it is impossible for the theory itself to be properly understood.

The necessity for this preliminary clearing of ideas which we call Economic Theory appears at once if we reflect how many ideas are used in the ordinary practice of business whose significance is not at all directly obvious. Some of these ideas are of a technical character, arising only in some particular industry, such as bootmaking or cotton manufacture; questions of technique are not in themselves of direct interest to the economist, although of course if he desires to make a special study of some particular kind of manufacture he will need to learn something about its technique. The ideas with which economics is concerned are chiefly those which arise, not in connection with one industry only, but with most or all industries; such ideas as 'capital', 'income', 'cost' arise in all business problems—these are the sort of ideas we have particularly to study. One of the main purposes of economic theory is to clear our minds about such terms as these. It turns out to be a more complicated matter than might at first sight be supposed. For one thing, these terms were originally invented by business men, for business purposes; but, as we have seen, the economist has to study the business world from a wider point of view than that of the business man; consequently it is necessary for him, not only to understand the business use of these terms, but also to appreciate their wider social significance. Further, when we try to work out this social significance, we find that all these ideas are very closely connected. It is impossible to understand 'income' fully without understanding 'capital' and vice versa. Economic theory therefore tends to shape itself into a system of thought, for the questions we want to ask turn out to be interrelated; answering one helps to answer others. We cannot fully understand any one of these ideas unless we have understood its neighbours as well. Answering one question shows us another question to ask, and so on almost indefinitely—but that is of course what always happens when we ask any of those key questions about the world which lead to the growth of a science.

In Part I of this book we shall start, as we have to, with a bit of Theory. Beginning from common sense and everyday experience, we shall sort out our ideas until we have reached a point where we can turn to some of the statistics and hope to learn something from them. In the later parts we shall run our Theory and our Applied Economics quite closely together.

PART I The Productive Process

CHAPTER I Production and Exchange

1. Economic affairs enter into the life of every one of us, the most important economic activity in the life of the ordinary man being the way he earns his living. People earn their living in all sorts of different ways—by manual work, by brain-work, in factories, in offices, and on farms, in dull ways, in interesting ways—but the thing which is common to all ways of earning one's living is the doing of work for which one is paid, doing work and being paid for doing it. In most countries the majority of people earn their living by working 'for' some particular employer; they receive their payment in the form of a wage or salary (which latter is only a word of Latin origin meaning *wage*, used instead of 'wage' so as to sound grander). But there are some people (it happens with dockers, gardeners, and journalists, for example) who may divide their time between two or three employers. And there are others (shopkeepers, doctors, farmers who deliver milk directly, and so on) who serve quite large numbers of different employers or *customers*—for it is really very much the same thing. Whatever sort of work it is that is done, whatever form the payment for doing it takes, the common element is always there: in order to earn his living a man has to work, and there has to be someone—an employer, or customer, or client—who is prepared to pay him for doing it.

Now why should the employer be prepared to pay? There are in fact several distinct cases. In the first place, an employer may be prepared to pay to have work done for him because the work is directly useful to him personally. A sick man goes to (that is, employs) a doctor because he hopes as a result to feel better in health; a traveller employs a taxi-driver to get him from one place to another when there is no public transport; a householder employs an electrician to mend a fuse. In all these instances, and in others of similar character, the work which is performed provides something which the employer or customer directly wants; whatever the nature of the want which is to be satisfied, the fact that he is to get something which he wants explains why he is prepared to pay for the work to be performed.

In many other cases the employer is prepared to pay, not because the work done is of any use to him personally, but because he expects it to result in something useful to a third person (the consumer) who will be willing to pay for it. The immediate employer is here nothing but an intermediary; he pays his employee, and the consumer pays him. The wants which are to be satisfied are the consumer's wants; the consumer is willing to pay because he gets something he wants; the employer is willing to pay because he expects to be paid by the consumer.

The necessity of having some sort of an employer-intermediary is made evident when one reflects how many workers there are whose work is in itself absolutely useless, though it becomes very useful when it is combined with the work of other people. The typical factory worker, nowadays, is engaged on some small specialized operation, which is only a stage in the making of some part of a useful article, a part like the lace of a shoe or the chain of a bicycle. Unless there are other workers to perform the other stages, and make the other parts, his work is utterly useless. There is no point in doing work of this kind unless there is someone to organize the different operations into a unity; to do this is the work of the employer-intermediary, the business manager or director, the professional employer, who brings together the different people who have the different sorts of skill needed to produce the complete article. Such an employer is not a consumer like the man who employs a doctor or a chimney-sweep; he is a worker or producer, contributing his own very important share to the process of producing goods which consumers want. Employer and employed are in fact co-operating together in the production of something useful to consumers; they each of them derive their earnings from the payments made by the consumers, who purchase the finished articles they have produced.

Every firm or business consists in essence of a co-operation of workers, organized in some way or another to produce saleable products. But it is not always the case that the products are sold directly to consumers; very often the product of one firm is sold to another firm, which performs some further operation upon it before it reaches the consumer's hands. Even when a firm has turned out the precise material product which the consumer wants—the jam, the tooth-paste, or the newspaper—there is still the further stage of providing it at the place and time where and when it is wanted; to do this is the function of the trader and the shopkeeper, who assist in satisfying people's wants just as much as other workers do. It often happens, on the other hand, that the product turned out by a firm has not yet reached the material form in which the consumer will finally want it; the products of steelworks and spinning-mills are only the raw materials of useful articles; they are usually sold to other firms, which use them as ingredients in further production. But even in these cases, although the chain connecting the particular firm with the ultimate consumer may be quite a long one, it is still there; if we take the trouble we can see for ourselves that the ultimate object of the work which is done is to assist in making something which some consumer will want, and will be willing to pay for. That consumer may be near at hand, or he may be at the other end of the earth; still he can always be found if we look for him. It is only because there is a prospect of finding a consumer at the end of the whole process, who will be prepared to pay for something he finds useful or desirable, that people can find employment in industry or in any sort of production at all.

2. Thus it appears that the whole of the economic activity of humanity (that vast complex of activities which we call the Economic System) consists of nothing else but an immense co-operation of workers or producers to make things and do things which consumers want. When it is described in this way, the economic system may sound quite an admirable thing—perhaps too admirable to agree with our experience of it. But in fact there is nothing necessarily admirable about a co-operation to satisfy the wants of consumers. The wants are usually harmless, but they may be deplorable; the methods of co-operating to satisfy even the most respectable wants are sometimes inefficient and stupid. Yet whether the wants are good or bad, whether production is organized efficiently or not, the description still holds. Economic life is an organization of producers to satisfy the wants of consumers.

Who are these consumers for whom the world is working? To a very large extent they are just the same people as the workers and producers themselves; the same people are workers and producers in one capacity and consumers in another. The consumer who spends his money upon the product of one industry (a bicycle or a suit of clothes) has earned that money by working in another occupation (say printing or market-gardening). The bicycle-makers and the clothing and textile workers spend their earnings in turn upon the products of other industries, the workers in these spend their earnings upon other products, and so on; among the various classes of workers and producers who come into the picture at one or other of these stages there will be some who will spend some part of their earnings upon the books and newspapers, the vegetables and flowers, which were the products of the printers and market-gardeners we started with.

The organization of production and consumption in the modern world is an immensely complicated affair; but if we turn our minds to the way it would be worked out in a simpler state of society, the general nature of the organization is at once apparent. Before the improvements in transport which have taken place in the last two centuries, the vast majority of the human race lived in fairly self-contained villages, villages which traded with one another in a few kinds of goods, but were in the main self-supporting. In such a village the principle upon which production has to be organized becomes clear at once. The whole thing is a system of exchanges. The farmer uses some part of his produce to satisfy his own wants, but sells some part to his neighbours. With the proceeds of that sale he buys other things which he needs—clothes from the weaver, woodwork from the carpenter, pottery from the potter. The weaver, in his turn, spends some of his time making his own clothes; but he sells most of his produce, using the proceeds to purchase the farmer's milk, or the potter's pots. And so on. 'You do this for me, and I will do that for you.' It is on bargains of this sort that the whole organization rests.

The advantage of organizing economic life in this way arises from the increased efficiency which comes from each person having a job, and sticking to it. 'The jack of all trades is master of none.' Although excessive specialization results in monotonous work, some degree of specialization is needed before any skill can be acquired. Instead of each person working so as to satisfy his own wants alone, which would mean wasting a great deal of time in continually shifting over from one job to another, everyone becomes to some extent a specialist, concentrating on one particular job or small range of jobs. The other things he wants done are done for him by other people, and in exchange for these services he uses his skill in serving them.

The main difference, from this point of view, between the primitive village organization and the economic system of the modern world is that in the modern world specialization has been carried immensely further. The wants of the ordinary person in the twentieth century are catered for by a system of exchanges in which an immensely larger number of people take part. The ordinary worker does not do more than assist in the production of some useful article. He joins together with a large number of other workers in producing something which will be useful to others, or perhaps to some of those he joins with; the things he gets in exchange are themselves the result of extensive, even world-wide, co-operation among producers. The reason for the adoption of this complicated system is still the technical advantage of specialization; subdividing productive processes has increased the efficiency of labour, enabling all sorts of more efficient methods (particularly mechanical methods) to be introduced into production. Nevertheless, in spite of the greater complexity of the specialization involved, the principle remains the same. 'You do this for me, and I will do that for you.'

3. We have now discovered two different ways of looking at the economic system. On the one hand, we can look upon it as a co-operation of producers to satisfy the wants of consumers; on the other hand, remembering that the producers and consumers are largely the same people, we can look upon it as a system of mutual exchanges. We shall find, as we go on, that it is very useful to have these two different points of view from which to approach our subject. Some things will be clearer from one of these standpoints, some from the other; and we can use one as a check against the other. It will be particularly useful when we come to making the fundamental classifications, which will occupy us in the next two chapters, to be able to check them up from each of these points of view. But before we proceed to that, we ought to satisfy ourselves that our treatment of the system as one of mutual exchanges is really correct, and not subject to qualifications. There are certain difficulties which do undoubtedly present themselves, and of which we ought to take proper account.

First of all, there is the question of money. Although the ultimate object of anyone who works or produces is to acquire useful things in exchange for his work, the immediate way he gets paid is not in the form of directly useful things, but in the form of money. The printer and journalist do not supply their customers with newspapers, getting bread and meat and clothes in direct exchange; they sell their newspapers for money, and then spend the money upon the things they want to buy as consumers. There is an obvious convenience in this arrangement. It must often happen that the people who supply the printers with clothes do not want to take newspapers to the full value of the clothes; if they had to take payment in newspapers, they would be obliged to re-sell the newspapers to another set of people; this would take time to arrange, and would be quite horribly inconvenient. To replace these complicated re-sales by a simple handing-on of tickets—for that is really what it amounts to—

saves an immense amount of trouble. The people who sell clothes to the printers do not take payment for them in newspapers but in tickets—that is, money; if they like, they can spend some of the money on newspapers, but if they prefer to spend it on bread and cheese, there is nothing to stop them. If they pass on the money to makers of bread or cheese, these people can spend it on newspapers, or they can hand it on to someone else to spend on newspapers, or it can be handed on again. The use of money enables indirect or roundabout exchanges to take place, without the goods which are exchanged having to be passed on unnecessarily from one person to another. That is the advantage we get from the use of money; it increases the flexibility of the system of exchanges to an extraordinary extent. But it remains a system of exchanges. Instead of newspapers being exchanged for clothes directly, the exchange takes place in two stages—the newspapers are sold for money, the money is spent on clothes. Yet the division into stages is important.

One of the advantages that are got from the use of money is that people do not have to pass it on immediately; they can choose the time of their purchases to suit their convenience. If they use this facility moderately, it is useful to them; and it does no harm to other people. But if they lose faith in the purchasing power of money, they may hurry to pass it on, so as not to get caught by rising prices; and if they lose confidence, in other ways, in what is going to happen to them, they may refrain from passing it on, trying to keep it as a nest-egg, or reserve. The former is what happens in a state of Inflation; the latter in a state of Deflation, or Depression. The world has had bad experiences of both sorts during the present century; they are to be regarded as monetary diseases. The Theory of Money, which is a special department of economics, is particularly concerned with studying these diseases; most of it lies outside the field which we shall study in the present volume. But it is impossible to study economic problems at all realistically without paying some attention to these matters, so that we shall be bound to encounter some aspects of these monetary diseases even here.

Another complication comes from the ownership of property. Most useful goods cannot be produced by human effort alone; the worker needs tools to work with and materials to work on. The products of agriculture are produced from the land; the products of mechanical industry are produced with machines; if agricultural land and industrial plant are in private ownership, the owners of these useful resources may be able to exact a price for their use. That is to say, people may acquire tickets which entitle them to purchase other people's products, not by contributing their labour to the productive process, but by allowing the use of their property. This is a matter of the most profound social significance, since some of the deepest divisions in society turn on the distinction between capitalist and worker; as we go on, we shall find that economics has to concern itself with these divisions to a very considerable extent. All the same, our double description of the economic system does not appear to be affected by the private ownership of property. The owner of property contributes to the productive process by allowing the use of his property in production; to this extent he has to be reckoned as a producer. He exchanges the use of his property for a share in the products of industry; in this way he enters into the system of exchanges. It is quite true that he gets these advantages much more easily than the worker does; or if (as is usually the case) he is also a worker, he gets a larger income than other workers get from the performance of similar work. If we decide, on the ground of convenience, to reckon the owner of property as a producer, we must not allow ourselves, in consequence of this decision, to beg any questions about the desirability of private property as an institution. The institution of private property has to be tried by more searching tests; but we shall find it easier to apply those tests if we begin by getting a clear idea about the working of the system in which private property functions.

The only real qualification to the rule that the economic system can be looked on as a system of exchanges comes from the economic activities of governments, national and local. Some part of the money which people receive, in return for the labour they have performed, or for the property they have allowed to be used, is taken away from them by public authorities in taxes and rates. In order to see how these taxes fit into the system, we must consider the purpose for which they are raised. Governments sometimes raise taxes in order to make presents to some of their own citizens or to foreigners; under this heading would come such things as tribute to a foreign power, pensions to the ex-soldiers of past wars, relief to the unemployed. All these things are just compulsory gifts from one set of persons to another; some of them are very sensible and desirable, some very undesirable. But some of the taxes which are raised by governments are raised for another purpose: they are raised in order to pay for the employment of people to do work for the good of the community in general—as, for example, soldiers or policemen or road-menders. These people work to satisfy the wants of consumers; their work is part of the Productive Process, but it does not result in the production of such things as can be bought by individual consumers, though consumers in general do undoubtedly desire that they should be provided. The wants which are satisfied by work of this sort are collective wants, not individual wants. During war-time a very large proportion of a nation's productive power is turned over to the satisfaction of collective wants, for the whole of the armed forces and of the munition industries must be reckoned as working to that end. Even in time of peace, the number of people whose work has to be reckoned as being directed to the satisfaction of collective wants is usually very considerable.

It might be supposed, at first sight, that the proportion of its population working for the satisfaction of collective wants would be a measure of the degree of socialization reached by a particular nation. But that is not so. Even in a completely socialized state, like Communist Russia, where the government is very nearly the only employer of labour, the proportion of persons working to satisfy collective wants need not be abnormally high. For in a socialist state the government does not only control the production of those things which are wanted collectively, it also controls the production of things wanted individually. (There are, of course, little bits of socialism in this sense in almost all countries—nationalized railways, municipal concert-halls, and so on.) In a socialist state people work for the government, whether they are producing collective goods, like roads and parks and military aeroplanes, or individual goods, like food and clothing. The roads and military aeroplanes are paid for by the public out of taxes, but the food and clothing are bought from the government, just as they would be bought from private producers in a community which was not organized in a socialist manner. Over the greater part of the field the socialist government merely acts as an intermediary, in the same way as the private employer. Thus there is nothing in socialism, as such, to prevent us from regarding the economic system as a system of exchanges. Indeed, most of the economic theory in this volume can be applied to a socialist state, just as much as to one which is based on a system of private enterprise. In either case we can look upon the economic system as a co-operation of producers to satisfy consumers' wants (including collective wants); or alternatively (apart from the qualification about taxation) we can look upon it as a system of mutual exchanges.

CHAPTER II Goods and Services

1. As soon as we have understood the double nature of the economic system, as it was explained in the previous chapter, we can see that it will be convenient to shape our further classifications in ways which will fit in with each of the two aspects. Henceforward we shall mean by *production* any activity directed to the satisfaction of other people's wants through exchange; we shall use the word *producer* to mean a person engaging in production in this sense. A person whose wants are satisfied by such production we shall call a *consumer*. Previously we have used these terms in a looser manner; from now on we shall try to confine them to these precise senses.

Let us see what we are committed to by these definitions. The words *producer* and *consumer* are widely used in ordinary speech and in business; but in practical life they do not need to be used very precisely or uniformly, so that they are often used in senses which do not square with our definitions. Farmers, for instance, are fond of drawing a contrast between their own activities as 'producers' of foodstuffs and those of the traders or retailers, who merely sell or 'distribute' them. On our definition the retailer is a producer just as much as the farmer. The work done by the retailer is a part of the process of satisfying consumers' wants, just as much as the work of the farmer. Milk on the farm and tobacco at the factory are of little use to anyone except the farmer and the manufacturer themselves; milk on the door-step and tobacco in the shop are provided, more or less, where and when the consumer wants them.

The reason why people have been able to persuade themselves that farmers are producers, while retailers are not, is of course that the word 'production', used in other senses than the economic, suggests the making of something material, something you can touch or handle, something you can cart about on a lorry or bring home in a paper bag. A very great part of economic production does consist in the making of material goods, but quite a large part does not. The trader and retailer deal with material goods, but they do not make them; their part is to take goods already made, and to make them more useful by supplying them at the places and times at which they are wanted. But there are many sorts of workers who are not concerned with the production of material goods at all; doctors, teachers, civil servants and administrators, passenger transport workers, entertainers, cleaners—all of these are producers in our sense, though they do not produce material products. They do useful work and are paid for it; consequently they count as producers. The things they produce are useful services, not material goods; it is convenient to say that the things produced by producers and consumed by consumers are of two kinds—Goods and Services, material goods and immaterial services.

The performance of such services as these is included in production; but if we are to be faithful to our definition, we may not say that all performance of services for other people reckons as production. Production is activity directed to the satisfaction of other people's wants through exchange; thus it is only those services which are paid for that have to be included. The most important kind of services which, on this test, have to be left out are the services performed within the family—the work done by wives for their husbands, by parents in looking after their children, and so on. These services are not to be reckoned as productive, because they are not paid for. It is of course not very convenient that we have to exclude this essential work from our definition of production, but there does not seem to be any help for it, if we are to have the advantage of using words in precise and well-defined ways.[1] The fact that we have excluded it from

[1] A further discussion of this, and of some related subjects, will be found in Appendix, Note A.

our definition does not absolve us from keeping the fundamental importance, the fundamental economic importance, of this sort of work very much in our minds.

2. There was a stage in the development of economic thought when the inclusion, in the definition of production, of those direct services which are paid for was not accepted even by economists. Adam Smith himself confined the term 'productive labour' to that labour which is devoted to the production of material goods. In a famous passage[1] he gave a list of such occupations as must be reckoned to be 'unproductive'. Beginning with 'menial servants', he goes on:

> The sovereign, for example, with all the officers both of justice and of war who serve under him, the whole army and navy, are unproductive labourers. . . . In the same class must be ranked, some both of the gravest and most important, and some of the most frivolous professions: churchmen, lawyers, physicians, men of letters of all kinds; players, buffoons, musicians, opera-singers, opera-dancers, &c.

This looks like the same fallacious, or at least uneconomic, way of thinking as is common among those who approach economic affairs from the standpoint of the technical processes of manufacture; it is strange to find it in the most famous of all economists. The manufacturer and the farmer naturally think of production as *making* something; we have seen that economics has to have a wider definition. Why did Adam Smith suppose the contrary? It was not because he supposed the distinction between material and immaterial products to have any economic significance; his reason was more subtle. Later economists have not been prepared to allow their definition of production to be influenced by it, but they have had to pay much attention to it in other parts of their economic theory. Adam Smith put it in this way:

> The labour of the menial servant does not fix or realise itself in any particular subject or vendible commodity. His services generally perish in the very instant of their performance. . . . Like the declamation of the actor, the harangue of the orator, or the

[1] *Wealth of Nations*, Book II, ch. 3 (vol. i, p. 314 in Cannan's edition).

tune of the musician, the work of all of them perishes in the very instant of its production.

The reason why Smith adopted his odd definition of production was because he was impressed by the fact that the production of most goods takes time, often a very long time, and the consumption of these goods comes afterwards. The significant thing about direct services is that the acts of performing the labour and of enjoying the results of the labour are contemporaneous and inseparable. Goods, on the other hand, have to be produced first and consumed afterwards. The production and consumption of services are, practically speaking, instantaneous; but the production and consumption of goods form a process. The further classifications, which will concern us in the rest of this chapter and in the next, are all concerned with the economic system considered as a process.

3. On a certain day (say in the spring of 1970) the reader of this book will probably have eaten a peice of bread for breakfast. Behind that piece of bread was a considerable history. Two or three days earlier it was baked by a baker, who for his stage in the process of bread-making used various ingredients, notably flour. Some weeks earlier the flour will have been milled out of wheat, various kinds of wheat being very probably mixed together, some imported from overseas, some produced at home. This wheat will have been harvested, probably during the year 1969, the precise date depending upon the part of the world from which it came. Some months before the time of the harvesting the wheat must have been sown, and before the sowing the land on which it was grown must have been ploughed. Taking this simple line of operations, from the ploughing of the land to the bread on the table, not much less than a year can have elapsed between the start and the finish. Often it will be a good deal more than a year. But this is by no means the whole of the history behind that piece of bread.

At every stage in the process described, ploughing, sowing, harvesting, threshing, milling, baking, power or fuel was needed. The power used for ploughing may have been nothing more modern than the traditional horse; if so, that horse had to be fed, its feeding-stuffs had to be grown, and the growth of the feeding-stuffs extends the process of production backwards for another series of months. Or the power may have been provided by a tractor; tractors use oil, so that the getting of the oil and its transport to the farm (another stage involving at least a month or two) have also to be reckoned into the process of production of the bread. The same will hold for the power (of whatever kind) used in harvesting, threshing, and milling; also for the oil or electricity used at the bakery. Of course many of these latter processes will be going on simultaneously, so that they do not lengthen the total time taken by the production. Nevertheless, when we have taken the power into account, the whole period looks more like two years than one.

Even this is not all. The tractor, the threshing-machine, the ships used for bringing the wheat from overseas, the elevator used for storing it, the milling machinery used for making the flour, even the baker's oven—all these had to be made at some time or other, and the reason why they were made was because they would be useful in the manufacture of bread. Not of course this particular piece of bread, which is far too humble an article to be able to claim for itself alone such mighty antecedents; but this piece of bread, and millions like it, are the reasons why the tractors and elevators and ovens and the rest of them were brought into being. All this elaborate equipment was in fact constructed as part of the process of manufacturing bread.

If at some date, three months or six months or a year before the bread appeared upon the table, we had examined how the process of producing it was getting on, we should have found that most of the equipment was already made and in use, while the raw material of the bread was still in the form of growing crops, or threshed wheat, or bags of flour. These things can all be looked upon as stages in the manufacture of the bread; whatever stage has been reached, even if it is only the making of the tractor, or the building of a tanker to transport the oil to feed the tractor, something has been done which will come in useful and help towards the final production of bread. The products which result from these early stages are useful products, but not products which are directly useful for satisfying the wants of consumers. Their use is to be found in their employment in the further stages, at the end of which a product which is directly wanted by consumers will emerge. It is convenient to use the term *goods* to cover the products of these earlier stages, as well as the final product which the consumer purchases. But the products of the earlier stages are called *producers' goods*, to distinguish them from the *consumers' goods*, which do satisfy the consumers' wants directly.

In our illustration the bread is a consumers' good; the wheat, the flour, the tractor, the ship, the oven (and so on) are producers' goods. A producers' good may be technically finished, in the sense that the particular operation needed to produce it is completed (the wheat has been harvested, or the tractor ready for use). Or it may not be technically finished, but still in process, even so far as its own stage is concerned (the corn may be standing in the field, or the ship still on the stocks). In either case it is a producers' good, because further stages are needed before the result of the whole process can pass into the consumers' hands. The consumers' good is the end of the whole process; producers' goods are stages on the road towards it.

4. The production of any consumers' good one cared to select could be similarly shown to consist of a process, occupying in all quite a considerable time, and involving the production of a number of producers' goods on the way. It has next to be noticed that with some consumers' goods, but only with some, consumption is also a process taking an appreciable time. Consumers' goods can be divided, from this point of view, into two classes.

In the first class we have goods, like the bread of our example (and foodstuffs generally), which are used and used up in a single act. The careful housewife may make a loaf of bread last two or three days, but only by dividing it into slices and consuming the slices at intervals. Each piece of bread is used up as soon as it is used at all. Other consumers' goods which are of the same type are fuel, tobacco, matches, and writing-paper. I shall call these goods *single-use goods*. From the point of view of consumption, services are similar in character to the single-use goods;[1] but, as we have noticed, they are different on the production side.

The other goods I shall call *durable-use goods*. Houses, furniture, clothes, radio sets, refrigerators, and motor-cars are examples of this second class. Their common characteristic is that they can go on being used for considerable periods. The fact that they have been used on one day does not prevent them from being used again on the next. The lengths of time for which they can go on being used vary of course a good deal. A pencil is probably to be reckoned as a durable-use good, in spite of the fact that it is bound to wear out after a few months of use. At the other extreme are such things as old furniture, which can go on being used almost indefinitely (apart from accidents), so long as it is properly looked after and kept in good repair.

The distinction between single-use goods and durable-use goods must not be confused with another distinction, of very similar character, which is commonly made in books on economics. It has been usual among economists to classify consumers' goods into *durable goods* and *perishable goods*; these classes are similar to ours, but they are not exactly the same. *Durable-use* goods are necessarily *durable*, but not all *single-use* goods are *perishable*. Coal, for example, is a very durable good; it can be stored almost indefinitely, and will not deteriorate seriously, so long as it is not used. But it cannot be used without being used up. Thus it is a single-use good. There are many other single-use goods which have a fair degree of durability; canned and otherwise preserved foods are instances. The fact that they are capable of being stored is an important characteristic of these goods, a characteristic with important economic consequences. But, for the present at least, it is not the characteristic we want to emphasize. The main classification of consumers' goods is into the single-use and durable-use varieties.

The goods which are purchased by a particular consumer belong partly to one of these varieties, partly to the other.

[1] It is of course true that the effects of consuming a particular service may last a long time through being stored in the memory; this, however, does not prevent the consumption itself being a single act. In the same way, the medicine which saves a man's life is a single-use good; but its effects remain as long as he lives.

Most of the single-use goods which are purchased have to go on being purchased, week after week, day after day. To have had a good meal yesterday does not prevent one from wanting another good meal today; to have been warm last night does not prevent one from needing to be warmed again this afternoon. Durable-use goods, on the other hand, may go on being useful for long periods after they have been bought; thus they do not need to be bought continuously, but only when the want for them first appears, or when an old one has broken down or become impossibly shabby. It follows that while the purchase of most sorts of single-use goods will take place at fairly regular intervals, purchases of durable-use goods may be very irregular. This is a matter of considerable importance for the running of the productive process. If all the goods which consumers wanted were single-use goods, it would be comparatively easy to organize the economic system so as to keep it running continuously at the same level of activity. The production of durable-use goods is much harder to stabilize, just because the need to purchase such goods is so much less regular. Nevertheless, durable-use goods are of great importance to the consumer; although food and warmth, the most urgent necessities, are single-use goods, some durable-use goods are essential at any standard of living, while at a higher standard they provide more solid satisfaction than single-use goods can do. Luxury single-use goods mainly take the form of entertainment; luxury durable-use goods range from good housing and good clothing to books and pictures and musical instruments and garden plants, the typical ingredients of a civilized life. People who buy these things can satisfy their wants for them without buying them so regularly as they would buy food; it is in consequence more difficult to arrange for their production in ways which may not involve economic disturbances. Very much the most difficult case is that of housing; we shall discuss it in more detail in another connection.[1]

5. A similar distinction between single-use and durable-use varieties can be made for producers' goods. Some producers' goods are used up—though this may only mean that they

[1] See Chapter VIII below.

have passed on to the next stage in their production—as soon as they are used at all; others can go on being used in the same way for long periods. In the illustration we gave, the wheat, the flour, and also the oil and the electricity were single-use goods in this sense; the tractor, the ship, and the baker's oven were durable-use goods. Generally speaking, single-use producers' goods are the materials used in industry; though half-finished products ought also to be reckoned as single-use goods which are at another stage. Durable-use producers' goods are the instruments of production—tools, machinery, industrial plant of all kinds. The production of durable-use producers' goods is perhaps even harder to stabilize than the production of durable-use consumers' goods—for much the same reasons. But we are not yet in a position to deal with such questions.

CHAPTER III Consumption and Investment

1. We have now got a general idea of the productive process; but before we can turn to the facts, and try to make sense of them, we need yet another set of definitions. The processes of production and exchange which we have been describing go on more or less indefinitely; they have gone on since the dawn of history, and will go on as long as the human race exists. Although it is true in one sense that particular processes come to an end every day with the completion and sale of finished consumers' goods, these goods have usually been produced along with many others (the durable-use producers' goods used in making them are for the most part still in existence, and being used again), so that it is very difficult to find a self-contained process which can ever be said to be really over, just as we have seen that it is very difficult to find a date when it can really be said to begin. The only way in which we can limit our investigations, so as not to have to deal with the whole of human history at once, is to select a particular period of time and to confine our attention to the working of the productive process during that period. Usually (though not always) the period which it is most convenient to take is a year.

The statistics of production which were described in the introductory chapter of this book usually refer to annual periods. They must of course always refer to some period. There is no point in saying that the number of aeroplanes produced is 100, unless one states the time to which this output refers. An output of 100 aeroplanes spread over two months is the same rate of output as 50 aeroplanes in one month. All measurements of the quantity of production have to refer to a stated period. If we are to use our definitions so as to square with these measurements, our definitions too must refer to a particular period of time.

Let us therefore fix our minds on the working of the productive process during a particular year—say 1970. We must think of the whole stream of time as being spread out before us, like a film which has been unwound. We take our scissors and cut out a particular section of the film. Or we may say that we put a spotlight upon this particular year, leaving everything before it and after it in the dark. What is the effect of this limitation upon the classifications we have given?

2. During the year producers will be turning out services and goods of all kinds, single-use goods, durable-use goods, producers' goods, consumers' goods. Most of the single-use goods will be used up in the course of the year, the consumers' goods in the direct satisfaction of consumers' wants, the producers' goods in the making of consumers' goods. It is fairly evident that single-use producers' goods, produced and used up during the year, ought not to be reckoned as part of the total production or output of the year. If we were to include both the bread and the flour out of which it is made, we should be reckoning the same productive effort twice; if we did this, there would be no reason why we should not include the wheat as well, and even the wheat standing in the field as well as the threshed wheat after it had been harvested. Once we allowed ourselves to reckon in both the single-use consumers' goods and the single-use producers' goods out of which they are made, there would be nothing to stop us from dividing the process of production into a large number of stages and counting what is essentially the same product as many times as we like. This would make the result of our calculation completely arbitrary. 'Double counting' of this sort has clearly got to be avoided.

Those single-use producers' goods which are produced and used up during the year must not be counted as part of the year's production. But does this mean that all producers' goods have got to be excluded? At first sight one might suppose so, but that is not the case. For the production we are concerned with is the production of the year 1970, and some of the durable producers' goods produced during 1970 will outlast 1970. We have to pay special attention to the hang-over from one year to another.

At the beginning of the year (the morning of 1 January 1970) there exists in the community a particular stock of goods, including some from all our four types, but among which the durable-use goods are no doubt predominant. These goods are inherited from the previous year; for the most part they are the result of production in that and in earlier years. The durable-use consumers' goods inherited from the previous year include the houses people are living in, the furniture they are using, the clothes they are wearing, and so on. The durable-use producers' goods will include the factories, the machinery standing in the factories, the railways, ships, lorries, tools, and so on which are available for use in production during the coming year. The single-use producers' goods which are inherited will include stocks of materials, goods undergoing processes that are still unfinished, finished goods waiting to be sold. The single-use consumers' goods (not so many of these) will include such things as foodstuffs already in the larder; remembering that the retailer is also a producer, foodstuffs in the shops ought to be reckoned as producers' goods.

This is the position at the beginning of the year. Then the wheel of time rolls on, and the wheels of production begin to turn. The goods in the larder are used up, and replaced by new goods out of the shops—that is to say, producers' goods pass into consumers' goods. At the same time, the vacant places in the shops are filled by new producers' goods coming forward—that is to say, the materials existing on 1 January are worked on by labour, with the help of durable-use producers' goods, and turned by degrees into finished products. At the same time, other workers, using other durable-use producers' goods, are preparing new materials. And other workers are making new durable-use goods. So the process goes on, with a continual stream of new consumers' goods passing into consumption, and new single-use producers' goods poking their heads out of the productive process, only to be tucked in again.

Those producers' goods which are produced during the year, and used up in further production within the year, do not reckon as part of the year's output. They are taken to be included in the consumers' goods of which they are the materials. If we were allowed to extend our gaze into the indefinite future, we should presumably find all the producers' goods incorporating themselves in consumers' goods in this way; but we are not allowed to look forward indefinitely. The year has an end as well as a beginning; many of the consumers' goods in which the producers' goods of this year will be incorporated belong to future years, not to this year. There will be producers' goods left over at the end of this year, just as there were producers' goods left over to this year from the year before.

There is no reason why the quantity of producers' goods bequeathed to 1971 should be the same as that inherited from 1969. The single-use producers' goods inherited from 1969 will, for the most part, have been used up in the production of 1970; new goods will have been produced to replace them, but these new goods may be greater or less in amount than the goods which have been used up. Some of the durable-use producers' goods inherited from 1969 will also have been used up, or worn out, during 1970; and even those which are not worn out will be a year older in January 1971 than they were in January 1970; this will often mean that they have a year's less 'life' left in them. Against this *depreciation* of the durable-use goods previously existing has to be set the production of new durable-use goods; but the depreciation may or may not be completely offset by the new production. If it is not completely offset, the quantity of such goods at the disposal of the community will be less at the end of the year than it was at the beginning; if it is more than offset, the quantity at the end of the year will be greater.[1]

The same process of using-up and replacing will occur with consumers' goods. Our year 1970 will have inherited from its predecessors certain quantities of consumers' goods (mainly

[1] For some qualifications to this statement, see Appendix, Note C.

durable-use goods, houses, and so on); it will hand on certain quantities to its successors. One of the tests of successful productive activity during the year is to be got by comparing the quantities at the end with those at the beginning.

3. The process of production during the year can therefore be described in summary fashion in the following way. At the beginning of the year there exists a certain stock of goods (all our four kinds) which we may call the Initial Equipment. During the year the initial equipment is worked upon by Labour, and there is produced from it a stream of goods. Some of these goods are producers' goods, used up again within the year, so that they do not reckon into the year's output; the goods which are included consist partly of consumers' goods, consumed within the year, partly of new equipment, added to the initial equipment as a result of the year's production. The equipment which exists at the end of the year becomes the initial equipment of the next year; it equals the initial equipment of the first year *plus* the new equipment which has been added *minus* the using-up of equipment which has taken place within the year. This is the scheme of the productive process which we need to have in our minds.

All the product or output of the year comes from labour and the initial equipment; these are therefore called the Factors of Production. The output of goods consists either of consumers' goods, consumed within the year (Consumption) or of New Equipment. We can therefore set out our scheme in the form of a table:

Factors of Production	Labour	Initial Equipment
Product or Output	Consumption	New Equipment

And for the effect on equipment of the year's production:

initial equipment 1971 = initial equipment 1970
+ new equipment produced in 1970
− using-up of equipment during 1970

The classification set out in this table is of fundamental importance for the whole of that part of economics which we shall study in this book. Everything further we have to say is nothing but elaboration of it and application of it to practical problems. For when theory has reached this point, it does begin to be capable of being applied.

4. Before we can proceed to these applications, it should first be noticed, however, that the table as it stands is not quite complete. In the first place, services have been left out of account, as Adam Smith left them out of account—and for what turns out to be substantially the same reason. Just as we have been learning to do, Adam Smith thought of the productive process as consisting of labour working on initial equipment, and making it grow into consumption goods and new equipment. And services did not fit into the picture properly; consequently he excluded them as 'unproductive'. We have decided not to take that way out, and so we must find some way of fitting services into our picture. We can really do so quite easily, if we include the services produced in the year as part of the consumption of the year, and allow for the possibility that these services may have been produced by labour alone, without making use of initial equipment to any important extent. (Of course—and this is even more true today than it was in Smith's time—services may require the assistance of durable-use goods from the initial equipment if they are to be produced; for instance, passenger transport workers provide direct services, but they use a great deal of equipment in providing these services.) This, then, is one of the adjustments which have to be made.

The other adjustment concerns the durable-use consumers' goods, which are included in the initial equipment and do in fact form an important part of it. Take, for example, houses. The houses which exist at the beginning of the year do for the most part go on being used during the year; they make themselves useful, very useful indeed. The use of a house is a thing for which people are prepared to pay; a man pays rent for the right to live in a particular house, just as he pays for the goods he (or his wife) purchases in the shops. We reckon the goods purchased in the shops as part of the consumption of the year, and, since house-room is purchased by consumers in the same sort of way, it is convenient (even if it means some stretching of terms) to reckon the use of house-room as part of the consumption of the year, and consequently even to reckon it as part of the production or output of the year. There is something to be said for doing the same with all the durable-use consumers' goods contained in the initial equipment (the motor-cars, for example). But, largely for the historical reason that there was a time when houses were usually rented by their occupiers, while motor-cars were generally bought outright, it has become usual to include in this way only the use of houses.[1] Houses are in any case the most important type of durable-use consumers' goods.

Our revised table may therefore be written as follows:

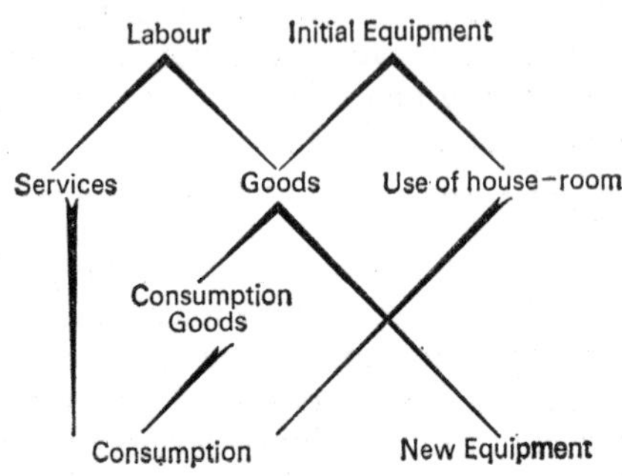

The new houses produced during the year are of course included in the new equipment.

5. Our table is now complete, but before we can use it we must introduce two new terms. Instead of our phrase 'Initial Equipment', economists usually employ the term 'Capital'; instead of our phrase 'New Equipment' the term 'Investment' is now generally used. We had better familiarize ourselves with these important words.

I have so far avoided talking about *Capital* and *Investment*, because these are such outstanding instances of the way in which economists have taken words used by business men and given new meanings to them, meanings which are not (at least on the surface) the same as the business meanings. There is a relation between the meanings of capital and

[1] See again Appendix, Note A.

investment in economics and their meanings in business practice; we shall try to get that relation cleared up before we are done. But for the moment it is only the economic meanings which concern us.

In economics the capital of a community consists in the stock of goods of all sorts possessed by the community (either by its individual members, or by associations of its members, such as governments) at a particular moment of time. Thus our 'initial equipment' is the capital possessed by our community on 1 January. In economics investment is the making of additions to capital. Thus the making of our 'new equipment' is investment.

In this terminology the factors of production are labour and capital.[1] The goods and services produced by the factors of production are partly consumed within the year (consumption), partly used to make additions to capital (investment). In order to produce these goods and services, some part of the capital possessed at the beginning of the year is used up (Depreciation[2] of Capital). The net addition to capital within the year is therefore the total production of additions to capital, with depreciation deducted. This net addition to capital is called Net Investment. Consumption *plus* Net Investment *equals* Net Product.

The definitions given in this last paragraph will become familiar enough as we go on. For the whole programme which lies before us is involved in these definitions. In the next two parts of this book we shall study the factors of production—labour and capital. In the last part we shall study the net product of the economic system; we shall discuss how it is measured, we shall examine some of the reasons for variations in its size, and we shall examine how it is divided up among different people, so that some are rich and some poor. All these things are developments of the fundamental classifications which we have been giving.

[1] Land, which nineteenth-century economics used to reckon as a third factor of production, is here included in capital. For the justification of this arrangement, see below, Chapter VIII.

[2] The business man employs the term 'depreciation' to include the using-up of durable-use goods only. Here we use it in the wider sense, more convenient in economics, which includes the using-up of such single-use goods as are not replaced during the year in identically the same form.

Let us then pass on to discuss the factor of production labour. The first problem to be discussed under that head is the problem of Population, for although not all the people living in a country are producers, it is the total population of the country which mainly governs the number of workers who are available to take part in the process of production.

PART II The Factors of Production—Labour

CHAPTER IV Population and its History

1. Let us begin by looking at some figures. The following table sets out, in round numbers, the population of a number of Western countries at various stages in modern history. Since the taking of censuses only began in the United States in 1790, in Great Britain in 1801, and in the other countries at various dates in the nineteenth century, it will be understood that the figures for 1650 are only guesses (though they are careful guesses),[1] while some even of the figures for 1800 and 1850 are not very much better. It is only for 1900 and 1950 that most of the figures are known at all precisely (the 1969 figures, the latest available at the time of writing, are only estimates). But it is not likely that any part of the table is seriously misleading. There have, of course, been some important changes in frontiers during the period; the most important changes have been allowed for.[2]

TABLE I

Population (in millions)

	1650	1800	1850	1900	1950	1969
Great Britain	6	10	21	37	49	54
France	16	27	35	41	41	50
Germany	14	20	35	54	70	78
Italy	13	17	24	32	46	53
U.S.A.	..	5	23	75	151	203
Ireland	1	5	6½	4½	4⅓	4½

[1] They are taken from G. N. Clark, *The Seventeenth Century*, ch. i.

[2] Thus France always includes Alsace-Lorraine, Ireland includes Northern Ireland, while the Germany of 1950 and 1969 includes East and West.

When a table of this sort is being examined, it is not the individual figures by themselves which deserve attention; it is the comparison of one figure with another. (This is why it is sufficient to work in round numbers; comparisons can be made more easily if the figures are given approximately; detail would distract the eye, without adding anything of importance.) In the table before us, at least two kinds of comparison can be made. By looking down the columns we can compare the populations of different countries at the same dates; the points which then emerge are mainly of political interest, though of very great political interest indeed. The greatness of France under Louis XIV and under Napoleon is reflected in the relatively high population of France in the 1650 and 1800 columns; the strength of Germany and Japan and the weight of the United States in the modern world are indicated in the columns for 1900 and 1950. Military strength is not by any means entirely a matter of population, but population has often been an important element in it.

From the economic point of view a study of the table by horizontal rows is more instructive. Every one of the countries in the list (with the exception of Ireland—included just because it is an exception) shows increases in population throughout the whole period; usually they show very large increases. The increase in population which has taken place in many countries during the last three centuries is one of the most stupendous facts in history; it is quite probable that nothing like it had ever been seen before. But when we look at the table more closely, it becomes apparent that the increase has not proceeded at all smoothly or regularly; it has been much faster at some times and places than at others. It will be useful to examine these variations in detail.

At first sight, the simplest way of comparing the rates of increase at different stages would seem to be by calculating the percentages at which the various populations increased between 1650 and 1800, 1800 and 1850, and so on. But since the intervals between our dates are of different lengths, these percentages would be less informative than one could wish. It is better to calculate the *average* rate of increase in each of the intervals—that is to say, the annual rate of increase which, if maintained over the whole interval, would have resulted in the actual increase of population which we find. Since the annual rates of increase are of course small (many of them less than 1 per cent), it is more convenient to express them as as rates per thousand than as rates per hundred (percentages).[1]

TABLE II

Average rates of population increase (per thousand) per annum

	1650–1800	1800–50	1850–1900	1900–50	1950–69
Great Britain	3	14	11	6	5
France	3	5	3	0	10
Germany	2	11	9	5	6
Italy	2	7	6	8	8
U.S.A.	..	31	24	15	16
Ireland	9	5	−16	−1	2

Apart from the special case of France, in 1950–69 (to which we shall be coming), the first thing which strikes one when looking at this new table is the rapid rate at which the populations of the Western countries were expanding during the interval 1800–50. Ireland, which again looks like an exception, is here less of an exception than it looks; the Irish population continued to increase at a rate of 9 per thousand until 1840, but between 1840 and 1850 it started falling, as a result of the potato famine. The general impression one gets from most of the table is that the history of population during the last two centuries has passed through two distinct phases, during the first of which there was a great acceleration in the rate of growth of population, while during the second the brake was put on more or less violently. This is in fact a correct impression, though in non-Western countries (as we shall be seeing) the upsurge has come much later; it is a phenomenon of the twentieth century, not of the nineteenth. The pattern which we have distinguished is very general; certainly it is something which needs to be explained.

Changes in population come about in two ways: by Natural

[1] In order to calculate the annual rate of increase which would turn a population of 6 million into one of 10 million in 150 years, we have to solve the equation $\left(1+\frac{x}{1,000}\right)^{150}=\frac{10}{6}$. Take logarithms of both sides and it comes out at once.

Increase or Decrease (excess of births over deaths, or vice versa), and by Migration. The figures in our tables are affected by migration to a considerable extent, but not sufficiently to disturb the general pattern. The population of the United States has been greatly increased by immigration; but the great mass of the nineteenth-century immigrants came in after 1850, so that the astounding rate of growth of American population during the early nineteenth century (31 per thousand per annum) was almost entirely a natural increase. What the immigrants did was to prevent the increase from slowing up as rapidly as it would have done without them. The decline in Irish population after 1840 was largely a result of emigration, but not entirely.

Some significant differences are made to our figures, when we allow for migration, in the cases of Italy and France. Especially from 1880 to 1910, there was a great emigration from Italy; so if one had figures for the Italian population, *whether living in Italy or not*, it is probable that its rates of increase would be something like 2, 7, 8, 11, 8 in successive periods, instead of the 2, 7, 6, 8, 8 that is shown. The natural increase has come down in the end, though the fall is rather late. In France, on the other hand, it is true that there has been an acceleration of natural increase in the last period 1950–69 (from the very low rates which were usual in the earlier periods); but it is not as large as it looks. For some part of the recent rise is due to exceptional immigration, chiefly from Algeria.

Let us take the two phases in turn and inquire (1) why the rate of population increase accelerated, and (2) why it slowed up.

2. The natural increase of population takes place by an excess of births over deaths; consequently the rate of natural increase (that is, the rate of growth in Table II adjusted for migration) equals the difference between the birth-rate (number of births per thousand of population per annum) and the death-rate (number of deaths per thousand per annum). A high rate of natural increase must be due to a wide gap between the birth-rate and the death-rate; but the gap may be wide because the birth-rate is exceptionally high or because the death-rate is exceptionally low. An increase rate of 10 per thousand (which is enough to cause quite a rapid expansion of population) may be due to a birth-rate of 35 and a death-rate of 25, or to a birth-rate of 25 and a death-rate of 15. It seems probable (though naturally one cannot say for certain) that the more or less stable-sized populations which seem to have been the general rule before 1750 were due to a combination of high birth-rate with high death-rate—both of them in the neighbourhood of 30 per thousand, with only a narrow gap between them. The principal development which upset this primitive equilibrium was a marked fall in the death-rate, due (beyond all doubt) to the improvements in sanitation and medical skill which were beginning to be effective in the north of Europe by the middle of the eighteenth century, though they failed to exercise any appreciable influence in other countries until much later.

Birth-rates and death-rates for England and Wales are set out in Chart I. It begins at 1850, which is near the date at which we commence to have reliable figures. At that date, as will be seen, there was already a wide gap between birth-rate and death-rate, so that population was increasing very rapidly. We must suppose that there had previously been a fall in the death-rate, though (as will be seen) the death-rate was not in fact falling in the mid nineteenth century. (The bad sanitary conditions in the early industrial towns are a possible explanation.) After 1870 the fall was resumed. As a result of the whole process the death-rate has been reduced, from the 30 per thousand at which it must have stood some time in the eighteenth century, to less than 12 per thousand today.

The rise in the rate of population growth (our first phase) was thus mainly due to a fall in the death-rate; the slowing-up in the second phase is undoubtedly due to a fall (a much more sudden fall) in the birth-rate. As appears from the chart, the English birth-rate turned definitely downwards after 1880; in fifty years it fell from 35 per thousand to 15. One can now see that the birth-rates of the nineteen-thirties were abnormally low, and since then there has been a recovery. But it was only in 1946 and 1947 that the birth-rate

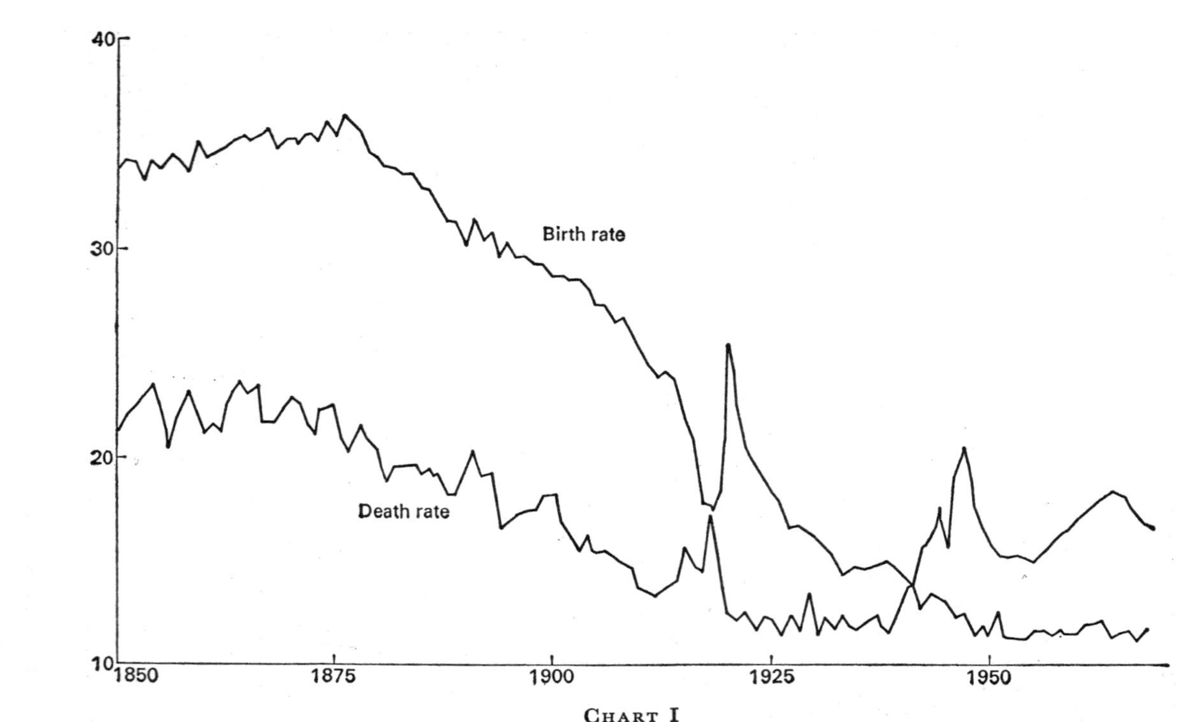

CHART I

exceeded 19 (the 'post-war bulge', quite obviously due, like that in 1920, to the postponement of births which, but for the war, would have taken place earlier). There have been fluctuations since then, but 15 and 18 have been the limits.

When we turn to the other countries, we find much the same story though there have been variations in timing. In all of the countries shown, death-rates were falling, at least by the late nineteenth century, and have now fallen to levels that are comparable with the British. And, usually well after the death-rate, the birth-rate fell. In France, alone, they kept nearly in step, which is why the French population (up to 1945) increased so little. The German birth-rate did not leave the 35 level until 1900, the Italian even later; but they end up (in the nineteen-sixties) within the same band (15–18) as the British. The American came down rather slowly (it was still at 25 in 1915), but in 1968 it is at 17, again in the same band. In France, we are not surprised to find, there has been a rise in the birth-rate since 1945; but it is just a rise *up to* that same level (17). Almost all 'developed' countries are now countries of fairly modest birth-rates; so that, in spite of their low death-rates, they have no more than a moderate rate of increase.

3. What are the causes of the great fall in the birth-rate? In spite of all the work which has been done on the subject, we do not altogether know. The explanation most commonly given is the practice of birth control, or contraception; but although the improvements in methods of birth control may explain how people *can* limit their families without undue difficulty, it does not explain why they should *want* to limit their families so very drastically. (Furthermore, it would appear that, in some of the countries where a fall in the birth-rate has taken place, the method most frequently used is not contraception but abortion; abortion is a repulsive method, often dangerous to health, often illegal and always immoral, so that the desire for family limitation must be very strong indeed for people to adopt it.) What has to be explained is the motive, or motives, which have led to so general a recourse to family limitation; naturally that is not a thing which can easily be discovered.

It is possible, however, that some light may be thrown on the matter if we look back at the period before 1870, when contraception is not likely to have been of much importance, and when, nevertheless, we do find considerable variations in birth-rates. As appears from our chart, the birth-rate in England was running at 35 or over until about 1870. This is a distinctly high rate, but even higher rates have occurred in North America, some as high as 50 per thousand. In France, on the other hand, the birth-rate ran at not much over 25 during the greater part of the nineteenth century. These variations are quite sufficient to make a large difference to the rate of population expansion; how are they to be explained?

The explanation which is usually given for the relatively low birth-rate in nineteenth-century France is to connect it with the system of landholding. A settled peasant population, owning its own farms, has a strong incentive to restrict the size of the family. Openings outside agriculture are limited; younger children can only be provided for by dividing the family holding—that is to say, at the expense of the elder.[1] Consider the contrast between this situation and that in the New World. American population could increase as rapidly as it did between 1800 and 1840 because parents needed to feel no responsibility for providing careers for their children; the career provided itself—'out West'. There was nothing to stop population from expanding at a fabulous pace.

Something of the same unlimited opportunity was provided in a more sordid way by the Industrial Revolution in England. Children became wage-earners at an early age; it cost parents very little trouble to ensure that their children had as good prospects in life as the parents had had themselves—though these prospects were often poor enough in all conscience. But as the standard of living (and in particular the standards of education) improved, the responsibilities of bringing up a family increased very markedly. The first dip in the English birth-rate is suspiciously contemporaneous with the early Factory Acts, which limited the employment

[1] This explanation may well be confirmed by the recent rise in the birth-rate in France. For with increasing industrialization, the proportion of the population to which it would apply has clearly been falling.

of children in industry. The later, and more permanent, decline follows upon the introduction of compulsory education. We cannot prove a connection, but it would not be surprising if the additional burden on the parents, due to their having to support their children up to the age of 14, without getting much in exchange even in the way of help about the home, had a good deal to do with the decline in the birth-rate. Elementary education may be free in itself, but children cannot take advantage even of elementary education unless they are properly brought up by their parents; it costs money (with the improvement in standards, it costs more than it did) to bring them up properly.

The reasons for the fall in the birth-rate still have a good deal of mystery about them, but this is at least one possible explanation so far as Britain is concerned. Something like it may hold for the other countries on our list, which (as we have seen) have had more or less the same experience. But we should notice that if this is the explanation, there is nothing inevitable about it; it will not enable us to say of any country that, because the death-rate has fallen, therefore the birth-rate *must* fall later on.

4. Discussion of population changes in terms of birth-rates and death-rates, though it remains useful for giving us a general idea of the problem, is nowadays thought to be a bit old-fashioned; and it is the fact that, without much trouble, one can do a good deal better. It is indeed more possible to make reasonably accurate prognostications about the future in matters of population than it is in most human affairs. This is because of the simple fact that all those people who will be over 20 years of age in twenty years' time are alive now; thus (apart from immigration) we can set an upper limit to the adult population of any country twenty years hence with complete confidence. On the basis of this known fact a good deal more about that future population can be guessed with some assurance. Thus we cannot tell how many babies will be born during the next twenty years; but we do know how many females, now living, are due to pass through the child-bearing age during the next twenty years—and that has a great deal to do with the number of births.

In order to estimate the future population of England, we do not just continue the birth-rate and death-rate curves in the way they are proceeding on the chart, and conclude that there is a prospect of a fairly slow increase, because the two curves are not far apart. We can do a great deal better than that, for we have additional information in the age-distribution of the present population.

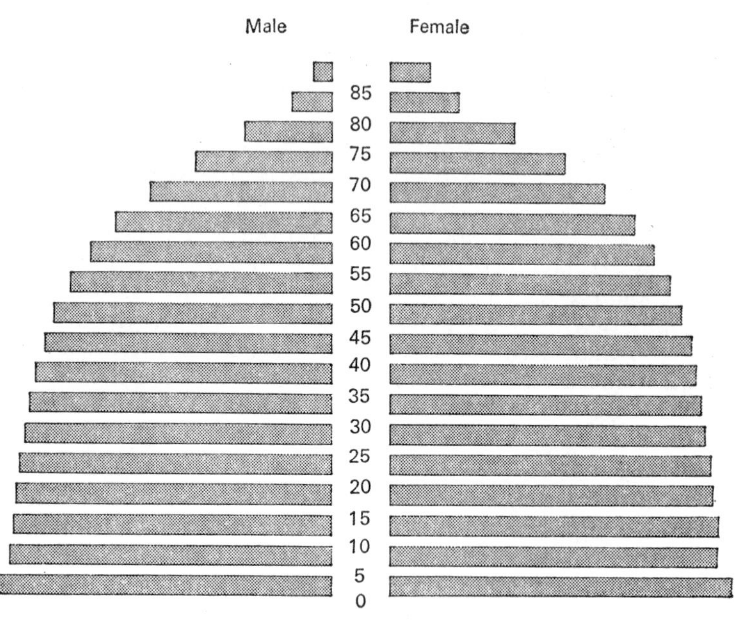

CHART IIA

The population of any country at any date can be divided into age-groups, so many 10-year-olds, so many 11-year-olds, and so on. In a completely stationary population with no migration, where the same number of births had taken place every year for the previous seventy years, these age-groups would form a descending series, with rather fewer persons in each age-group than in the one before it (because a certain number of people die at every age). A typical age-distribution for a stationary population of this sort is shown in Chart IIA.

If now this population began to increase by extra births, the new generations coming into the junior age-groups would be larger than the older generations were when they came in; consequently the beehive would begin to swell at the bottom, the lower strips growing in size relatively to the others. As time went on, this swelling would travel upwards; but if the

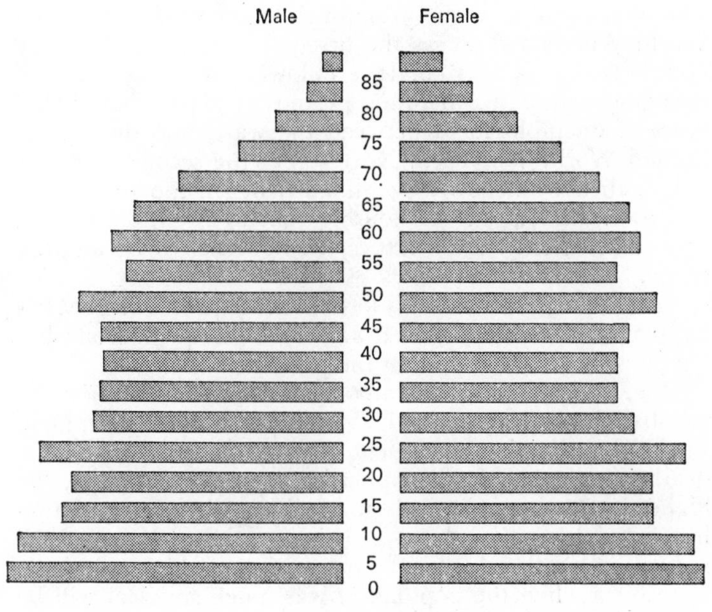

CHART IIB

number of births went on increasing, the numbers in the lower age-groups would still be disproportionately high relatively to those in the higher age-groups. The slope of the beehive would be distinctly flattened as compared with the stationary case, so that the beehive would be more like a regular pyramid.

Chart IIB shows the actual age-distribution of the English population in 1969. Some of the upper age-groups show this 'flattening' effect quite clearly, for they still reflect the rapid increase of population before 1910. But the fall in the birth-rate has diminished the numbers in the other age-groups; though the two lowest age-groups are quite large enough to support a stationary population of the present size, some of those in the middle are relatively rather small. The English age-distribution is far from being a beehive or pyramid; it bulges in some places and is dented in others. There is a dent for the people in the 50–55 age-group; these are the people who were born between 1914 and 1919, the years of the First World War. Then comes the first post-war bulge, aged by now between 45 and 50. It is followed by a big dent, all the age-groups between 25 and 45; those who were born in the years of unemployment between the wars, and during the Second World War itself. Next comes the second post-war bulge; then what now looks like a dent (in the 10–20 age-group)—was this due to housing shortage?—while finally, with those born in the sixties, there seems to be another bulge.

An age-distribution of this sort is a consequence of what has happened in the past; but it has its own consequences on what happens, or may happen, in the present.

One, which is of great importance in some countries (as we shall be seeing) and which was probably important in England earlier in the present century, is an effect on the death-rate. The older a population is, on the average, the higher its death-rate is likely to be. Thus when a population has for a long time been growing rapidly, that in itself reduces its death-rate; for the proportion of old people (who were born when the population was much smaller) will be abnormally low. And this continues to be so for some time after the rapid rise slows up. Later on, it may well be that there is a contrary tendency; but even that, in the English case, is probably past (or passing). For the date in English history when the number of births was at its maximum was 1900; and people who were born in 1900, and are still alive, are 70 years old.

A much more important effect—a still important effect—is the effect on the birth-rate. The number of births in any period depends upon the number of potential mothers then living, and on the average number of births from each potential mother. Consequently even if the ordinary size of the family remains the same, the number of births will be low if the number of potential mothers is low; and this is probably one of the reasons for the low level of births in the fifties. The number of women in England and Wales between 20 and 40 was 6·7 million in 1930 and 6·8 million in 1940; but in 1951 it was only 6·3 million, and it had fallen to less than 6 million in 1960. (This, of course, was a result of the 'dent'.) In the later sixties—twenty years after the post-war bulge—there has been a (presumably temporary) recovery; but it comes too late to explain the larger births of the sixties, which started a good deal earlier.

What are we to make of these considerations? During the nineteen-thirties, when the birth-rate was at its lowest (and even later, when it was reasonable to suspect that the post-war bulge was a mere flash in the pan), the conclusion which was widely drawn was rather startling. The gap between birth-rate and death-rate was already narrow; age-distribution indicated that a rise in the death-rate and a fall in the birth-rate were in prospect; surely, under their combined effect, the pincers would close, the rise in population (already slow) would stop, and even (for that is what the figures seemed to show) would pass over to a decline. That is how things looked when earlier editions of this book were written; it was in that expectation that I originally wrote this chapter. But now (1970) things look different. For the fact is that we have already come to the time when, according to the earlier 'projections', the death-rate should be exceeding the birth-rate, and population should be falling. And it has not happened. The forces pulling down the birth-rate (on account of age-distribution) are at work; they are making the birth-rate lower than it would be otherwise. But they have not been strong enough to make the curves cross over, and it does not now seem likely that they will be. Improvements in medical skill have prevented the death-rate from rising; a slight increase in family size has kept the birth-rate above what it was in the thirties and fifties, in spite of the low number of potential mothers. Thus the outlook is now for a continuance of increase—not at all rapid in the seventies—rather more rapid thereafter. Of course, the further ahead one looks, the more doubtful these guesses become. All one can say is that on present tendencies, decline no longer looks probable; but neither is there the slightest reason to expect a return to the headlong increase which occurred in the nineteenth century.[1]

That is the British story; it peters out, it may perhaps be thought, into something which does not seem so very interesting. The British population, after a great disturbance, seems to be settling down not to stationariness, but to a rate of increase that is fairly moderate. The same would hold, more or less, for many others of the 'developed' countries also. But there are other parts of the world where the settling down is far less advanced, or indeed has hardly begun. These are the countries where population is (now) a real problem.

5. I can do no more than give a few examples. Table III gives the same (twentieth century) information as Tables I and II, for three of the more populous countries not so far

TABLE III

	Population (in millions)			*Annual rate of increase (per thousand)*	
	1900	1950	1969	1900–50	1950–69
Japan	44	83	102	13	11
India, Pakistan	280	433	660	9	25
Mexico	14	25	47	10	34

considered. I have chosen countries where frontier changes are not considerable (the partition of India can be dealt with by taking India and Pakistan together), where migration has not been considerable (emigration from India and Pakistan has been minute in comparison with the enormous populations of those countries), and where the figures are fairly reliable. (There must indeed be reservations about the 1969 figure for India and Pakistan; but it can hardly be sufficiently in error for the rate of increase since 1950 to be seriously wrong.)

[1] The official prognostication is that England and Wales which had a population of 49 million in 1969 will reach 60 million by 2000. That is how things seem to look at present.

The Japanese expansion, over the whole period since 1900, has been rapid by European standards (though not quite so rapid as the increase, during the same time, in the United States). But there is an appreciable slowing up after 1950; and this is in fact a more important change than it looks. The rise from 1900 to 1950 was of the same type as the (much earlier) rise in England, a fall in the death-rate with a birth-rate which for a while did not follow; but the fall in the birth-rate did come, and when it came it was rather sudden. As late as 1950, the Japanese birth-rate was at 27; by 1960, it was no more than 17; actually within the European 'band'. But because of the rapid increase in the past, the still fairly recent past, the proportion of old people is low, so that the death-rate is low (only 7 against 11 in England). We may be fairly sure that that will not last; but the gap between birth-rate and death-rate is still sufficient, for the present, to keep up an expansion at what, in 'Western' terms, is a more than normal rate.

Little that is reliable is known about Indian death-rates, but it would certainly appear that they are still quite high (perhaps about 20). Yet there has been a fall, from something much higher; a fall which has occurred since 1945, with improvements in medicine, especially in the control of malaria. This is a *new* thing in India, so India is at the stage (if it is a stage) when the death-rate has fallen, but the birth-rate has not come down. In India, as in Mexico, the birth-rate seems still to be running at 40 or over. But in Mexico, a much richer country, the death-rate is rather low (it is supposed to be no more than 11 per thousand, showing the 'old people' effect very clearly). So the rate of increase in Mexico is even greater than the Indian.

It is indeed in countries such as these last—and there are many that are more or less like them—that the population problem of the world is at its most acute. Death is 'controlled', but birth is 'uncontrolled'; so population spurts. The death-rate has been brought down by a (really very sudden) medical revolution; but of the fall in the birth-rate, which should restore a balance, there is (so far) little sign. It is much to be hoped that it will follow on the same lines as elsewhere, but it is by no means certain that we can count on the same process working itself out. And even if it does, it will still be necessary to reckon with the hangover, such as is being experienced in Japan. The consequences which may be expected from this are one of the matters which we shall be exploring in the next chapter.

CHAPTER V The Economics of Population

1. There have been two occasions in history when economists have found themselves devoting particular attention to the problem of population. One was at the beginning of the nineteenth century, when it was first possible to recognize that the population of some countries (especially Britain) was growing at a remarkably rapid rate; the other a generation ago, when the populations of most Western countries seemed to have finished their upward surge, and it was suddenly recognized that there was a possibility of decline. Though the decline has not occurred (and does not now seem so likely to occur), it was a stimulus to thinking when it was thought that it might happen. So it is easy to understand that T. R. Malthus, with whose *Essay on Population* (1798) serious discussion of the population problem really begins, should have been profoundly troubled by the perils of population becoming too large, through a rise in numbers proceeding unchecked; while the 'stagnationists' of the nineteen-thirties were more inclined to emphasize the opposite danger, of population becoming too small, or getting smaller. One can also understand how in more recent years, with the prospects of population change in Western countries becoming less dramatic, and the focus of interest shifting to the expansion of population that is going on in the tropics, Malthus has returned to his own. There are possible dangers in each direction; each has to be considered.

Long before systematic economic thought began to develop, these dangers were noted: 'the one part through the small number of inhabitants becometh desolate, and the other being overcharged, oppressed with poverty.'[1] The dangers of under-population (too small a population for economic efficiency) and of over-population (too large a population) are both real dangers, though they arise from different causes. The studies which have been made in the subject, both in the time of Malthus and in our own day, have enabled us to appreciate these dangers much more precisely.

2. To begin with the case of under-population. It is easy to appreciate how it is possible for a country to be under-populated if one considers the case of a small colony, with few people and poor communications. Such a colony, obliged to satisfy its own wants by its own labour, could hardly fail to be miserably poor; for the organization of its economic system would be inevitably rudimentary and unproductive. It would be hampered by fewness of numbers in two different ways. In the first place, there might be things which would badly need doing, but could not possibly be done by a small number of workers. Such things as the building of bridges over large rivers would be physically impossible; the building of a railway between two distant places might not be impossible physically, but would be impossible practically, because it would take so long that the makers could hardly hope to live to see the fruit of their labours. But a much more important disadvantage would be the limit imposed upon specialization. The high efficiency of modern industry comes about very largely as a result of specialization; workers are specialized to particular jobs, and as a result they acquire great dexterity at those jobs; their efficiency is further increased by their use of highly specialized equipment. Very little of this specialization would be possible in a small colony with a few thousand inhabitants. It would be useless for people to specialize themselves on the sort of operations needed to produce motor-cars on a large scale if the maximum number of motor-cars which could be sold in a year was a few dozen. With so limited a market for their products, the motor-car manufacturers would spend most of their time standing idle,

[1] Machiavelli, *History of Florence* (in Tudor Translations series, p. 70).

with the result that they would actually use their time more productively if they spent it in tilling the soil. But for the same reason the methods of cultivation used would have to be of a primitive character; modern agriculture, with its use of machinery and fertilizers, is itself dependent upon large-scale industry; tractors and harvesters could not be produced if only a few could be sold in a year. The same would be the case for nearly every specialized occupation one could think of; a small isolated community could only produce in unspecialized and consequently primitive ways. In the technical language of economic theory, it would be unable to take advantage of the *economies of large-scale production*.

These disadvantages of under-population are in fact experienced even today by small communities in out-of-the-way places, though they are greatly moderated by the opportunity of trading with the outside world. Trading enables the small community to specialize in suitable lines, even although it is unable to sell at home all it produces in these lines; for it can sell its surpluses abroad, receiving in exchange for them things which it would have been unable to produce at home, or (and this is even more important) larger quantities of things which it could have produced at home in smaller quantities if it had not sought for the advantages of employing its labour in specialized ways. Sometimes the disadvantages of a small population can be completely overcome by this means; but the cost of transporting goods to and from distant countries is sometimes too great for it to be possible to carry specialization through foreign trading very far. The costs of transporting goods from one area to another are often artificially increased by the protective policies of governments. For the sake of national security governments may not like their peoples to become too specialized; but specialization is a condition of maximum productivity, so that the division of the world into an increasing number of national states (whatever may or may not be its political advantages) is liable to be a considerable drag on economic progress.

3. The dangers of over-population spring from a different source. As we have seen, the greater part of production takes place by the combination of labour with capital equipment. If population increases, the factor of production labour becomes more plentiful; and this will usually enable the total amount of goods and services produced to be increased. But the increase in population also involves an increase in the wants which have to be satisfied; the extra workers have to be fed and clothed and housed, so that unless the increase in production is proportional to the increase in population, the average standard of living will fall. (That is to say, if population increases by 2 per cent, the people will be poorer *on the average*, unless total production increases by at least 2 per cent at the same time. If production increases by less than 2 per cent, the *average productivity* of the workers is diminished by the increase in their numbers.)

It is probable that an increase in population will be attended by a fall in average productivity, if the increase in the factor of production labour is not accompanied by an increase in the factor of production capital. For if this happens, the same amount of capital equipment will have to be shared out amongst a larger number of workers; each of them, therefore, will have on the average a smaller amount of equipment to work with. Sharing specialized equipment is of course a very awkward business; it is probable that in the first instance many of the extra workers could only be taken on as 'helpers'. At a later stage, when equipment wears out and comes to be replaced, it may be possible to replace it in forms which make better use of the extra labour. But so long as it is a matter of squeezing the extra workers into a productive system which is not really any better provided with equipment, the amount of goods produced is not likely to increase in the same proportion as the labour force has increased—excepting in cases when the larger supply of labour enables new economies of exceptional importance to be derived from specialization.

This is in principle the way in which the danger of over-population arises; as population increases, its average productivity may fall, because of the lack of a similar expansion in capital equipment. But over-population will arise only if capital equipment fails to expand sufficiently. Quite apart from the question of specialization, it is often possible to overcome the shortage of equipment by increasing the supply. If this can be done, the danger of over-population disappears.

There is, however, one particular sort of capital equipment which is not capable of being increased by human agency to any appreciable extent; it is agricultural land.[1] A community which runs short of land can sometimes overcome the shortage by seizing land from its neighbours; apart from military action of that sort, very little can be done to remedy a shortage of land, though up to a point the evil can be moderated by using the land more economically, or by making improvements in its quality. So long as a country's population remains small, relatively to the size of its territory, there is not likely to be any shortage of land; there may be land of good quality which remains uncultivated. The danger of over-population arises when the best land is already being intensively cultivated, so that extra food for extra mouths can only be secured by scratching at stony soils, or pushing the boundary of cultivation higher and higher up mountain-sides. The reality of such over-population (at least within certain localities) will be appreciated by anyone who has seen the congested districts of western Ireland, or watched the Italian peasant cultivating a little pocket of ground perched among cliffs in his congested area near Naples. India and China contain between them one-half of the human race; large parts of their peoples are living in abject poverty, because immense populations are concentrated in small areas, and have to feed themselves from those areas. Over-population through shortage of land is one of the great causes of the poverty there is in the world.

4. In the light of this terrible possibility, the over-population scare of the early nineteenth century becomes readily intelligible. The British population was increasing at an alarming rate, doubling itself in half a century; how (asked Malthus and his followers) would it be possible to feed so vast a population from the limited area of the island? At that time little assistance was got from imports; the shortage of

[1] It was for this reason that nineteenth-century economists used to reckon lands as a third factor of production, alongside labour and capital, instead of regarding it as a particular kind of capital equipment, which is what we have decided to do.

land was a real nightmare. There seemed to be no way of avoiding a future in which all the luxuries and conveniences of life would have to be sacrificed to the dire necessity of getting bread; and when at last even bread might be lacking. If the rise in population continued, that was the fate which appeared to be in store sooner or later.

As we know, this fate has been avoided. The British population is now more than five times what it was in 1800, yet it is in less danger than it was at that time of suffering from want of food. But the fact that the fears of the Malthusians were not realized does not mean that they were idle. Malthus had discerned a real peril; England avoided it, but it was not avoided in another case closely parallel to England's—in the case of Ireland.

At the time when Malthus was writing, the Irish population was half the size of the English, and it was growing at much the same rate. But in the Irish case the growth of population began to be checked after 1820, and checked by shortage of food. Ireland experienced a series of famines, which culminated in the great famine of 1846. Today the Irish population is less than one-tenth of the size of the English.

How was it that England avoided the danger to which Ireland succumbed? If England had been obliged to support her population entirely from her own soil, there can be little doubt that England would have experienced a similar disaster before the nineteenth century was over. In fact, in the years before improvements in ocean transport made it easy to import foodstuffs on a great scale, food in England was very scarce; the Corn Law agitation was the sign of a real scarcity, the premonitory symptom of what might have grown into a much greater calamity. As it was, the cheapening of transport made it possible for the English people to draw upon the ample supplies of agricultural land in the New Worlds of America and Australia, and so to remedy their own shortage. But how was it possible for the English people to save themselves in this way, and not possible for the Irish to do so as well?

The reason is that imports have to be paid for. If the agricultural land available in England was becoming small relatively to the population, England possessed other natural resources, in the form of coal and other minerals, which were absent in Ireland, and she was continually adding to her man-made equipment, her factories and mines, her ships and her railways. All these resources enabled her to produce a plenty of goods which she could exchange against foodstuffs from overseas. Although she was short of agricultural land, her capital equipment as a whole was continually increasing. The things which she could produce with this equipment were most of them unsuitable for satisfying the basic need for food, but that difficulty could be removed by trading with other countries. Yet she would have been unable to remove it so easily if her general productive power had not been increasing at such a rapid pace.

5. When the matter is looked at in this way, it suggests a conclusion of very wide significance. As the problem appeared to the Malthusians, shortage of agricultural land was an insuperable obstacle; when once the population of any country had reached the point where shortage of land becomes acute, the people would be bound to suffer from poverty, poverty which could only be remedied by the population becoming smaller.[1] Today, as a result of the improvements in transport which have taken place, it is no longer so serious as it was that the population of a particular country has grown very large in relation to its land supply. Such over-population can be remedied by industrialization, by an increase in the amount of capital equipment—in those kinds of equipment that can be increased by human effort. The food which cannot be grown at home can then be imported in exchange for manufactured exports.

Nevertheless, so far as the major over-populated countries of the world are concerned, this is hardly a likely solution. It is of much more importance, for them, that there have been other improvements, as well as improvements in transport. There have been direct improvements in agriculture—improvements in breeding, of plants and animals, and a notable improvement in the control of pests; these have made it fairly easy to raise far more food from a fixed supply

[1] A more modern version of this Malthusian argument is discussed in Appendix, Note B.

of land than was possible in the nineteenth century or in the early twentieth. These improvements are available to everyone; it is the more advanced countries which (as might be expected) have gone furthest in their use, but their impact on the rest has also been considerable. They could provide a way out.

So far, indeed, that has rarely happened. All that has so often happened is that more people are being supported on the same land. Their total production is greater, but their average production is no greater or very little greater. This is what must have been happening in countries such as India and Mexico (for which I gave figures). The improvements do explain why population has been able to increase, as we have seen that it has increased, without being checked by sheer starvation. But they do no more than that.

It is indeed by no means clear that in order to produce the extra food, the extra people are needed. Sometimes, no doubt, their labour is needed; the better methods require extra care, and that means more labour. But one suspects that there are very many cases in which this is not so, so that the extra people are mere hangers-on. Now in an increasing population, the extra people will at first be children, whom their parents will expect to support; later on, they will be brothers and sisters, who (in countries where family feeling is very strong) will also be, fairly readily, supported; but, even then, will the same be true when they are no more than cousins? This passage of generations is going on all the time; so that a continuing rise in population, even while there is some continuing agricultural improvement, is likely to lead in the end to unemployment and destitution.

There is a race—between productivity and population. When population wins, or when neither of them draws ahead, what has just been described is very likely to happen; only when productivity draws decisively ahead (either by very rapid increase in productivity, or by a slowing-up of the population increase) can we be sure that the vicious circle will be broken. For once the point is reached when those remaining in agriculture are producing enough for their own needs and have something over, there is a surplus which can be sold to people outside agriculture; people can then be employed outside agriculture, for the food will be there, on which they can spend that essential part of their wages. Until this point is reached they cannot be so employed, on any considerable scale. Only when it is reached does the increase in population cease to be a menace.

In the more advanced countries, this point has, of course, been reached; in most of them it was already reached many decades ago. In Japan (and perhaps in Italy) it has not been reached for very long; but that they are past it now there can be no doubt. Either from their own production, or from what they can import (and can pay for), their food supplies are ample; not merely sufficient to support their farmers, but enough to support, outside agriculture, what has become the greater part of their populations. Their rates of increase are now, as we have seen, no more than moderate; the feeding of that moderate increase presents no problem.

Against the background of what is happening in countries such as India, the increase of population in Britain (or in Western Europe as a whole) is a matter of secondary importance. So far as it goes, we can even admit some truth in the view that was commonly expressed at the time of the 'declining population' scare of the thirties—that, for a country which can easily feed itself (by production or trade) and is rich enough to be able to increase its equipment at a rapid rate from its own resources, the balance of advantage (from that country's point of view) may well be on the side of an increasing population. Quite apart from the economies of large-scale production, the increase in population affords a stimulus to investment; new houses have to be produced for the extra people to live in, new machines to make clothes and other conveniences for them, and so on. A considerable part of the labour force in such progressive countries will be specialized on the production of such investment goods; this means (paradoxically enough) that it is actually easier to maintain employment (prevent unemployment) when population is increasing. It is not impossible that slowing-up of population increase may have been one of the things responsible for the exceptional unemployment which occurred during the nineteen-thirties; this is particularly plausible in the case of the United States. Declining population might actually involve such a country in greater difficulties on the side of production than would arise from further increase.

Such narrowly economic considerations are of course not the only ones which have to be taken into account. Although, in the case of England, we are not seriously incommoded in peace-time by the limited amount of agricultural land available in our island, we are incommoded by pressure of population in other ways. Great Britain can only support her present population of 54 million people if at least half of those people will live in great cities, enjoying certain advantages (it is true) from being so close together, but in other ways being decidedly cramped. I was already asking, in the first edition of this book (1942), whether it would still be true, if the bulk of the people possessed motor-cars, that there was room for 50 million people on the island. Now (in 1970) that point has just about been reached; and we manage. But we are becoming very well aware that we are faced, in that way and in several other ways, with what we call 'congestion'. This itself is a population problem; but it does not compare with what was here in the past, and over so much of the world is still in the present, rightly regarded as the problem of population.

CHAPTER VI The Specialization of Labour

1. Population is only the first of the economic problems connected with labour as a factor of production. The contribution of labour to the productive process depends in the first place upon the number of workers, secondly on the kinds of work they can do, and thirdly on the effort they put into their work. We shall consider the second of these questions in the present chapter, and the third in the chapter that follows it.

We must begin, however, with some further remarks about numbers. The number of persons who work, or earn their living, in a particular country is always much less than the total population. Idleness (voluntary or involuntary) is responsible for no more than a small fraction of the difference; most of it is due to age and sex. One must begin by subtracting the children (in Britain no one under 15 can legally be working); then those over 65, most of whom in one way or another will be pensioned; so the main source of supply of the 'labour force' is to be found in those of ages 15–64. But from these there are also to be deducted those who are continuing their education, as well as a substantial proportion of the women in the middle age-group who have something else to do with their time than to spend it in earning their living.

Table IV shows the numbers of persons (male and female) in these three age-groups, as they have been[1] in Great

[1] These are the official figures, but it should be noticed that in strictness they are no more than estimates, derived from applying information about births, deaths, and migration to the censuses of 1951 and 1961. There is however no doubt that they are reliable, at least to the degree of approximation that we are using.

Britain (not including Northern Ireland) in 1957 and 1969. It also shows the numbers of both sexes who were reckoned as belonging to the 'working population' in the middle of each year (this includes those who happened to be unemployed at the date when the count was taken). As so often happens, there is much more to be learned from the comparison of two years than from the figures for a single year in isolation.

TABLE IV

Population of Great Britain (millions)

	1957		1969	
	Males	Females	Males	Females
Under 15	5·9	5·6	6·6	6·2
15–64	15·9	16·8	17·0	17·2
65 and over	2·3	3·5	2·6	4·2
Working population	16·2	8·0	16·2	9·0

It will be seen, first of all, that the number of persons in the important 15–64 age-group has behaved in what looks a very curious manner. The number of males has increased, over the twelve years, by more than a million; but the number of females by less than half as much. This is principally (but not entirely) a consequence of the wars, especially of the very heavy casualties in the First World War. It resulted from these casualties that the men between 55 and 65 in 1957 were abnormally few. But by 1969 these men had passed into the upper age-group; they had been replaced by men of an age which did not suffer these losses. So the balance of men and women in the group 15–64 was more normal in 1969 than it was in 1957.

It is still more remarkable, when this is understood, to find that the *working population* has moved in quite a different way. There has been no increase in the number of males in the working population, while the number of females has increased by a million. When we look at 1957, we find that there were actually more males in the working population than there were in the age-group 15–64; those who were continuing their education must have been more than matched by those over 65 who were continuing working.

In 1969 this is totally changed. With the expansion of secondary and higher education, the number of those whose entry into the labour force is delayed has increased; while the number of those who continue working beyond a pensionable age has clearly diminished.[1] These checks to the supply of men to the working population have indeed been matched by an increase in the supply of women (many of whom, however, will have been part-timers). Men and women do not, at all conveniently, do just the same jobs; though there are many that can be done by either, there are some where men are clearly better, and some where women are clearly better. Since the proportion of women in the labour force has thus been rising, we should not be surprised to find that the proportion of women's jobs has been rising too.

2. To give a complete list of all the occupations pursued by different people in a country like Great Britain would require a volume considerably larger than the present.[2] But it will be useful to indicate some broad groups, such as are shown (for 1957 and, in this case, 1968) in Table V.

There are several important facts about the British economy (both about its permanent characteristics and about the way in which it is changing) which emerge from this table.

One is impressed, first of all, by the smallness of the numbers engaged in the 'extractive' industries—agriculture and mining. Even in 1957 they represented *together* no more than 8 per cent of the total; since then they have fallen further,

[1] Closer examination suggests that these fairly obvious considerations are by no means the whole story. There is a curious tendency for much of the fall in the *proportion* of the male population which is recorded as working (or seeking work) to be concentrated in the age-groups 25–39 (not in 20–24, or in 40–60). A fall in these age-groups cannot be explained by continuing education, or by early retirement. It is not easy to find an explanation which does not reflect upon the reliability of the figures. While the numbers of (normally) employed persons in the working population are known fairly accurately, from the records of National Insurance, the numbers of the 'self-employed' can only be estimated and the estimates are to some extent uncertain. It would not be surprising if it should turn out (when the Census of 1971 has been analysed) that the numbers of the self-employed are larger than has been supposed. The apparent stationariness of the male working population might then be changed into a small increase. But the increase could hardly be large enough to affect the general impression.

[2] The most complete list is that given in the 'Occupations' volume of the Census report.

TABLE V

Estimated[1] distribution of working population (hundreds of thousands)

	1957	1968
Agriculture	10	8
Mining (chiefly coal-mining)	9	5
Manufacturing	88	87
Building and contracting	15	16
Gas, water, electricity	4	4
Transport (including post office)	17	16
Administration (national and local)	13	14
Armed forces	7	4
Distributive trades	30	33
Other services (including professions)	47	60
Unemployed	3	5
Total	242	252

to little more than 5 per cent. A fall in the proportion of the population which is engaged in agriculture is a common experience; one finds it in many countries, all over the continent of Europe, in the United States, and in Japan. It is chiefly a consequence of mechanization. It has actually been less rapid in Britain, during the last ten years, than in many other countries; for the contraction in the agricultural population which is occurring now on the continent, had occurred in Britain previously. But the smallness of the farm population in Britain was not only due to the efficiency of British agriculture (though that was a factor); it was also due to the British practice of importing a large part of the nation's food. There was a time when that food was paid for by exporting another of the products of the land—namely coal; but coal has been displaced by oil, so that fuel

[1] I have based this table on the 'Distribution of Working Population' tables in the *Annual Abstracts of Statistics*; but the reader should be warned that some adjustments have had to be made to the tables there published, in order that the figures for the two years should be comparable. Thus the published figures for 1968 give employees only divided among the industries, 1,600,000 'employers and self-employed' being shown as a separate entry; in 1957 these people were attributed to the industries in which they were supposed to be working. I have divided them up, for 1968 also, on the basis of such indications as were available. One also finds, when one looks at the figures closely, that 300,000 people working in garages were reckoned as belonging to the motor trades (and so manufacturing)in 1957, but have been moved to 'other services' in 1968. I have put them (and some others that have been similary re-classified) in 'other services' at both dates. These are typical trials of those who work with published statistics.

as well as food comes in as an import. The great manufacturing sector, exports from which have to pay for the food and the fuel that are imported, is now itself very largely dependent on imported materials.

There appears, from the table, to be a (much smaller) reduction, between our two dates, in the number of people working in the manufacturing sector itself. It should however be noticed that industry was much more prosperous in 1957 than in 1968, as is indicated (in the table) by the number of unemployed. In 1957 the number of unemployed was very low—nearly as low as it has been in any year since 1945. (It will never vanish altogether, in the statistics, for people reckon as unemployed when they are only changing jobs.) If one just deals out the extra unemployed among the various groups, in proportion to those shown in the groups, one raises the number in the manufacturing group from 87 to 88, but has little visible effect on most of the smaller sectors.

The fact is, indeed, that when all the 'middle' industries (manufacturing, building, transport, and so on) are taken together, the labour force engaged in them is very steady. There is a (relatively) large reduction in the number in the forces—but we need not discuss that, for it is a political not an economic story. The striking *rises* are in the Distributive Trades, and (much more) in the final entry, which I have labelled 'other services'.

That there should be *some* rises in these occupations is (to the economist) not at all surprising. There is a tendency in this direction in all advanced countries, especially when they are experiencing rapid technical improvements. The general reason is that as productivity increases, in manufacturing as in agriculture, more goods can be produced even though less labour is employed in producing them. But though there are such technical improvements in the service trades, which are not to be overlooked (the telephone and the typewriter, at least, have undoubtedly effected great technical improvements), such improvements are much less important than they are in manufacturing industry. So the supply of services does not increase, to match the increase in the supply of goods, unless more people are employed in the service trades.

This probably accounts for a part of the expansion in the

service trades that is shown in the table. But it cannot account for more than a part of it, perhaps quite a small part. There are quite clearly, other forces at work.

One of them is easily identified. Much the largest part of the expansion in employment in 'other services' is an expansion in the *social* services—education and health. We have seen that the remarkable change-round in the number of males, in the 15–64 age-group, who are *not* in the working population, is partly to be explained by the expansion in education; if they are being taught, someone must be teaching them. When we look for the teachers, here they are. The number of persons employed in educational services has risen by 500,000 between our two dates; those employed in medical services by 400,000. So these, when taken together, actually account for most of the rise in 'other services'. We are left with a rise of about 400,000, not much more than the rise in the Distributive Trades.

Even with regard to this remaining rise, there is a further point. We saw (it will be remembered) that the whole of the rise in the total labour force between our two dates was a rise of one million in female labour. Must it not be here, in the expansion of the Distributive Trades, and in the remaining 'other services', that a large part of that additional female labour has found employment? Some of them, no doubt, will be teachers, some nurses; some will have found employment in other industries. But it is here, at this end of the table, that 'women's jobs' are likely to be come by most easily. This is where we should expect to find that most of the women have been fitted in.[1]

3. What we have just been doing is what used to be called (during the Second World War) 'man-power budgeting'.

[1] From information at present available, this is only a conjecture. But it is curiously confirmed by the figures that are given in the Abstract of Statistics for the age-distribution of female labour. The striking increase is in the number of older women (40–65) who are now in the working population. Useful as these ladies doubtless are, most of them must surely be part-time workers, and the range of jobs for which they are suited must be rather narrow.

If it is the case (as it seems consistent with the figures that it should be) that the expansion of employment in the Distributive Trades has taken the form of replacing full-time men by part-time elderly women, the expansion itself would be rather illusory.

Like the other budgets to which we shall be coming in Part IV, it is a useful way of summarizing the resources (or a part of the resources) that are at the disposal of the nation, and which can be devoted, in various ways, to its various purposes. It is the simplest of all the budgets, and by no means the least revealing.

Yet less is heard of it in peace than in war-time; and one can see why. For it is only in war, in modern war, that the size of the working population, and its distribution among occupations, has been directly controlled. It is only in war that governments have taken power to say to their people 'you shall work at this—you shall not work at that'; and that is what is needed if the distribution of labour among occupations is to be a thing that government can decide. Even Communist governments, which take great power to themselves, have usually avoided taking this extreme power, in conditions of peace. If it does not have this power, a government can only influence occupational distribution indirectly; it is then through other budgets that it must mainly work.

It is nevertheless at all times a matter of great importance for the economic organization of a community that its working population should be divided among occupations in an efficient, or at least fairly efficient, way. This means not only that there should be the right number of workers in each occupation, but that the qualities of the workers in each occupation should be as appropriate as possible—that people having particular capabilities should be in the positions where they can make the best use of their powers. Now it is obvious that if each person worked in the occupation which he himself preferred to follow, just because he had a liking for that particular sort of work, this desirable distribution would not be reached; there would be far too many people in the more popular occupations, far too few in the unpopular ones. Some sorts of goods or services would be produced in much larger amounts than were wanted, while the supplies of others (some of which might be necessities of life) would be grievously short. The distribution of labour among occupations cannot be left to be settled according to the preference of producers alone; the desires of consumers must also be taken into account. Since every producer is also a consumer, it is to everyone's interest that such an adjustment should be made.

There are two known methods of making the adjustment. One is the war-time method, the method of *compulsion*. The government just decides that more people are needed to work in a particular occupation; it then picks on certain people and compels them to transfer themselves where it wants them to go. There may well be no other way of coping with the immense *temporary* redistribution of occupations which is necessary in an emergency such as a modern war. But in more normal conditions, and for the making of more permanent adjustments, it is not simply oppressive; it is also inefficient.

What is the alternative? There is only one alternative, the method of *incentive*. People must be given an incentive, an incentive to transfer themselves—voluntarily—to those occupations where the supply of labour is short. The incentive may take various forms; certain kinds of labour have been attracted into the British Civil Service by the prospect of honours (such as knighthoods), while in Soviet Russia the 'shock brigades' used to be said to have the best chance of theatre tickets or of being sent on holidays. But the simplest form of incentive is to offer higher wages in those occupations where there is a scarcity of labour; people are encouraged to look for employment in those occupations where extra labour is wanted more urgently, in preference to occupations where extra labour is wanted less urgently, because they will be offered better wages in the former occupations.

Thus the use of the incentive method makes it almost inevitable that some people should get higher wages than others; but before we allow our sense of fairness to be outraged by these differences, we ought to look at the method of compulsion again. The method of compulsion is itself not beyond criticism on the score of fairness; and on other grounds it is distinctly inferior. Suppose that it is decided that 1,000 additional workers are wanted for some new trade, say the manufacture of computers; out of all the 20 million or so, who are working (with more or less regularity) at other occupations, which thousand is it that ought to be transferred? The ideal solution would be to find those particular 1,000 people who will at once be the most useful in the new occupation and the least useful in their old occupations, and who can also be transferred from one occupation to the other at least trouble to themselves. These three tests (it should be observed that they are distinct and different tests) will not always be satisfied by the same people; yet clearly there will be some people who will satisfy the tests reasonably well, and some who will satisfy them very badly indeed. Clearly it is desirable that the people who are to be transferred should satisfy the tests reasonably well—but how are such people to be discovered? If the method of compulsion is used without any adequate system of selection, then although the numbers transferred may be right, the choice of the particular people to be transferred will often be unsatisfactory. People will be transferred who would have been more useful at their old occupation, and also people for whom the transference involves exceptional hardship.[1] A means of selection is needed which will reduce the danger of these sorts of waste.

4. The great advantage of the incentive method is that it contains a means of selection within itself. When our computer manufacturer is looking for his 1,000 workers, he estimates first of all what wages will be necessary to attract 1,000 suitable people. The rates offered will of course have to be high enough to attract a good many more than 1,000 persons altogether; the suitable people will have to be picked out of a longer list. But this is the only part of the work of selection which has to be performed by the radio manufacturer himself and by his managers; all they have to do is to select, out of the applicants who present themselves, those who seem best fitted to do the work which is to be done. Of course even this is not an easy job; but it is a job which people who are themselves specialized in the management of that particular kind of work will be specially competent to perform.

[1] When the method of compulsion is used in war-time this sort of thing does of course happen; various more or less adquate devices have to be introduced in order to mitigate its consequences. Even so, these effects of compulsion are only tolerable because of the overmastering necessity of the tasks to which the labour is being transferred; they would be less tolerable in cases of less urgency.

They do not have to pay any attention to the other side of the selection; for the only people who will put in an application for work at a stated level of wages are people who consider that they will benefit themselves by getting employment on those conditions. There is thus no possibility of people being selected who would be involved in exceptional hardship by having to work at this job rather than at some other job which is open to them; such people will not apply. Nor is there much danger of people applying who are essential workers at other occupations; for if a worker who was really essential in his old job sought to change his occupation, his old employer would probably raise his wages, so as to make it worth his while to remain. It may indeed sometimes happen that a worker possesses some exceptional skill which makes both employers want him very badly; in that case he may be enticed away by the new employer offering even higher wages than the old employer would be prepared to offer. But if the new employer can only get this particular man by offering him exceptionally high wages, he has a strong inducement to do without him, if he can find any means of doing so; the method of incentive does give him an inducement to weigh up the urgency of his need against the need of the other employer, and not to take on a worker who is specially useful elsewhere unless he is also very specially useful in the new occupation.

The method of incentive has these advantages; if we consider how continually adjustments of this sort require to be made in a modern community, we shall appreciate how important these advantages are. Yet we must never forget that the use of the incentive method does involve inequality of incomes; it means that those people whose abilities are more urgently demanded will earn higher wages than those whose abilities are less urgently demanded. And this is not all; since there are frequent changes in the urgency of the demand for particular kinds of labour—sometimes it is one industry that is seeking to expand, and sometimes another—the differences in wages, which occur as a result of this competition for labour, do not stay put. Sometimes it is one group that is forging ahead, sometimes it is another. Now though it may well be maintained, on abstract grounds, or grounds of principle, that people *ought* to have equal wages, there is no doubt that people are more sensitive, in practice, to changes in inequality than they are to inequality itself. The man who earns £20 a week is more disturbed when his neighbour, who used to earn the same as himself, goes up to £25, than he is by the fact of the professional man earning five times as much as he does—a difference to which he is accustomed. Yet it is the former kind of inequality, the changing inequalities between not such very different incomes, which is probably the more important for the efficient working of the method of incentive.

For this and other reasons, modern communities rarely allow the incentive method of distributing labour to work unchecked, or without qualification; it only operates very roughly, and it sometimes seems that it is seizing up, hardly working at all. Nevertheless, as we have seen, even in the nineteen-sixties, there has been a quite considerable redistribution of labour in the British economy; it has clearly not come by compulsion, so it must have come about by some form of the incentive method.

5. The differences in individual skill, which are mainly responsible for the larger differences in wages and salaries, come about in three ways—from differences in natural ability, in training, and in experience. A man can only be made into a first-class doctor or a first-class engineer if he has natural gifts for that sort of work, and if he has been properly trained; but even then he will only be able to use his gifts and his training to the best advantage when he has had experience in using them. Both training and experience take time to acquire, shorter and longer times in different occupations; in 'semi-skilled' jobs a worker can become proficient in a few months, while in professional and administrative work even those people who have the best natural endowments may not reach the height of their powers save after years of training and longer years of practice.

When a man's skill has been built up by years of training or experience, it is probable that he will be very much better at doing the work for which he has been trained, or which he has learned by practice, than he will be for doing any other sort of work; unless he is given a very strong inducement to the contrary, the work to which he is accustomed is the work he will prefer to do. At any particular time a large part of the working population is specialized in this way on particular jobs; and the specialization looks so firm that the problem of distributing labour among right occupations hardly looks a real one. But that is not always so, since the number of people who are specialized in a particular occupation at a particular time may be greater or less than the number wanted. In England, already in the nineteen-twenties, there were too many coal-miners; as a result of the invention of more economical methods of using coal (by converting it into electricity, and so on) less coal was needed than before, and consequently fewer miners were needed. But while the coal industry was contracting somewhat, other industries were expanding; as a result of the improvements in motor-car manufacture, for example, more workers were needed in the motor industry than at any previous time. Not much could be done towards the necessary adjustment by transferring workers directly from mining to motor manufacture (the sorts of skill which were needed were too different); but workers were drawn into the motor trade from neighbouring industries, workers who did possess kinds of skill more or less similar; these in their turn were replaced by others, and so, by a long process of shifting round, the supply of labour was fitted to the demand, the incentive to transference operating, in spite of specialization. Economic history is full of transformations such as this; they involve apparent wastage of what looks like valuable skill, but they are one of the ways in which the economic system has adjusted itself to economic progress, and has therefore made that progress possible.

When the number of workers requiring to be transferred from one occupation to another is relatively small, the adjustment can, however, be made in a smoother and simpler manner. The people who are working in any occupation at any time will include beginners, as well as experienced workers; if it is only necessary for the beginners to move, a smaller amount of acquired skill has to be sacrificed. A smaller incentive will often be sufficient to induce beginners to move, than will be needed if mature workers have to be uprooted. It is by influencing the decisions of beginners, and of new entrants to industry, that the most painless method of adjusting the supply of trained labour to the demand for it is to to be found.

It is the most painless method, but it is necessarily a slow method; and it may well be questioned whether the British economy during the sixties (the period of the figures with which we began this chapter) has not been relying upon it overmuch. There has again, as we have seen, been a great reduction in the numbers of coal-miners, but it has not come about, to a similar extent, by transference; it has come by stoppage of intake, and by early retirement, removing the more elderly miners from the work force altogether. This is, of course, much better, for many of the people immediately concerned, than the alternative; but if it had been those who could be most useful elsewhere who had removed, the economy in general might well have been in a healthier—certainly a more productive—state. And the case of coal-mining is only one of the many cases in which something of the same kind appears to have been happening.

Nevertheless, slow as it is, redistribution of labour by re-direction of new entrants does work. When a boy is deciding what occupation to take up, he will certainly be influenced to a considerable extent by the sort of natural abilities he possesses (we most of us know very well that there are occupations we should never make a hand at, even in the most favourable circumstances); but in most cases he will also be influenced (or his parents will see that he is influenced) by the 'prospects' offered by the possible occupations—which 'prospect' is not only a matter of the wage which is offered at the moment, but is also concerned with the assurance of better wages when the job has been fully learned, and with the assurance of regular employment. These things are more likely to be secured in a trade where the demand for labour is expanding than in one where it is contracting; consequently careful decisions made on this basis do have the effect of directing labour towards those occupations where extra workers are most wanted.

There is, however, one other thing which has to be taken

into account. The occupations which offer the best 'prospects' are usually occupations which require a long training; it is not surprising that this should be so, since most of the highest degrees of skill can only be acquired by the combination of long training with natural ability, and the necessity of a long period of training is itself a reason why the supply of such kinds of labour should be scarce. As things were until a generation ago, the opportunity of undergoing the longer periods of education and training was only open to the children of wealthy parents—and this limitation made the supply of such trained labour even scarcer than it would have been otherwise. The expansion in secondary and higher education (which showed up so strongly in the figures we were examining) has, of course, done, and is doing, a great deal to widen these opportunities. As a result it will doubtless become less common for people to possess exceptional abilities but to be prevented from making use of those abilities by lack of training. But it will still be the case that the supply of persons with exceptional abilities will be less than what is needed for the most skilled and responsible positions; so that the gaps will be made up by people whose skill is mainly derived from their experience, and so, ultimately, from the luck that they have had in getting into positions from which they can derive that experience. This is not to deny that the greater availability of trained people will have a great effect—in the direction of greater equality; but the reorganization which will be needed, before that effect can work itself out, will not be an easy matter. The need for this reorganization is concealed, in the present, by the internal momentum of the educational expansion; however many graduates are turned out, there is always a demand for them, as teachers if as nothing else. But an expansion of this sort cannot continue indefinitely; it is bound, at the least, to have pauses. The time is bound to come when other openings, on a large scale, will have to be found.

6. The questions which we have been discussing in this chapter are obviously controversial; they are also difficult, and it is not pretended that they are by any means exhausted by what has been said here. A large part of that more advanced part of economics which is called the Theory of Value is taken up with the closer analysis of issues such as those we have been raising. But although we shall have to return to such issues now and again, a systematic study of the Theory of Value lies outside the scope of this book.

CHAPTER VII The Effort of Labour

1. We have now discussed the numbers of the working population and their skill; one further element in the contribution made by labour to the productive process remains to be dealt with—the effort which people put into their work. This is partly a question of the Hours of Labour, the proportion of their time which people spend in working; partly it is a question of effort in the narrower sense, of the energy and attention with which people work during their working hours. There are several economic questions which fall under each of these heads, questions which are particularly interesting from the standpoints of Industrial Relations and Labour Management. Only a few of them can be indicated very briefly here.

2. It is usually the case that people will produce more if they work harder, but this does not mean that they will necessarily produce more if they work longer hours. After a certain point the additional fatigue diminishes output. For any particular kind of work there will be a certain length of working day from which a greater output can be secured than from any other length. If the number of hours worked is less than this critical number, production will be cut down because the workers have less time to work in; if it is greater, production will also suffer, because the additional time is offset by the fatigue.

The possibility that the working day may be too long for efficiency of production was demonstrated in a fairly unmistakable manner at the time of the early Factory Acts; it is a lesson which continues to impress the modern student of economic history, as it impressed Karl Marx.[1] The modern industrialist rarely makes any mistake about the matter, except under the pressure of a sudden emergency. It has occasionally happened in war-time that those who are responsible for the direction of industry are unable to resist the temptation of endeavouring to increase production by lengthening hours, even when there is in reality nothing more to be gained in that direction; but it is unlikely that mistakes of this sort are often made when pressure is less extreme.

The number of hours actually worked in normal conditions is usually appreciably less than the number which would give the maximum output. For this there is a very good reason. When the working day is at its most productive length the fatigue which is imposed upon the worker is already nearly sufficient to cause a reduction in his output; it must therefore be already very considerable. It is not surprising that from their own point of view most workers would prefer to work rather shorter hours than this, and that they are even prepared to make some sacrifice in wages in order to get such a reduction in hours.

There has in fact been a notable shortening of the working week in most industrial countries during the last hundred years. During the eighteen-forties and -fifties it was the Ten-Hour Day which was the objective of labour pressure; by the time of the First World War it was the Eight-Hour Day; by the nineteen-thirties, the Eight-Hour Day having been widely secured, the objective had moved on to the Forty-Hour Week. It seems highly probable that the main explanation of this long-continued tendency towards shorter hours is to be found in the general rise in the standard of living which has taken place, more or less rapidly, over the whole period. As wages rise, people become prepared to make some sacrifice in wages in order to get a little more time in which to enjoy the fruits of their labour. An increased supply of amenities, and even luxuries, can give little satisfaction if there is a shortage of time in which to enjoy them. Time and again, as the process of rising standards goes on, a further shortening

[1] Marx, *Capital*, vol. i, ch. 10.

of the working week has become a thing which is even more urgently desired than a further rise in wages.

It is clear, on the other hand, that the conditions in which most industrial workers have to work are such as to make long hours particularly tiresome and trying. Those fortunate people whose work admits of much variety are not likely to mind very much how long they work; the only disadvantage which they get from working long hours is physical weariness. But when a man's work is very uniform and monotonous, his desire to have less of it may be very strong. It is not impossible that as people have become better educated, the irksomeness of factory labour has increased.

However this may be, there can be no doubt that the shortening of hours which has taken place during the last century (with some temporary set-backs during war emergencies) has been a great gain to labour; it is a gain which needs to be taken into account when measuring the economic progress achieved. The quantity of goods and services produced is not a sufficient measure of economic progress; if the same quantity of goods can be produced with a smaller expenditure of undesired effort, people will on the average be better off. Sometimes, even if there is a decline in the quantity of goods produced, the decline may be offset by a gain in leisure.

Instances of this sort do in fact occur. In 1919, at the end of the First World War, there was in most British industries a rather sudden reduction in the length of the working week, a reduction which generally proved to be lasting. (The typical change was from a working week of about 52 hours before 1914 to one of about 48 hours in 1919–39.) This reduction has to be taken into account when we are assessing the effect of the war upon the productivity of British industry. When we find, as we do find, that the quantity of goods produced per head was in all probability just a shade lower in 1924 than it was in 1911, we must not conclude that productivity was really any lower at the later date. If there was any decline in the amount produced, it was certainly less than what might have been expected from the reduction in hours. Economic progress had taken place, in spite of the war; but during those particular years the gain from economic progress had been deliberately taken out in the form of increased leisure.[1]

3. Much the same fundamental issues as arise in connection with the length of the working day arise also in connection with the effort and application of labour during working hours; but the form which they take in practice is somewhat different. Just as the worker, looking (quite properly) at the strain which is imposed upon him, will usually prefer to work for rather shorter hours than those which would best suit his employer from the point of view of production, so he will often (though not always) prefer to work during his working time with less intensity than his employer might desire. There is a real conflict here, which inevitably causes trouble, though we can see (when we look at the matter fairly) that it is not in the least discreditable to either party; it is a conflict more difficult to deal with than the parallel question about hours. For it is possible to make an agreement about hours, and to stick to that agreement over long periods; but the effort which a man puts into his work is liable to vary, even from day to day, for all sorts of personal reasons, so that it is much more difficult to come to an agreement about it. The resulting situation can be dealt with, more or less satisfactorily, in one or other of the following ways.

The best way is to awaken the worker's interest in his work to such an extent that the conflict of interest is reduced to a minimum. We have seen that when a man is interested in his work, and feels a responsibility towards it, he is not likely to mind very much how long he works; similarly, he will not mind how much trouble he takes when he is working. A good employer may be very successful in awakening such a sense of responsibility, though usually he will only do so if he himself takes a good deal of trouble in watching over the welfare of his employees. Nevertheless, the success with which this policy is likely to be attended depends very much upon the character of the work which is to be done; even the best

[1] The same thing has happened again, though in a rather less striking fashion, in the nineteen-sixties; there has been a reduction from the old 48, which was still the rule for full-time workers in the fifties, to about 46. The effect on production (as we shall see in a later chapter) was again quite marked.

employer will rarely succeed in arousing much interest when the work to be done is dull and monotonous.

The next best solution—in the case of repetitive work it is usually the best solution open—is to establish a connection between the intensity of work and the wages paid. This is called Payment by Results. The simplest form of payment by results is piece-work, according to which the worker is paid so much for each unit of the product which he turns out. The drawback to simple piece-work is that the amount of product turned out does not always measure the intensity of work very satisfactorily; quality may be important as well as quantity; a man's output may go up or down for reasons outside his own control; one man's output may be larger than another's, simply because of a difference in the equipment they are using. The methods of payment by results which are adopted in practice have often to be adjusted so as to allow for these discrepancies; in the process of adjustment they may become very complicated indeed. Now complication is itself a disadvantage; complicated methods are liable to rouse the suspicions of workers, who feel that they may be cheated by them; while it is not unknown for both employers and workers to be cheated in these mazes, the system adopted having characteristics which damage the interests of both parties! The more complicated a system of payment by results has to become, the less satisfactory (in most cases) it is; but the simpler systems will not fit the technique of production in more than a certain number of occupations without causing unfairness.[1] There is thus a limit to the number of cases where the method of payment by results can be conveniently applied.

If neither of these two solutions is open—if the work to be done is in its nature uninteresting, and yet it is unsuited for payment by results—then there may be nothing for it but to pay the worker by time (at a fixed rate per hour or per day,

[1] Another difficulty which besets the system of payment by results is the necessity of making an adjustment in rates of pay whenever the method of production, or the character of the product, changes. It may well take some negotiation to establish a rate which is accepted as being fair to both parties; in industries where technical changes occur frequently, there may be no time for such negotiations, and the feeling of unfairness which arises in consequence makes the system work badly.

irrespective of output), and to bridge over the conflict of interests by the supervision of foremen or other managers. Obviously this method is less satisfactory than either of the others; it is only too likely to degenerate into petty tyranny, and it depends too much upon the sanction of dismissal. But there remains a considerable range of occupations (in the field of unskilled labour, for example) where no better incentive has been devised. It is highly desirable that this range should be narrowed; the best way to narrow it is by making improvements in the other methods, so that their application can be extended.

PART III The Factors of Production—Capital

CHAPTER VIII Capital Goods and their Varieties

1. Capital, as we saw when we were making our earlier study of the Productive Process, consists of all those goods, existing at a particular time, which can be used in any way so as to satisfy wants during the subsequent period. Some of these goods are consumers' goods, which can be used to satisfy consumers' wants directly; some of them are producers' goods, which co-operate with labour to produce further goods and services. When we are studying capital as a factor of production, it is mainly the producers' goods which interest us; in the present chapter and in that which follows it we shall concentrate most of our attention upon producers' capital.

So far we have divided producers' capital goods into two classes—durable-use goods and single-use goods. We shall now proceed to make a further subdivision. The purpose of this further classification is in part to improve our understanding of the nature of capital; but at the same time we shall find that it throws a good deal of light upon one of the most important of practical economic questions—on the causes of fluctuation in employment. Unemployment is of course itself a problem of labour; but its causes have more to do with the factor of production capital than with the factor of production labour. Most of what can be said about the causes of fluctuation within the framework of an introductory volume such as this will be found in the present chapter.

2. Durable-use producers' goods have generally been divided by economists into two classes, called (1) Land, (2) Fixed Capital. Land includes agricultural land and urban land (used for building sites and similar purposes); it also includes mines. Fixed capital includes buildings, machines, tools, transport equipment, and so on.[1] The distinction between these two varieties of producers' goods received a great deal of attention from nineteenth-century economists, who used to mark their sense of its importance by classifying land as a separate factor of production, instead of treating it as a particular species of capital, which is the more modern practice followed here. All are agreed, however, that there is a distinction between land and fixed capital; what is the exact basis of the distinction?

Broadly speaking, we may say that land (in its economic sense) consists of all those durable-use goods which are given by nature;[2] fixed capital consists of those which are made by man. There are some kinds of durable-use equipment whose supply can be readily increased, if we so desire, by the production of new units; these are called fixed capital. There are other kinds which are inherited from the past, but their supply cannot be readily increased if we want more of them; these we call land.

It is not necessary to suppose that we could mark off, at all precisely, out of the whole equipment of a community existing at any particular time, just which items ought to be reckoned as land and which as fixed capital. Certainly if we attempted to do so by inquiring into the ultimate origin of each particular piece of equipment we should raise some awkward historical questions, and should often be hard put to it to say what was man-made and what not. The agricultural land

[1] Thus fixed capital does not mean fixed in location. The term is rather a curious one, having been borrowed by economists from accounting practice. Accountants, who have to look at economic problems from the point of view of an individual firm, think of the firm's 'capital' as the sum of money which has been put at its disposal. (We shall see in the next chapter how this fits in with the economic conception.) If a part of this money is spent upon durable-use equipment, it becomes 'fixed' for a long period—in contrast with money spent in purchasing materials, which is released again as soon as the materials are sold; thus the materials get the name 'circulating capital'.

[2] It should be noticed that land includes some consumers' capital, as well as producers' capital. If land is used for gardens, or parks, or sites for dwelling-houses, it is a consumers' good.

of England is presumably, for the most part, a free gift of nature; yet how much does it not owe to the improvements which have been made in it by successive generations of farmers, to the hedging and ditching carried out in the eighteenth century, and even to the clearing-away of the primitive forest by the ancient Mercians? The rich soil of Burgundy, on which the famous French wines are produced, is said by some of the best authorities to have been literally compounded out of the debris left by two thousand years of vine-growing.[1] But for purposes of economic discussion, it is doubtful whether such historical questions as these need to be raised at all. However the soil of England came into existence in the past, it is not possible to produce any more of it in the present; the most that can be done is to make improvements in its quality to a limited extent. Thus we may agree that in the economic sense it is land. The important thing about fixed capital, on the other hand, is that it is capable of being increased by human effort at the present time.

There is another distinction which is sometimes confused with that we have just been making; although it divides the whole class of durable-use producers' goods in a rather similar way, it is really not the same distinction at all. There are some durable-use goods which wear out as they are used; there are some which do not. Most of the goods which do not wear out are such as we have previously classified as land; most of those which do wear out are fixed capital. Yet the two distinctions do not exactly correspond, as can be seen at once from the case of mines. Mines are a gift of nature, yet they undoubtedly give out after they have been worked for a certain time.

Here again we must be careful not to push the distinction too far. In a phrase which has become more famous than its author would probably have desired, the great economist Ricardo described land, in its economic sense, as 'the original and indestructible powers of the soil'.[2] If land is a free gift of

[1] 'C'est en fin de compte, non les vertus du minéral, mais les rudes labeurs humains, les misères et les peines de multiples générations de vignerons, qui ont fait, de ces sols ingrats entre tous, des terres de choix, de nobles crus, des lieux élus.' (G. Roupnel, *Histoire de la campagne française*, p. 249.)

[2] *Principles of Political Economy and Taxation* (1817), ch. 2.

nature, its powers are presumably original; but there are many parts of the world where farmers have learned from bitter experience that the powers of agricultural land are by no means indestructible. If the fertility of land is to be maintained, it requires to be cultivated in a suitable way; and the finding of a way to 'put back into the soil what you have taken out of it' may not be an easy matter. The word 'indestructible' was a bad one; it is, however, characteristic of agricultural land that it can usually be cultivated in such a way that it does not deteriorate. If it is properly looked after, the land will be just as good in fifty or a hundred years' time as it is now.

The opposite is clearly true with many sorts of fixed capital. However well they are looked after, they are unlikely to be usable for more than a certain length of time; besides, they are liable to accidents, which may cut them off when they are relatively new. The necessity for replacement can often be postponed by making repairs; but when repairs have to pass a certain point, it will often be simpler to replace the article altogether. In any case, repairs are often nothing else but replacements of individual parts.

It has become clear that the distinctions we have been trying to draw in the field of durable-use producers' goods are not easy to define very precisely. But they do enable us to distinguish an important class of durable-use producers' goods, which are such that a proportion of the existing supply must be expected to wear out every year, and which are also such that new units can be produced, as additions to the total supply, or as replacements for those which have worn out. Modern society is dependent upon the existence of such goods, but it is just this dependence which makes it so difficult to keep the economic system running smoothly. Let us see how that is.

3. The trades which are specialized upon the production of new fixed capital goods are called the constructional trades. These are, of course, much more extensive than the group which we labelled 'building and contracting' in the table on p. 74; they also include large parts of 'manufacture' (engineering and other metal trades for instance). Perhaps as many as 6 million out of the British working population of 25 million can be regarded as belonging to the constructional trades in the present sense. But it should be noted that this figure is swollen by the great importance of the engineering trades in British exports. A rather lower proportion (say 15–20 per cent of the total) would be characteristic of other industrial countries.

The constructional trades have the double task of constructing new fixed capital and of replacing old fixed capital when it wears out. Let us take a numerical example in order to see how these two functions fit together. A certain community possesses, let us suppose, 1,000 ships; and let us say that a ship lasts, on the average, about twenty years. Then it would be possible, in completely steady conditions, to keep 1,000 ships constantly available by producing a steady output of 50 ships per year. Every year 50 ships would wear out, and every year there would be a new 50 ships coming forward to replace them. In twenty years the whole fleet would have been replaced—which is just the time it would take to wear out and to need replacing.

Now suppose that the community ceases to be contented with this constant number of 1,000 ships; in order to cope with the demands of an increasing population or of an expanding trade, the number of ships needed begins to expand at an even rate—say 3 per cent per annum. In order to have 1,030 ships in the second year, the number of new ships produced must be raised from 50 to 80. If 80 ships were produced every year, the total number of ships available would go on increasing in a regular manner.

This is more like the situation as it has usually existed in the actual world; but it should be observed that steadiness in the output of the shipbuilding industry now depends upon the expansion of the total demand for ships proceeding at a steady rate. And steadiness in the *rate of expansion* is obviously very difficult to attain. Population itself has not expanded at all steadily, though it has (up to the present) gone on expanding; but there are other things to be taken into account which are even less reliable. Inventions and changes in wants cause sudden accelerations and retardations in the demand for particular sorts of fixed capital; political changes (particularly wars and their consequences) are even more disturbing. Even when economic progress is continuing without serious intermission, the rate of progress is liable to be speeded up or slowed down for all sorts of reasons.

Even when these changes in the rate of progress are themselves quite moderate, they will have a considerable effect upon the activity of the constructional trades. We have seen that with 80 ships produced every year, the numbers of ships available would go on increasing from 1,000 to 1,030 and 1,060, and so on. Now suppose that in the second year the number of ships needed was a little larger than this; for the number of ships needed to be 1,050 instead of 1,030 would not imply any great disturbance in the demand for shipping. But if 1,050 ships were to be made available in that year, the number of ships produced would have to be 100 instead of 80. If in the third year no more than the normal 1,060 were needed, the number of ships produced in that year would only be 60 (10 as an addition to the total supply, and the usual 50 replacements). This means that if there were enough people specialized to ship-building to be able to produce 100 ships in the rush year, in the year after 40 per cent of them would be unemployed.

Nor is this all. We have so far been assuming that the existing supply of ships can be relied upon to wear out at a regular rate. If anything were to happen (as for example a war) which caused them to wear out, or to be destroyed, more rapidly than usual, the demand for new ships would probably be further disturbed. There is also a more subtle reason why the rate of wearing-out may not be regular. If there have in the past been irregularities in the rate of production of ships, so that an abnormally large proportion of the existing ships were built in certain particular past years, the wearing-out of these ships is likely to be 'bunched'. (It is just the same problem as with the age-distribution of a human population; if the age-distribution of the existing ships is bunched, just as the present age-distribution of the British population is bunched, abnormally large numbers of ships will be ready for replacement in those particular years when the bunched ships are most rapidly wearing out.) We can now see a good many reasons why demand for the products of the constructional trades is liable to fluctuate. It is in fact notoriously liable to fluctuate. It is probable that in these fluctuations we have a main cause of the boom and slumps, the years of good trade followed by years of bad trade, which have afflicted industrial countries since the very beginning of the Industrial Revolution.

4. There is no doubt, as a matter of experience, that in years of bad trade it is the constructional trades which are usually the hardest hit. But it is not only the constructional trades that are depressed; the unemployment which arises out of the instability of the constructional trades does not affect the constructional trades only; it spreads to other industries as well. For when the constructional trades are slack, the people working in them have less to spend; and the result is a slackening in the demand for the products of other industries too. The unemployment disease is infectious; some trades get the infection first, others catch it from them; the trades from which the infection originates are usually (though not always) the constructional trades.

The mechanism by which the unemployment virus is passed on is a very simple one. The incomes which most people spend are the incomes which they earn by working; if fewer people are working, there are fewer incomes to be spent, and fewer goods can be sold. Since fewer goods can be sold, fewer people are needed to make those goods, so that fewer people can be employed in those industries. This mechanism is not the fundamental cause of unemployment; it is the way unemployment spreads from one trade to another.

The spreading of unemployment is not impeded by national frontiers. Most people spend some of their earnings upon imported goods; when they have less to spend, they will buy smaller amounts of imported goods as well as of other goods, and that will affect the foreign producers of these goods, causing unemployment in the countries where the foreign producers live. Even if the goods which are bought appear to be produced at home, they will often include some materials imported from abroad; thus if home production is slowed up, fewer materials will be imported, and this again leads to unemployment among the foreign producers of those materials. If we look at the matter from the point of view of those foreign producers, we can see how it will often happen that the unemployment infection may come into a particular nation from outside; so far as that particular nation is concerned, it is not its constructional trades which are primarily hit, but its export trades. Something of that kind has frequently been our experience in Great Britain.[1]

Most of these troubles can be removed if a way is found of achieving a greater regularity in the output of the constructional trades. There are ways by which this can be done; to replace equipment at times when trade is slack, rather than at the time when it is technically most convenient to replace it, is one of the mildest and most obvious. This, in principle, is in these days well understood; it is sufficiently understood for really severe slumps, like that of 1930–2, to have become unlikely. (In those days, the student must realize, it was not understood; it only became understood as a result of the work of Keynes and his contemporaries, which was itself in large measure prompted by the experience of the Slump; the date of Keynes's book is 1936.) It is chiefly because of this greater understanding that the fluctuations in trade, which have occurred in the fifties and sixties, have been so much less severe than those of the twenties and thirties; but though they have been less severe, they have indeed occurred. For though governments, and their advisers, now know what to do—they know in general what to do—it is still by no means easy to find the right moment at which to take action, and by no means easy to find how much action it is wise to take. Besides, they have other things to attend to; when the moment for action comes they may well be

[1] At the time of the great unemployment in 1930–2 it was the experience of nearly all countries that their export trades were some of the worst sufferers. This was a direct result of the protective policies so generally introduced. The government of each nation, finding that its people had less to spend, and that unemployment was therefore increasing among them, did all it could to induce them to economize on imports, rather than on goods produced at home; the result was to push the unemployment off on to foreigners, on to the exporting industries of foreign countries. With almost all countries behaving in this way, the exporting industries of all alike suffered. Now that so large a part of our export trade is itself a trade in constructional goods, we have become even more vulnerable than we were before. Fluctuations in the rate of construction *in other countries* will now hit British exports even more drastically and directly than in the past.

subjected to other pressures; so the need to keep the economy running smoothly takes a back place. The way in which this has worked, in the case of Britain, will be considered in a later chapter.[1]

5. Our classification of durable-use producers' goods has taken us far afield; let us now see where we shall be led by the single-use goods. The distinction we have to make among single-use goods is also concerned with problems of the regularity of output; but naturally it takes a different form. The single-use goods in the hands of producers at any particular time are partly goods actually undergoing production—'goods in process'—and goods being handed on from one stage of production to another. These we call *Working Capital*.[2] Partly they are stocks of materials which are not undergoing production at the moment, though they have been produced previously, and are expected to be used in further production later on; these we call *Stocks*, or Reserve Stocks.[3] We may think of working capital as symbolizing the regularity with which the greater part of the productive process does go on all the time, in spite of the ups and downs we have been discussing; but when we come to reserve stocks we encounter some new sorts of irregularity.

If the wants of consumers never changed, but remained the same from day to day and from year to year, and if the outputs of goods never changed, it would be unnecessary for businesses to keep reserve stocks to any important extent. But since a manufacturer is often ignorant of the exact form which the next order coming to him will take, and since he usually needs rather different materials (different qualities, for instance) for dealing with different sorts of orders, he will need to keep stocks on hand, so as to be able to deal quickly with the orders that come in. (Alternatively, the stocks may be kept, not by manufacturers themselves, but by merchants,

[1] Chapter XVI below.

[2] The older name was *Circulating Capital* (see above, p. 96, note).

[3] The word *Stock* is listed in the *Oxford English Dictionary* as having fifty-eight distinct meanings; quite a number of these meanings are of economic importance. (We shall encounter another one in the next chapter.) The Americans are therefore very wise to use another word (Inventories) for Reserve Stocks; but Inventories has another meaning in England, so we get no advantage from following them.

who are ready to sell without delay to any manufacturer who needs a supply.) It is a very delicate problem of business management to decide what amount of stocks need to be held for this purpose. If more stocks are held, orders can be fulfilled more quickly; it is a good thing for a firm's reputation to fulfil orders quickly, for by doing so it satisfies the consumer's wants better; but the holding of large stocks is very expensive. One of the easiest ways of economizing may be to let your stocks run down.

Let us suppose that in a certain industry manufacturers (or merchants) are in the habit of keeping stocks of materials equal to the amount which is normally used in production during a period of three months. They may keep this stock by them for long periods, or they may 'turn over their stock'—that is to say, every month they take one month's supply from their stock, and replace it by the same quantity newly supplied by the raw material producers. So long as this continued there would be no dislocation. But now suppose that these manufacturers decided to content themselves with smaller stocks, and that from now on two months' supply would be sufficient. In the month when this happened, they would take the usual amount from their stocks, but they would not give the usual order to replace what they had taken. During that month the demand for the raw material would be interrupted, although after the interruption it would continue as usual.

This sort of dislocation is worth considering, because it shows us that changes in the demand for the products of raw-material producing industries do not necessarily correspond at all exactly with changes in the purchasing of the ultimate consumer. The stocks which are held by merchants and manufacturers form a kind of buffer between the raw-material producer and the consumer for whom he is ultimately working. It is an elastic buffer, and it is liable to certain swellings and contractings of its own. But the most important economic consequences of stock-holding arise when there has already been some disturbance in the production of the raw materials.

There are many materials (for example, wheat and cotton) which are the result of agricultural operations, so that supplies inevitably come in at certain particular times of the year. Since they are needed continuously, and can be kept until they are wanted, merchants have built up a very delicate and ingenious organization to facilitate the holding of stocks on a large scale, so that supplies which only come in at particular seasons can be used at an even rate throughout the year.[1] But it sometimes happens that this organization is subjected to exceptional strains. It can cope fairly well with the strain which is caused by a bumper crop, to which it reacts in the obviously desirable way of holding over the surplus, in the expectation that on some future occasion there will be a shortage. But suppose (as is not unknown) that two bumper crops come in succession, what then? As warehouses become overcrowded, the costs of holding even larger stocks amount very rapidly, so that a signal has to be given to the farmers to cut down production. The same thing happens (and this has been a frequent occurrence in the modern world) if the demand for the product has been increasing very rapidly, but farmers have over-estimated the rate at which it is increasing, so that they have produced more than the consumer is at the moment prepared to take. In either case the warehouses become loaded with *surplus stocks*.

It will be well for us to reflect for a moment on the situation which then arises, for there are few economic problems which are liable to cause more misunderstanding. Either as a result of the vagaries of nature, or as a result of miscalaculation, producers have turned out more than they would have desired to produce, and more than they would be willing to produce as a long-term policy in later years. If the commodity produced is a perishable one, there may be nothing for it but to destroy the surplus; thus when there is an overproduction of fruit, the surplus has to be left on the trees, because the labour needed to convey it to market is not available. If the commodity could be stored very easily, it would be possible to hold over the surplus supply for a long period, releasing it very slowly in small quantities so that little disturbance would be created as it was sold. Between these two extremes is the common case when the commodity can be stored, but storage is expensive; stocks can then be held over,

[1] This organization consists of the Organized Produce Markets, whose market reports were referred to above, p. 7.

but anyone holding a stock will desire to dispose of it as soon as he conveniently can. In this case there will generally be a period of two or three years after the surplus first occurred, during which it is being disposed of; and during those years the demand for new supplies will be less than normal, since the wants of consumers are being satisfied to a considerable extent out of the surplus stocks. Thus these years are bound to be years of unemployment or under-employment for the producers. It is not surprising that in some such cases (as in the famous case of Brazilian coffee after 1931) the producers should prefer to adopt the solution which would have to be adopted in the case of a perishable commodity—that is, to destroy the surplus! For by so doing they escape the awkward process of digesting surplus stocks, which would otherwise hang over them for some time.

During the nineteen-forties the world was confronted with the opposite problem—that of a persistent shortage of materials, with which producers were unable to catch up. In such conditions the market organization does not greatly help; for once stocks have been run down to a minimum, they can no longer act as a buffer. Governments endeavoured to meet this situation by themselves taking over the control of stocks; this did not in any way enable supplies to be increased, but it facilitated the introduction of allocation and rationing, by which the available supplies could be distributed among manufacturers and consumers in a more equitable, but not necessarily more efficient, manner. There is no reason to suppose that this machinery, necessary as it is in times of great scarcity, has any superiority over the market mechanism in more normal conditions. In fact, when scarcities diminished, there was a general return to distribution through the market. Governments are doubtless readier, than they were in the past, to step in when the market mechanism does not seem to be functioning; but on the whole, as long as things are going fairly smoothly, the market is left to do the job.

The problems which we have studied in this chapter are very difficult problems; there is much more to be said about them than we have been able to say here. But further discussion of them would soon lead us into very advanced economics. It is sufficient for the present if we have appreciated some of the difficulties which inevitably attend the organization of a productive process which uses elaborate equipment. It should be observed that most of these difficulties are inherent in the productive process itself; they do not depend on the private ownership of capital. Some of the consequences of private ownership will be considered in the next chapter.

CHAPTER IX Private Property in Capital

1. If capital goods are to play their part in the ordinary running of the productive process, they need to be looked after; some one has to be responsible for seeing that the durable-use varieties are kept in good condition, and that all kinds are used to advantage. In a socialist system the duty of looking after the community's capital equipment must be exercised by public officials; in a system of private property it is supposed to be performed by the private people who own the capital. There are some kinds of society for which the case that can be made along these lines for the institution of private property is extremely convincing; for instance, the great strength of peasant proprietorship as a form of land tenure is to be found in the loving care which a peasant bestows upon land when it belongs to him. If capital is used to better advantage as a result of private ownership, and if the profits which are received by the owners are on the whole not more than a reasonable return for the care which they take of their property, then it may be more to the interest of the whole community (including those who are not owners of property) to have capital administered by owners rather than by public officials (who would also require to be paid). But it is only possible to make out a good case for private ownership along these lines if the owners of property do actually look after the capital goods which they own; in practice it has become less and less true that they do so. The case for private ownership is in consequence considerably weakened; or at the least it is obliged to shift its ground. We shall give an outline in this chapter of the remarkable way in which the

nature of capital ownership has been transformed during the course of the last two hundred years.

2. The principal influence which has brought about this transformation is the growing advantage of producing on a large scale. New ways of producing on a large scale have continually been invented, and some of them have offered great gains in efficiency; thus in many industries the size of the firm has had to keep on growing in order to take advantage of these more productive methods. In the middle of the eighteenth century a firm which employed a few dozen men was a large firm; by 1815 there were a few monster concerns whose employees were running into thousands. Although it was of course impossible for this rate of expansion to continue, we have today reached a point where firms with over a thousand employees are fairly numerous, while a few of the largest combines are well past the 10,000 mark. Since the amount of capital used has generally increased more rapidly than the number of employees, even these figures do not fully reflect the change which has taken place. A change of this magnitude was bound to affect the whole problem of the control of capital.[1]

So long as the typical firm was only a small workshop with a handful of employees, the capital goods needed for production could usually be acquired by a single person out of his own possessions, though some part of them (perhaps the building itself) might be hired from someone else. If the business was successful, and earned good profits, some part of these profits might be used for the acquisition of more capital goods, and so the size of the business would grow. But, except in very favourable conditions (such as did exist in the early days of the cotton industry, for example), the rate at which growth could proceed along these lines would be very moderate. The firm began small, and, even if successful, it usually stayed small.

[1] It should be noticed that such changes in the scale of production, however they occur, are always likely to have repercussions on ownership. Many examples can be found in the history of agriculture. The English enclosure movement of the late eighteenth century is one of them; the collectivization of agriculture in Russia (the Communist revolution began on a basis of peasant proprietorship) was almost certainly another.

In this primitive organization of business the manager and controller of the firm and the owner of the capital goods employed were one and the same person. (Our ancestors originally referred to him as the 'undertaker' of the business. Nineteenth-century economists, fearing misunderstanding, preferred the French equivalent 'entrepreneur'.) But when the advantages of producing on a larger scale began to develop, the capital goods needed for starting one of these larger businesses became too costly for a single person to be able to acquire them out of his own possessions—or rather, few of those people who possessed the right kind of ability were able to do so. A solution might, however, be found if a number of people clubbed together so as to provide the necessary capital equipment out of their joint resources. The legal form of this association was the Partnership.

Partnership is a system whereby a small number of persons hold capital equipment in joint ownership, and legally joint ownership is supposed to imply joint management. But it will often happen that some of the partners take a more active share in the administration of the capital than the others can do—the partnership is divided into active partners and 'sleeping partners'. Now the sleeping partner is putting himself very completely into the hands of his associates; he is allowing them to manage his capital for him, and on the success of their management depends, not merely whether he makes a good income or not, but whether he preserves his capital or loses it completely. To enter into a partnership when one does not intend to take an active part in its management is a very risky thing to do; it means imposing a very high degree of trust in one's associates.

3. It can readily be understood that there must always have existed owners of capital who would be reluctant to enter into partnerships; but there has always been an alternative method by which the property of such people can be made available for use in businesses which they do not control—the method of borrowing. When an entrepreneur acquires control over capital by borrowing it, his obligations to the lender are set down in the contract, which states that certain definite sums of money are to be paid at particular dates, and so on. The lender has no right to anything beyond what is laid down, but to that he has a firm legal right. It is not surprising that owners of property should often prefer to have a definite contract of this sort instead of the close association involved in a partnership.

Capital may be lent in the form of goods or in the form of money. In the case of land or buildings, it is possible to arrange for a particular capital good to be leased or hired, subject to a precise undertaking that it is to be returned in satisfactory condition; but (at least in ordinary business dealings) it is not possible for single-use goods to be hired in this way, since they are going to be used up in the process of using them. There is therefore nothing for it but to express the loan in the form of a certain sum of money value, to be returned in money at an agreed date in the future; even in the case of durable-use goods it is often more convenient for the loan to take this form. Instead of the borrower being lent capital goods directly, he is lent a sum of money with which he can acquire the capital goods he needs.

The situation which arises as the result of a money loan such as this deserves very careful attention. If capital goods are owned by a partnership, then it is clear that the partners own those capital goods in joint ownership. If a landlord leases land or buildings to a tenant, then it is clear that the landlord still owns the property which has been leased; the tenant simply acquires the right to make use of the property. But if an entrepreneur borrows £1,000, and uses that £1,000 to make an addition to the capital goods under his control, these capital goods do not belong to the lender, nor to the lender and borrower in joint ownership; they belong to the borrower, and he has every right to dispose of them exactly as he wishes. But he does not personally become any richer as a result of this increase in the capital goods which he possesses (though of course he may become so in the end if he uses these additional resources advantageously); the increase in the capital at his disposal is offset by the debt of £1,000 which he owes. Similarly, if the lender has sold capital goods (say house property) in order to be able to lend the £1,000, he is not made poorer as a result of his having a smaller amount of capital goods in his possession; the £1,000 debt owing to him stands in the place of the capital goods he sold. When we are considering the personal 'capital' of particular people, we have to regard the debts owing to them as part of their 'capital', and the debts which they owe as deductions from their 'capital'. This is the reason for the distinction between *capital* in its economic sense (capital goods) and *capital* in its business sense (when it may mean nothing but pieces of paper acknowledging claims). The claims are indications that the control over capital goods has been transferred in return for the promise of an agreed annual payment.

If we contrast the position of a lender (who, after he has made his loan, is better described as a creditor or a bond-holder)[1] with that of a sleeping partner, we see that while the receipts of the sleeping partner are entirely dependent upon the way the business he participates in is managed, the bond-holder is bound to receive exactly what he has been promised, so long as the borrower is able to pay at all. The only risk to which the bond-holder is exposed is that the debtor will default on his obligation, and (at least so far as debts arising within a country are concerned) there is always legal machinery to ensure that debtors must pay if they can. But there is always the possibility that a debtor will not be able to pay (or not be able to pay fully), and a lender will therefore be more willing to lend if he has good reason for confidence in the *solvency* of the borrower. Since there are many cases in which the lender would himself be unable to acquire the requisite knowledge of the borrower's affairs, there is great scope for intermediaries between borrower and lender—intermediaries in whose own solvency the ordinary lender has confidence, and who can make the necessary inquiries before passing on the funds which have been entrusted to them. The work of these intermediaries is called Finance; there are various kinds of financial firms, but the most important are the banks.[2]

One of the main considerations which a lender has to take into account when estimating whether it is safe to lend to a

[1] The distinction between these being, broadly, that a creditor has lent money for a short period, a bondholder for a long period.

[2] The mutual relations of different kinds of financial intermediaries will occupy a good deal of the attention of a student of economics when he comes to the subject of Money.

particular borrower is the amount of other capital which that borrower possesses. If a person who possessed no capital of his own tried to borrow £1,000, he would be unlikely to have much success in his endeavours; for even if the way in which he proposed to use the money appeared to be promising, the least mishap to his enterprise would leave him with capital goods worth less than £1,000, so that circumstances in which he would be unable to honour his obligation in full would be exceedingly likely to occur. Even if he possessed £1,000 of his own, the risk of losing half the capital invested in the enterprise might be quite considerable, so that a lender might still think that the security was not good enough. But if he already possessed a capital of £10,000, he would usually have little difficulty in borrowing an extra £1,000 for some promising purpose; for if capital goods to the value of £11,000 were used in a particular business, the chance of so much being lost that a debt of £1,000 could not be met would be relatively small. Whether it is a rule of economic affairs that 'to him that hath shall be given' may be disputed; but there can be no doubt that it is a rule of borrowing and lending that *to him that hath shall be lent.*

4. These two methods—Partnership and Borrowing—were the only legal methods of increasing the capital at the disposal of a single firm which were available in England (in ordinary cases) up to the middle of the last century. Even when they were both used to the utmost, there were limits to the amounts of capital which could be brought together in these ways. Partnerships did not work smoothly if they had more than half a dozen members or so; and the amount of money which could be borrowed by a partnership depended on the capital which the partners themselves were putting up. If, say, the partners themselves had contributed £10,000 and £10,000 had been borrowed, further borrowing might become very difficult, for the reason we have mentioned. The way in which these difficulties have finally been surmounted is by the formation of companies, instead of partnerships, as a more convenient way of organizing large businesses; but before the eighteen-fifties the only legal ways of forming a company were by Royal Charter, or by special legislation (as was done for the early railways), and these were expensive. So-called companies were also formed in a less regular way, but these were in law nothing but extended partnerships, so that their legal position remained anomalous and dangerous to their members.

The particular danger to which the members of these companies were exposed (the same danger beset all sleeping partners) was the danger of Unlimited Liability. The law declined to make an absolute distinction between the private property of a partner and the capital which he had contributed to the partnership. If the partnership was unable to meet its obligations, the whole of the property of the partners could be drawn upon to satisfy the demands of creditors. Thus there was many a sleeping partner who experienced a rude awakening; the business in which he had been mildly 'interested' suddenly collapsed and engulfed his whole fortune.[1]

The great change in the English law on this matter was brought about by a series of Company Acts (culminating in the Act of 1862), which made it easy to form Joint Stock Companies with Limited Liability. A shareholder in such a company is ordinarily not liable for the debts of the company to any greater amount than the capital which he has contributed; thus if he has bought shares to the value of £100, he may lose that £100 if the company is a complete failure, but he cannot lose any more. The shareholder is therefore in a much less risky position than the sleeping partner (whose role he in a sense inherits). There is nothing to prevent the formation of companies with hundreds (or even thousands) of shareholders, so that the amounts of capital which can be brought together by the company form of organization are much larger than what could have been brought together by partnerships.

It was perhaps not unreasonable for the law to assume that the members of a partnership would all be actively engaged in the management of their joint capital; but it would be

[1] The potentialities of such a catastrophe as a source of domestic drama were a godsend to novelists; but there was one novelist (Sir Walter Scott) who experienced them in his own person. He had used the profits of the Waverley novels to become a sleeping Partner in a publishing house, which failed, leaving him personally in debt to the amount of £130,000.

obviously absurd to pretend that a crowd of shareholders could take any active part in the management of a giant concern, in which many of them would have no more than a few shares. The legal theory of the joint stock company is that the shareholders elect representatives—the directors—who administer their capital for them. In order to protect the shareholders against directors who might abuse their position, the law insists on safeguards, such as a certain degree of publicity in accounts, and imposes penalties for the raising of capital on false pretences (mis-statements in prospectuses, and so on). The history of company legislation is a long story of guerrilla warfare between the law and a small fringe of ingenious rascals whose activities form the shady side of company promotion; there is no doubt that in England the law has had the better of the struggle. Provision has also been made in one of the later Company Acts (1908) for the institution of a hybrid between the partnership and the old joint stock company—the Private Company. Thus there are now three main legal forms taken by English businesses. (1) The partnership still exists with its unlimited liability, but its main stronghold is in the professions where little capital is used. (2) Small firms are largely organized as private companies, with limited liability, but not allowed to have more than fifty shareholders, and (since it is supposed that a small group of shareholders will usually have personal knowledge of the business) without the obligation to publish accounts. (3) When a business desires to have more shareholders than this, it has to become a Public Company, whose number of shareholders is unrestricted, but which is subject to regulations about publicity. (These regulations have been continually tightened up, as, for instance, by the Companies Act of 1967, which was mentioned above.)[1] Most of the largest companies naturally take this form.

5. Thus the modern company has two ways of securing the capital goods which it needs in order to commence, or to expand, its operations: one by borrowing, and one by the issue of shares. The shareholders who have purchased the

[1] p. 7.

shares are in a certain sense part-owners of the company; they elect the directors, who are their representatives. But it is impossible for any legal provisions to give to shareholders the knowledge which they would need in order to elect competent directors;[1] so that in practice the directors of a new company are usually nominated before the shares are issued—before the shareholders have become shareholders—and they perpetuate themselves by co-opting others, whose selection is merely ratified by the dumb herd. It therefore corresponds much more with the facts if we consider the directors of a company as themselves forming a kind of partnership, putting up some part of the capital themselves, and acquiring extra capital (often far in excess of what they have put up), partly by borrowing, partly by issuing shares. If we look at the matter in this way, we see that the issue of shares has itself developed into a kind of borrowing, distinguished from the other kind in just one significant way—that the bondholder has the right to a fixed annual payment (expressed as a fixed rate of *interest*), while the shareholder has no more than the right to a share in whatever *profits* are left over each year after other claims have been met.[2]

The shareholder has the protection of limited liability; but otherwise he puts himself into the hands of his directors, just as the sleeping partner put himself into the hands of his associates. He gives over his property to the directors and lets them manage it for him, so that it depends on their ability and their diligence whether or not he gets a good return, or whether indeed he loses it altogether. At first sight it seems astonishing that shareholders should be found who will have such confidence in the directors of public companies, people with whom they are most unlikely to have any close acquain-

[1] Just the same problem arises with political democracy. It is impossible for important officers, requiring specialized capacities, to be elected directly; for instance, a democracy which attempted to appoint its ambassadors to foreign states by direct election would soon be in a sorry plight. The method of electing general-purposes politicians whose business it is to make appointments, or to select those who are to make appointments, is not available in an association such as a company, itself formed for one specialized purpose.

[2] Another thing which indicates that this is the right way of looking at the matter is the creation of various sorts of obligation intermediate between the bond (or debenture) and the *ordinary* share—preference shares and so on.

tance. The explanation is partly to be found in another consequence of limited liability. Since the shareholder cannot lose more than he has put in, whatever happens to the company in which he has invested, he will be in a safer position if he has small holdings of shares in a number of different companies than if he has 'all his eggs in one basket'. This the sleeping partner could not do without adding to his risks, but it is the common practice of the modern capitalist.

Another way in which the shareholder in a public company is protected is by the facility with which he can dispose of his shares whenever he desires. Shares in private companies cannot be sold except to persons approved by the directors of the company; but shares in public companies can usually be bought and sold quite freely, without the company's officials being consulted in any way. In order to facilitate such transactions, there has grown up a body of dealers, who are organized in the Stock Exchange.[1] The ability to sell his shares on the Stock Exchange does not indeed safeguard the shareholder against loss; if he gets bad news about the company, and so wants to dispose of his shares, the chances are that other people will have heard it as well, so that buyers will be hard to find, except at a reduced price. But the pessimist does get a chance of withdrawing his fingers before they get burnt too badly.

6. The final result of the transformation we have been describing in this chapter (a transformation, similar in outline, but with many tiresome differences in detail, has been going on in most other countries) is that the capital equipment of the community has, in the main, ceased to be owned directly by private people. The main exceptions to this rule (and they are only partial exceptions) are land and houses; it is a curious commentary on the attitude often taken by social reformers towards land ownership that the modern landlord still performs a real function in looking after the capital goods

[1] So called because the dealers trade in stocks and shares. This is the other sense of *stock*, to which we alluded in the last chapter. The difference between stocks and shares is of no economic importance, except that stocks may include bonds. ('Stock' in *Joint Stock Company* is yet a third sense, the now obsolete sense whose place has been taken by the modern 'capital'.)

in his ownership, while most other property-owners hardly do so any longer. They have mostly given up their direct command over capital goods and have acquired titles to ownership, which are only pieces of paper, without any particular goods being identifiable to which they correspond. Since the shares owned by the modern shareholder are usually spread over a number of different companies, his connection with any particular capital goods has practically disappeared.

This is indeed less true for company directors themselves, who are usually important shareholders in the companies they control, and it is to some extent less true for the shareholders in private companies. In these cases something of the original function of ownership remains. But if we ask what economic function is retained by the purely passive shareholder, it can be no more than the function of enabling the active directors and controllers of business to get command over capital. Now it is a real advantage that they should be able to do this easily, because it enables new opportunities for the expansion of business to satisfy consumers' wants to be seized upon easily, and (above all) to be seized upon without delay. The facility of raising capital is actually increased by the looseness of the connection between the particular capitalist and any particular set of capital goods. For, if a business desires to raise more capital, it is not obliged to appeal to those particular people who happen at the moment to have spare money available; it has much the wider choice of applying to anyone who possesses shares which can be sold on the Stock Exchange, and who would be willing to sell some of these shares and lend the proceeds to the business in question. This facility of raising capital is a real social gain, though the full possible advantage is not always taken of it. But perhaps it is not a large gain to set against the considerable part of the Social Product which has to be set aside for the payment of interest and dividends.

We shall be returning to this point when we come to consider the Distribution of Income;[1] it will suffice for the present if we have got some idea of the remarkable evolution

[1] See below, Chapters XIV and XVIII.

which has been taking place in the institution of Private Property—an evolution which is probably not yet finished, and which may yet have some surprising turns in store.[1]

[1] There is one 'surprising turn' which has occurred since the above chapter (which I have been able to leave substantially unchanged from earlier editions) was first written, and on which a word would seem to be in place. This is the appearance of 'take-over bids' and suchlike, which have become rather common in the fifties and sixties: something of a revolt, on the part of the dumb shareholder, against the passive role, for which we were (still, I think, on the whole quite justly) casting him.

What may be said to have happened is that, although a 'change of government'—shareholders turning out directors by democratic election—is not much more practicable than it was, the market has provided an alternative. The prices at which a company's shares are *normally* valued are based upon the expectation that the company will continue under the same management; for the sale of a few shares by one individual and their purchase by another cannot significantly affect any voting. If, however, a company's policy is such that an outsider can feel very sure that it is not doing its best for its shareholders, it will become worth his while to pay higher prices for large blocks of shares—in order to acquire enough voting power to change the management (either in person or in policy). Having brought about this revolution, the shares can again be sold; and if the revolution has been successful, they will be sold at a profit. When directors get themselves into the state of mind (the origin of which has been explained in this chapter) of thinking that they are working for the interest of the 'company', or of the 'public', or for anything distinct from the interest of their shareholders, they have now been shown to lay themselves open to a flank attack along these lines.

CHAPTER X

The National Capital

1. We have now examined the nature of capital under two aspects: (1) its aspect as a factor of production, consisting of real goods being used in the productive process; (2) its aspect as a superstructure of rights and titles to ownership, by means of which the real goods are attributed to their ultimate owners. The general way in which these two aspects are fitted together is becoming clear. The capital possessed by an individual capitalist will usually include some actual goods (houses, land, durable-use consumers' goods, and so on), but for the most part it is likely to consist of paper titles, shares, and bonds. These latter cannot be associated with particular pieces of real equipment, but are claims against the equipment used by firms; usually they entitle their holders to receive interest or dividends out of the profits which the firms earn by using that equipment. Now since a company, from the point of view of ownership, is simply a means whereby a number of people can hold capital goods in common, the capital equipment of the company, after other obligations have been met, belongs to its shareholders. The conventional way of expressing this when drawing up a company's accounts is to reckon the shares as *Liabilities* of the company, and to bring out the company's liabilities as equal in value to its *assets*. (The assets of a company—like those of an individual person—consist of the property it possesses, plus the debts due to it; its liabilities are the debts which it owes, or the claims which are set against its assets.) This would work out in a concrete case in the following way.

Suppose that a company has been formed in the year 1960, and its capital was then got together by issuing ordinary shares to the value of £100,000 and by borrowing £30,000 on debentures or bonds. Let us suppose that we are considering its position at the beginning of the year 1970. At that time it also owes £10,000 to a bank, and £5,000 to various trade creditors (goods have been delivered to it, but not yet paid for). On the other side it is owed £5,000 by customers who have not yet paid for the goods which have been delivered to them; and it possesses equipment, consisting of the various sorts of real goods, valued at £150,000. The resulting situation would be expressed on a balance-sheet more or less as follows:

Liabilities	£	*Assets*	£
Capital issued:		Equipment (land, buildings, plant, goods in process, stock in trade)	150,000
Ordinary shares	100,000		
Bonds	30,000		
Bank debt	10,000	Trade Debtors	5,000
Trade Creditors	5,000		
Balance	10,000		
	155,000		155,000

The firm has been a moderately successful one, so that the total value of its assets exceeds the value of its debts *plus* the original value of its share capital. This leaves a balance of £10,000, which is put on the liabilities side, because any such surplus accrues to the ordinary shareholders, and is available to be distributed to them in dividends (though a prudent management will not begin to distribute any such surplus until it has grown fairly large). Nevertheless, we may say that the ordinary shareholders, who originally contributed £100,000, now have claims worth £110,000. (If the firm had been unsuccessful, the balance might have gone the other way, and the claims of the ordinary shareholders would be worth less than what they had originally contributed.)

When the balance-sheet of a company is understood in this way, it will be seen that it is quite proper for the two sides of the account to add up to the same figure; for if the claims of shareholders are treated as liabilities, the *net assets* of the company (assets *minus* liabilities) must of course be nil. In the case of a private individual, on the other hand, net assets are normally a positive amount. A private person may owe some money to his bank (having an overdraft), and he may have bills owing to shopkeepers which at a particular moment he had not yet paid; but these liabilities are nearly always a good deal less than his assets, for the very good reason that he would be unable to give adequate security for loans to any larger amount. We shall be considering one exception to this rule a little later on;[1] but such exceptions are of little practical importance.

2. Let us now take a simple case, and see how the two aspects of capital fit together. Suppose that we have a company like that we have been considering, but with no trade debts either way, and no debt to a bank. Let us further suppose that its shareholders (including bondholders) have no investments in other companies. Then we can take the company and its shareholders together, and can treat them as a self-contained group. The total capital of the group can be added up in two different ways, either of which will give the same result.

On the one hand, we can look at the capital from the side of ownership. The shareholders will have in their private possession certain capital goods (houses and so on) which have no connection with their investments in the company. Let us say that the value of these personal possessions is £20,000. They also own shares and bonds to the value of £150,000. If we assume that they have no personal debts, their total net assets come to £170,000. The net assets of the company are, as we saw, nil. Therefore the net assets of the whole group are £170,000.

On the other hand, we may look at the real goods. The shares and bonds worth £150,000 correspond, in the company's books, to real equipment worth £150,000. Writing the company's balance-sheet in an abbreviated form, and subjoining a similar account for the shareholders' private possessions, we get the table opposite.

When company and shareholders are taken together, the paper claims (marked *a*) cancel out, giving us as the sum of

[1] See below, p. 125.

	Liabilities		*Assets*	
		£		£
Company:	[a]Shares and bonds	150,000	Capital goods	150,000
Shareholders:	..	..	Capital goods	20,000
			[a]Shares and bonds	150,000
Company and shareholders together:	..	..	Capital goods	170,000

the possessions of the whole group, nothing but the real equipment, which is worth £170,000, the same as the total value of the net assets.

The reason why the paper claims cancel out is that we have added together the capital of the company (for which the claims are liabilities) and the capital of the shareholders (for whom they are assets). If we were to take any group of individuals and institutions, and were to perform a similar addition, we should find that all debts and obligations *between members of the group* cancelled out in the same way, appearing as positive items in the accounts of some members and negative items in the accounts of others. If the group were a self-contained group, not having any debts or claims excepting between its members, the total capital of the group could be estimated, either by adding together the net assets of all members, or by adding up the values of all the real capital goods possessed. The two totals would have to come out to the same figure.

3. The particular group for which it is most interesting to make such a calculation is, of course, the Nation. When we add together all the assets and liabilities of all the persons and institutions which compose a nation, most of the paper claims (being owed by firms to persons, or persons to firms, or firms to firms, or persons to persons, all of which are included in the nation) cancel out in the way we have described. If the nation were completely self-contained, we should find that when we had made the cancelling-out properly, the sum of the net assets of all the persons and institutions in the country gave us the same total as the total value of all the capital goods possessed by the nation and its citizens. Very roughly, this is what we do find; but there are a few snags in the cancelling-out process which need a little attention.

First of all, a modern nation is not a completely self-contained group in the sense which would be needed for the cancelling-out to be perfect. Firms engaging in foreign trade will generally have debts owing to foreigners, and will be owed debts by foreigners; while some of the nations' citizens will be shareholders in foreign companies, and some of the companies operating within the country may have foreign shareholders. In consequence, if we were to add together the net assets of all the members of a national group, we should find that the cancelling-out process was not complete. There would be loose ends in the form of paper claims owed to or by persons outside the nation. Since the accounts of these outsiders would not be added in to the national reckoning, the claims to which they were parties would only appear on one side of the national balance-sheet, instead of cancelling-out by appearing on both.

The Balance-sheet of a Nation would thus have to be written in the following form:

Liabilities	*Assets*
[a]Obligations due to fellow nationals	Real capital goods
Obligations due to outsiders	[a]Obligations due by fellow nationals
	Obligations due by outsiders

The National Capital of a country equals the sum of the net assets of all individuals and institutions within it. This is the difference between total assets and total liabilities. Since the obligations (*a*) to fellow nationals cancel out, the national capital (as appears from the above table) equals the total value of all capital goods possessed by members of the nation, *plus* the excess of obligations due from outsiders over obligations due to outsiders. Thus most of the national capital consists of real goods; but in the case of a creditor country (such as Great Britain has usually been) something has to be added on to the value of these real goods to allow for the investments which its citizens have made abroad; while in the case of a debtor country such as Britain was for a while after 1945, something has to be subtracted from the value of the capital goods owned by British subjects or by the British Government in order to allow for the balance of debts owed overseas.[1]

[1] We shall be returning to the subject of foreign investment in Chapter XII.

4. The other main snag in the cancelling-out process arises over the National Debt. In order to see how this fits into the calculation, let us begin by taking another rather similar case, of infinitely less importance, but easier to understand.[1] A young man, who expects to inherit some property on the death of an elderly relative, can sometimes succeed in borrowing money from a money-lender without any security but his 'expectations'. The practice is not a wise one, and it is probably much less common today than it was in the aristocratic society of earlier times. But how does it fit into our accounting? The loan, when it has been made and spent upon riotous living, is an asset to the money-lender and a liability to the gilded youth who borrowed it. It is not a liability to the elderly relative, from whose estate it is expected to be paid; he has not been consulted about it at all, and would be within his rights if he cut the spendthrift off 'with a shilling'. Thus there are no capital goods outstanding against the loan; we cannot regard it as a claim possessed by the money-lender against any of the real capital goods of the community. But, being a debt from one member of the nation to another, it has to be cancelled out when we are adding up the national capital. There is nothing for it but to regard the net assets of the spendthrift as a minus quantity, a state of affairs which is only possible because he has the expectation of getting an addition to his assets at some future date which will enable him to pay his debts.

Apart from a few special cases such as this, no individual or firm can have negative net assets. If a person's liabilities became greater than his assets, he would be adjudged bankrupt, and his assets would be divided up among his creditors, each of them receiving so many pence in the pound as the assets would provide. Governments, however, can have negative net assets without going bankrupt, and can carry on in that situation for an indefinite period; the reason being that they have the power of raising taxes to cover the interest on their debts.

The national debts of governments have been mostly accumulated by past wars; however necessary these wars may have been, they are unlikely to have resulted in the

[1] This is the case to which we referred above, p. 122.

acquisition of capital goods as industrial borrowing would do; there is nothing to show but the immaterial gains of freedom and independence. Whatever may be the case from a higher standpoint, the situation of the government, when the war is over, is from the standpoint of National Accounting just like that of the spendthrift. It owes a vast debt, and has no equivalent assets to set against it. Its net assets are negative.

When we are setting out the National Balance-sheet, the national debt has to be reckoned as a liability of the government. If the people to whom the debt is owed are themselves citizens of the country, it will appear as an asset in their accounts; and so, when the accounts are added together, the national debt cancels out, like other internal debts. It is only when some part of the debt is due to foreigners that there is no cancelling out; external debt of this sort is a genuine deduction from national capital. From all points of view, a large external debt is much more damaging to a nation than a large internal debt.

5. Now that we have discovered how the capital of a nation is made up, we should like to turn and see what the national balance-sheet looks like in a particular case. That is what we shall do in a moment, but before we can even approach such figures, it is necessary to utter a most solemn warning. The information which is available for the construction of a national balance-sheet is much less good than that which can be used for most other large-scale economic calculations. (It is much less good than that which we shall use for the calculation of the national income in Part IV below.) The proportion of guesswork in calculations of the national capital is abnormally high. This is partly because of defects in our information which could conceivably be remedied; direct information about many of the items is lacking, so that estimates have to be made by roundabout and imperfect methods. But the fundamental cause lies deeper, and can hardly be removed in the nature of the case.

The greater part of the national capital consists of durable-use goods, land and buildings, vehicles, and machines. What value is to be put upon these goods? It should be noticed, in the first place, that any one of these goods has, in ordinary practice, two sorts of values: (1) its *capital value*, the value at which it could be sold outright; (2) its *annual value*, the price which would be paid for the right to *use* it during a year, the article to be returned in good condition when the year is over. Since most of these durable-use goods are expected to last for much more than a year, their capital values will usually be much higher than their annual values. The selling price of a house, for instance (which is its capital value), may well be from 10 to 15 times as high as the rent, which is its annual value.[1]

For the purpose of calculating the national capital, the values which are used are capital values, not annual values.[2] But to arrive at the capital value of a durable-use good is often not an easy matter. When a house is sold for £3,000, we can say without any hesitation that its capital value is £3,000; but many of the durable-use goods which are included in the national capital will not have been sold since long before the date to which the calculation refers, and their owners will not be proposing to sell them (if at all) until long after that date. What value is to be put upon such goods? There are several purposes (in connection with the inheritance of property and with certain kinds of taxation) for which it is necessary to value these goods; skilled valuers are trained to do the job, but the methods which they use vary according to the purpose for which the valuation is wanted. The fixed capital used by a manufacturing firm may have half a dozen different values which can plausibly be put upon it. Different values may be put (1) by the directors and managers of the firm, (2) by their shareholders, (3) by another firm which might consider purchasing the whole equipment

[1] The relation between the capital value of an article and its annual value does not depend entirely upon the number of years the article is expected to last. Even in the case of land, which is more or less expected to last for ever, the selling price is rarely more than 20 times the rent, which the owner can expect to receive. If it is more than 20 times the *current* rent (as does happen in times of inflation) that is a sign that the rent is expected to rise. The selling price of a promise by the British Government to pay the same sum in interest every year for ever is now (end of 1970) about 10 times the interest (or annual value); that is, the rate of interest (annual value÷capital value) is about 10 per cent, but this (again) is a phenomenon of inflation.

[2] The annual values of capital goods reckon into the national output, not the national capital. We have seen that the rents of houses (the price paid for the use of house-room) are part of the value of the social output.

'as a going concern', (4) by yet other firms who would only be willing to purchase the equipment bit by bit. In addition to these there are the values at which the same capital might be assessed for purposes of taxation, central and local, which are not necessarily the same as any of the preceding. In any estimates of the national capital these last values, made for taxation purposes, have to be drawn upon to a large extent, because they are the most readily available; but it should be noticed that they may have less economic significance than some of the others.

The same problem of valuation arises, to a lesser but still significant extent, with some of the paper claims themselves. If, for instance, the government has borrowed £1,000 from a certain person, under promise to repay that £1,000 at some date in the future (say 1990) and to pay 3 per cent interest per annum meanwhile; then this debt should stand, and does stand, in the books of the government, at its face value of £1,000, for that is the sum which the government will have to pay out in order to pay back the loan when the time comes. This is all right from the point of view of the government, but from the point of view of the bondholder it is not at all clear that the asset he possesses should be reckoned by him at its face value. The most important value for him to use in his reckoning would be that at which he could sell the bond now, if he chose to sell it to another investor; and this may be more or less than the face value, depending on the relation between the 3 per cent offered and the interest which could be earned in alternative investments. (In fact, at the time of writing, a government bond, such as that described, could not be sold for more than £400.) The same difficulty arises with company debentures. We must therefore expect that there will be many cases where the same obligation, which appears on the liabilities side of one balance-sheet and on the assets side of another, will be assessed at different values in the two accounts, so that it will fail to cancel out, as it ought to do, when the two accounts are taken together. Difficulties of this kind can be overcome to some extent, but they are bound to make the national balance-sheet a less informative document than we should like to make it.

6. In spite of these troubles, it is useful to put down a sketch of the national balance-sheet of Great Britain, as it would appear at some recent date (at some date, in fact, during the year 1966, being the period to which the calculation by Mr. A. Roe, from which these figures are drawn, refers). This is shown in the table on p. 133. Since it is desirable to bring out the very peculiar position which is occupied, especially since 1940, by Government Debt, the owners of property are divided, for the purposes of this table, into two groups or 'sectors', which are shown separately, and then brought together. The first sector, called 'Private', shows property that belongs, directly or indirectly, to private persons; thus as well as property which is owned by persons directly, it includes property which is owned by groups of persons (such as churches or trade unions), and property which is possessed, in the first place, by joint-stock companies (whether they are 'private' or 'public' in the legal sense). The other sector, called 'Public', shows property possessed by all organs of government, not only the central government, but also local government, and also those publicly owned concerns—the nationalized industries. All of the property in each sector is British owned—the persons are British, the companies are British, the government organs are, of course, British; though there is some property in each sector which is situated abroad, and there are debts which are owed between British and non-British owners of property (who may be persons, companies, or governments on either side).

Though, for the purposes of this balance-sheet, the sectors are shown separately, the numerous distinct units which are included in each sector have been taken together. This implies, as we have seen, that debts which are owing from one unit to another within the same sector must be cancelled out. Mr. Brown has a mortgage on his house, owed to a building society; since both Mr. Brown and the building society belong to the private sector, Mr. Brown's liability will cancel out against the building society's asset, and in our table that mortgage will not appear. (What will appear is the house; whether we have left the house belonging to Mr. Brown or have turned a part of it over to the building society is a question we do not need to ask.) In just the same way we shall cancel out the shares which his neighbour owns in Marks & Spencer; the same share is an asset to the shareholder and a liability to the company (both within the private sector) so it will not appear. Similar claims will nevertheless appear if they run outside the private sector; if Mr. Brown had borrowed from a local authority, that would appear as a liability of the private and an asset of the public sector; if his neighbour had shares in an American company, that would appear as an external asset (of the private sector).

There is quite a lot of cancelling to be done in the public sector also. Rather surprisingly, the central government turns out to owe quite a bit of national debt to itself; for there are many departments and offices of government with funds of their own, and they are very liable to hold spare funds in the form of government debt, like other people. (Such holdings will, of course, be cancelled out straight off.) The same must happen with debt which is owed by local authorities and nationalized industries to the central government—the loans which have been raised by these authorities 'through the Treasury'; but, of course, it will not happen with the loans which they have raised 'on the market'. These result in debts from public sector bodies to private sector bodies, so they will be shown.

Most of the items in our table should make sense along these lines; there is, however, one item which may still look curious—the 'notes and coin' which have been included among the liabilities of the public sector. In order to understand why they are treated in this way, it will be well to look first at the other part of the nation's money holdings—the money which people have 'in the bank'. That, it is fairly clear, can be nothing else but a debt from the bank to the depositor; it has no more 'real' existence. If we were reckoning the banks and their (private) depositors as belonging to different sectors, the bank money would appear as an asset of the depositor and a liability of the bank; there would clearly be no other way in which we could treat it. On our reckoning, however, both belong to the private sector; so the bank money does not appear. Like other debts that are wholly within the private sector, it cancels out in our table.

Since 1946 the Bank of England has been nationalized; so

in our table it belongs to the public sector. Debts from the Bank of England to persons (and other bodies) within the private sector must accordingly be shown. The notes which are issued by the Bank of England are nothing else but statements of such debt. (If the reader doubts this, he can just look at a pound note and see!) They are undoubtedly assets to the holders; they appear as liabilities in the account of the Bank of England (though it must be admitted that they are an odd sort of liability, since they carry no interest, and cannot be paid off excepting in themselves). They are basically the same kind of thing as bank deposits—cheaper and easier to transfer, but on the other hand more easily stolen. For the purposes of our table we want to treat them (as we are treating them, excepting for the Bank of England being in the public sector) in exactly the same way as the bank money.

Paper money does not look like anything more than a certificate of debt; metal coins are made to look as if they were much more solid. But since the metal which is contained in modern token coinage is worth much less than the face value of the coins, they also are best regarded as a kind of note, printed on metal instead of paper in order to wear better. The value of the metal which they contain is a quite minor matter. The important thing (one of the most important things which emerges from the national balance-sheet) is that the money which circulates in the country is simply a part of the system of debts from one part of the national economy to another.

The whole of the internal monetary circulation has to be regarded in this manner; but there is another part of the nation's money supply, which does not circulate within the country. This is the reserve of international money, mainly kept in the form of gold. The gold reserve used to be kept in the Bank of England, but since 1939 it has been kept in the hands of the government directly. In any case it will reckon among the assets of the public sector, where it will be found in the table. The functions of this reserve will be considered in Chapter XII.

7. Let us now look again at Table VI, and this time let us follow it through. (The figures in the table are in hundreds of millions of pounds; one can just put it like that in a table, but here, so as not to get drowned in noughts, I shall invent a symbol £H for that same astronomical unit.)

The assets of the private sector comprise, in the first place, 1024£H of real goods: these include the real goods (houses and so on) owned by private persons, as well as all the capital goods (land and buildings, machinery and stocks) owned by non-nationalized business. All debts and credits *within the private sector* have been cancelled out, as will be remembered; there nevertheless remains, as well as the quite small 27£H of notes and coin, the large figure of 305£H which is owing to the private sector in government debt of other sorts (local authority and nationalized industry debt, as well as national debt proper). The particular parts of the private sector which owns this debt cannot, of course, be shown in our table; a substantial part is owing to financial institutions (banks and such like), but the amount which was still held, in 1966, by private persons, not only by small savers, appears also to have been very considerable.

The external assets, shown as the remaining item on the assets side of the private sector, include (as well as some buildings and other equipment owned abroad) the value of overseas branches of British companies, shares owned by British companies in overseas companies, and overseas investments by British persons. These, it will be observed, are to a considerable extent offset by external liabilities (such as shares in British companies owned outside the United Kingdom, and deposits in British banks owned externally). When the private sector is taken alone, it is a substantial net creditor on external account.

Turning to the public sector, the real goods which appear on the assets side include those which are owned by the nationalized industries; but they also include such things as military equipment and the road system, though it is very doubtful what value should be put on things of that kind. But it is only by putting a substantial value upon them that the assets of the public sector are brought to exceed its liabilities as they do in this table. On external account, unquestionably, the public sector is a net debtor (even if we reckon the gold reserve as belonging to the external account, as it is rather useful to do, since the government could always reduce its external liabilities by paying out gold, or it could turn its gold into another form of external asset, as, for instance, by increasing its subscription to the International Monetary Fund). The external liabilities of the public sector include, on the one hand, the 21£H owed to the governments of the United States and Canada as a result of the loans which were given by those governments in 1945–6; and on the other, the holdings of ordinary British government debt by outsiders (largely banks).

If we allow ourselves to add up these items, and to offset liabilities against assets, we find that the private sector has

TABLE VI

Estimated Balance-sheet of the National Capital of the United Kingdom (1966) (£ Hundred millions)[1]

Liabilities		Assets		Net Assets
Private Sector				
		Real Goods	1024	
		Govt. Debt	305	
		Notes and Coin	27	
External	116	External	159	
Total	116	Total	1515	1399
Public Sector				
		Real Goods	412	
Internal Debt	305			
Notes and Coin	27			
External	64	Gold and currency reserve	11	
		Other external assets	20	
Total	396	Total	443	47
Whole Economy				
		Real Goods	1436	
		Gold reserve	11	
External liabilities	180	Other external assets	179	
Total	180	Total	1626	1446

[1] The figures in this table were provided for me by Mr. A. Roe, of the Department of Applied Economics, University of Cambridge; they come from his forthcoming publication *The Financial Interdependence of the Economy 1957–1966* (to be published by Chapman and Hall) which is a continuation of the study made by Professor J. R. S. Revell (*The Wealth of the Nation*, Cambridge University Press, 1967). For some further discussion see below, Appendix, Note D.

net assets to the extent of 1399£H, while the public sector (as shown) has net assets of 47£H. Offsetting again, we find that the value of the national capital, taken as a whole, comes out at 1446£H. Adding up the real goods separately, they come to 1436£H; the difference is, of course, explained by the net credit on external account—which (as it turned out in this particular year) was almost equal to the reserve of gold and foreign currency.

PART IV The Social Product

CHAPTER XI The Social Product and the Social Income

1. The general picture of the productive process during any period, which we worked out in Part I of this book, and have needed to keep at the back of our minds throughout our later discussions, can be briefly described as Labour working on Capital to produce Output. In Parts II and III we have discussed the Factors of Production—Labour and Capital; now we come to the study of Output—the Social Product. We shall devote a good deal of our attention to the problem of measuring the social (or national) product, mainly in order that we should have a clear idea of what it consists, and what are its component parts. When we have done this, we shall be in a position to say something about changes in the social product, how they are caused, and how people's economic welfare is affected by them.

There are many similarities between the problem of measuring output and the problem of measuring capital; we shall meet again over our new problem some of the same difficulties as we have met already. But it is very important that we should keep the two problems clearly distinct. Both the output of a community and its capital consist, for the most part, of a collection of goods (though output contains services as well, while capital does not). But the goods which are included in the one collection are not the same as the goods included in the other. The goods included in capital are those which exist at a particular moment of time; the goods included in output are those produced during a period of time. Some of the goods contained in output are durable goods, which will also reckon as parts of the community's capital at any time when they are simultaneously in existence. A house finished in April and a house finished in June are both in existence in July, and will reckon as parts of the community's capital in July. But a loaf of bread baked in April has been eaten before a loaf baked in June comes into existence; both loaves are part of the year's output, but there is no date at which they are both of them parts of capital.

Thus the social product consists of a different collection of commodities from that which makes up the social capital; but they are both of them collections of commodities including many different sorts. Because of the different sorts of commodities included in capital, the only feasible way of reducing them to a common basis, so as to get a single figure for the national capital, was to take their values in terms of money (this quite apart from the question of foreign debts). We gave our figure for the national capital as so many pounds sterling, and just the same has to be done for the national product. We must always think of the social output as consisting of goods and services, things useful for satisfying wants; but when it comes to measurement, the only way of adding together an output consisting of so much bread, so many bicycles, so many ships, so many hours' teaching and so on, is to take the value in terms of money. There are serious defects in the money measure, so that it has to be used very carefully. But we shall find it convenient to begin by taking the money measure for granted, leaving its defects, and how far they can be remedied, for later discussion.[1]

2. The methods of computing the social product which are commonly employed depend on a very important economic principle, which is concerned with the close relationship between the value of the net social product and the total of the incomes of members of the community. When this principle is applied, as we usually want to apply it, to calculating the national product of a nation, there are a couple of snags which complicate the argument; after our study of the national capital, the reader will not be surprised to learn

[1] See below, Chapter XV.

that these snags are due (1) to economic dealings with persons outside the nation, (2) to the economic activities of the government. We shall deal with these snags in due time,[1] but for the present it will simplify things if we leave them out of account. In the rest of this chapter we shall make the unreal assumptions that there are no economic relations with persons or bodies outside our community, and that the economic activities of the State can be neglected. When these assumptions are made, the argument is easier to follow; there is not much harm in making simplifications of this sort if we propose to fill in the gaps later on.

Subject to these assumptions, the principle we have to establish is very simple. It states that the value of the net social product of the community and the sum of the incomes of its members are exactly equal. The net social product and the social income are one and the same thing.

It will be convenient to begin with a special case in which this principle is directly obvious. Let us suppose that the whole of the productive system of our community is organized in a single giant Firm, which controls all the capital equipment, and employs all the labour. This is very much the situation which would exist in a perfectly socialist community; the whole economic system of such a community would consist of a single firm, in which the State would own all the shares. We need not here suppose that the State owns the shares, as we do not want to bring the State into the picture just yet; we will suppose that the shares belong to a body of private shareholders, who may thus be regarded as the indirect owners of the capital equipment.

The net social product and the net product of our Firm are then one and the same thing. It consists, as we know, of the total amount of consumption goods and services produced, *plus* net investment, which is the increase in capital equipment brought about by the year's production. The wages of labour have to be paid out of the value of this output; but all the rest is profit, belonging to the shareholders.[2] The wages of labour are the incomes of the labourers; the

[1] See below, Chapters XII and XIII.

[2] Since our firm controls the whole of production, there can be no purchasing of materials from other firms.

profit left over is the income of the shareholders. The value of the net social product is thus equal to wages *plus* profits; and wages *plus* profits equals the sum of incomes. The net social product equals the social income.

The same equality can be tested out along another route, by considering the way in which the incomes are spent. People will spend part of their incomes on buying consumption goods and services (buying them, of course, from the Firm, so that a part of its output is accounted for in this way); the rest they will save. Now when we say that a person saves a part of his income, we do not mean that this part of his income is not spent; saving is the opposite of consumption, not the opposite of spending. When a person saves, he uses a part of his income to make an addition to his assets; he is still saving, whatever form the additional assets take. Thus one possible way for a person to save would be by purchasing new equipment directly, and adding it to the assets in his possession at the end of the year. If we supposed that all the savings took this form, then it would be easy to see that the social income would purchase the social product. The part of the social product which consisted of consumption goods and services would be bought out of consumption expenditure; the part which consisted of the net investment would be purchased out of savings. Income as a whole would purchase output as a whole; we should have social income equalling net social product along this route too.

Further, it is obvious that the equality would not be disturbed if we were to suppose that the savers, after acquiring the new equipment in this way, did not retain it in their possession, but lent it back to the Firm. The social income would still have purchased the social product; but the Firm would retain control of the new equipment, issuing shares in exchange for it. The additional assets of the savers would now take the form of shares; the shares would be a liability to the Firm, but the Firm's assets and liabilities would still be equal, as they should be, because the Firm would have the new equipment, equal in value to the shares, added on to its assets. The Firm's balance-sheet would still balance.

In order to arrive at this last situation it would obviously be unnecessary for the actual goods, which constitute the new equipment, ever to pass directly into the hands of the savers. The savers might use their savings to acquire shares directly, and the Firm might issue the shares for them to acquire, without the new equipment ever changing hands. If the value of the shares issued was equal to the value of the savings, it would also be equal to the value of the net investment. The Firm's assets and liabilities would still balance; the savers would have acquired shares to the amount of their savings, while the goods which constitute the net investment would be retained by the Firm and added to its capital equipment.

So long as we assume that the whole of the capital equipment of the community is controlled by the single Firm, it is this last form which we ought to suppose the saving to take. People save by acquiring shares in the Firm; but the creation of the shares is only the reverse side of the accumulation of additional equipment by the Firm. When a person saves, he acquires the right to receive some part of the profit which will be earned by using the additional equipment which is being produced. He uses a part of his income to acquire a share in the indirect ownership of that new capital equipment.[1]

Let us look back at the combined balance-sheet of firm and shareholders, which was given in the last chapter,[2] and see how it is affected by saving. Taking figures more appropriate for a giant Firm, we should have, at the beginning of the year

	Liabilities	*Assets*	
Firm:	Shares £1,000 million	Real Equipment	£1,000 million
Shareholders:	..	Shares	£1,000 million

At the end of the year

	Liabilities	*Assets*	
Firm:	Shares £1,050 million	Real Equipment	£1,050 million
Shareholders:	..	Shares	£1,050 million

[1] A particular person may indeed dispose of his savings in another way than by lending them to the Firm: he may lend them to another private person and so enable that other person to consume in excess of his income. But we need not pay much attention to lending of this sort, for when the borrower and lender are taken together, the saving obviously cancels out. There is no excess of total income over total consumption. It is only savings which generate such an excess which are net savings; under our assumption of the single Firm which owns all the capital equipment such net savings must be lent to the Firm.

[2] p. 123.

The extra £50 million of shares held by the shareholders are their savings; the extra £50 millions' worth of Real Equipment is the Net Investment. Since the Firm's assets and liabilities must be equal *at both dates*, the savings must be equal in value to the net investment.

Thus the fact that people save by acquiring titles to the ownership of parts of the new equipment, instead of by acquiring new equipment directly, does not disturb the relationship between the social product and the social income. That relation can be summed up in the following very important table.

On the earning side

Net Social Product	=	Wages + Profits	=	Social Income

On the spending side

Social Income	=	Consumption + Saving	=	Consumption + Net Investment	=	Net Social Product

These equations will remain valid in spite of all the further complications which we shall take into account in the rest of this chapter. But in the following chapters we shall encounter certain points where it is necessary to take some care over the interpretation of these equations.

3. It will be convenient, as a next step, to take into account some complications which can be allowed for while still supposing that industry is organized in a giant Firm.

In the first place, we have hitherto been assuming that the Firm pays out to its shareholders the whole of the profits which it earns, that the shareholders then save part of the incomes they get in this way, and that they lend these savings back to the Firm. In practice, a firm might be inclined to short-circuit this process, and to keep back part of its profits, instead of distributing all the profits to the shareholders directly. In such a case, what effectively happens is that the shareholders are compelled to save a part of the incomes which are due to them; additional shares may not be issued, but the shares previously outstanding will increase in value, because of the additional capital goods which they represent. The undistributed profits have to be reckoned as part of the social income; they are really part of the incomes of the shareholders, although they are not usually reckoned as such, because shareholders do not get them into their own hands. They have to be reckoned into that part of the social income which is saved; there is a part of net investment corresponding to them, as there should be.

Secondly, we have been assuming hitherto that private people can hold in their personal possession no sort of capital goods, not even consumers' capital goods, such as houses. If we allow them to possess such things as houses, then the rents of these houses have to be reckoned as part of the social income, income derived from a form of capital which is not in the possession of the Firm. (It will be remembered that we are reckoning the use of the houses as part of the social product.) Expenditure on paying the rents of houses is of course a part of consumption. The building of new houses is a part of investment; we may suppose that the actual building is carried out by the Firm, but the part of its output which consists of new houses is sold off to private people, just as the consumption goods are sold off, and not lent back to the Firm, like other investment goods. If private people spend some part of their incomes in buying new houses, they are adding to the assets which they will have in their possession at the end of the year, just as they would do if they acquired shares; consequently income spent in buying new houses is a part of saving. The new houses are to be looked on as a part of new equipment, which is retained in direct private ownership, and not handed back to the Firm in return for shares.

Thirdly, we have been assuming that all labour is employed by the Firm. This is not very convenient in the case of some of the direct personal services. If we allow some of the people who provide direct services to be working on their own account, not for the Firm, we have to distinguish a part of the social product, consisting of these services, which is not part of the product of the Firm, and also to distinguish a part of the earnings of labour which are not wages paid by the Firm. The income spent on these services is a part of consumption, so it finds its place in the table without any difficulty.

Let us now consider what alterations have to be made in our equations to allow for these three complications which we have been discussing. On the earning side, instead of wages *plus* profits, we must write earnings of labour *plus* profits *plus* house rents; and these in turn can be further divided up. So we have the following equivalent columns:

Social product				Social income
Net product of Firm*	Wages earned in Firm*	Wages paid by Firm*	Earnings of labour	Personal incomes
	plus Profits earned by Firm*	*plus* Profits paid out in interest and dividends*	*plus* Interest and dividends	*plus* Undistributed profits
		plus Undistributed profits*	*plus* Rents	
plus Services of labour not employed by Firm	*plus* Earnings of labour not employed by Firm	*plus* Earnings of labour not employed by Firm	*plus* Undistributed profits	
plus Use of house-room	*plus* House rents	*plus* House rents		

On the spending side, consumption and saving can be similarly divided up, so that we have as our other set of equivalent columns:

Social income	Consumption of* goods produced by Firm	Output of consumption goods and services	Consumption	Social product
	plus Consumption of other labour services			
	plus Consumption of house-room			
	plus Saving spent on buying new houses*	*plus* Output of new houses sold to savers		
	plus Saving lent to Firm*		*plus* Net investment	
	plus Saving in the form of undistributed profits*	*plus* Net new equipment of Firm		

This expanded table has exactly the same significance as our earlier table, which it in no way supersedes. If we interpret wages to mean all earnings of labour, and profits to mean all earnings of capital, it is still true that the social income consists of wages plus profits, and that these wages and profits are earned in producing the social product. If we interpret saving to include undistributed profits, and investment to include the purchase of durable-use goods by consumers, it is still true that saving equals net investment; it is the equality between saving and investment which establishes the equality between income and product on the spending side. Understood in this way, the fundamental equations of p. 142 remain completely true.

4. We are now in a position to drop our assumption of the giant Firm. In the tables we have just given, the part played by the giant Firm is exactly the same as that played in reality by all the firms which compose industry and commerce, when they are taken all together. Our Firm is simply the whole collection of actual firms rolled into one. And we can see the part which this whole collection of firms actually plays in the earning and spending of the social income, by looking at the place of the single Firm (marked out by the starred items) in the tables opposite. On the earning side, the net product of the Firm is equal to the wages it pays out, *plus* its profits (distributed and undistributed). On the spending side, the net product of the Firm is purchased (1) out of consumption expenditure, so far as it consists of consumption goods; (2) out of saving, so far as it consists of new consumer's capital goods, such as houses; (3) out of saving, so far as it is offset by lending to the Firm; (4) out of saving, so far as it corresponds to undistributed profits. This is the position of the single giant Firm, as it appears in the tables; but this is also the position of the whole collection of firms, which composed the real world of industry and commerce, *when they are all taken together*. This we shall now proceed to show.

The new points which emerge when we pull apart our giant Firm into the multitudinous separate firms, large and small, which correspond to it in reality, are only two in number. On the one hand, we have to take account of the materials[1] which are produced by one firm and sold to another, which uses them in its own production. These materials do not come into the picture, so long as industry and commerce are supposed to be amalgamated into one single Firm, because the passing on of materials from one stage of production to another is then a purely internal matter within the Firm. When the firms are pulled apart, the sale of materials looks just the same to the firm which sells them as any other sort of sale does. But since we have also to take into account the purchase of the materials by the firm which uses them, the sale and purchase of such materials will cancel out when all firms are taken together.

The other point which has to be taken into account when we have more firms than one is the possibility that part of the shares (or other obligations) of one firm may be owned, not by private persons who are shareholders, but by another firm. If this happens, a part of the profits of the one firm will be paid out to the other firm; but here again, when all the firms are taken together, these transferences of profits will cancel out. The only profits left will be those which are actually paid out to private persons, or which remain as undistributed profits. A further consequence of this possibility is that savings lent to one firm may not be used as a means of increasing the capital goods in the possession of that firm, but may be lent again to some other firm. (An obvious example of this is the case of the banks.) These re-lendings, too, will cancel out when all firms are taken together.

5. Thus the separation of firms makes absolutely no difference to our general argument. All transactions between firms cancel out, when all firms are taken together, as they have to be for calculation of the *social* income or product. But it will, nevertheless, be instructive to show in detail how the cancellation proceeds, by looking at the way in which firms do actually calculate their profits in practice. We shall continue to simplify by leaving out all reference to questions of taxation; but even so it may be that the fitting together of

[1] There are also certain services, such as transport and insurance, which are performed by one firm for another, so that their role is similar to that of materials.

the firms will be found a little bewildering. It is therefore wise to insist that no new principle is involved beyond those which have been set out in the preceding section.

The profits which are earned by a firm from the production of a particular year equal the value of its output *minus* the expenses to which it has been put to produce that output. These expenses include (1) wages and salaries, (2) cost of materials used up in order to produce the output, (3) cost of services, such as transport and insurance, provided by other firms, (4) depreciation of the *fixed* capital equipment.[1] Thus for any firm

Value of output = Wages + Cost of materials and services + Depreciation + Profits

This is the basic equation which expresses the part played by the Firm in the earning of the social income.[2]

We shall have to use this basic equation in many ways; it will therefore be convenient to define some terms which enable us to break it up into steps. In what follows we shall be careful to call the output (or sales) of the firm, in the sense ordinarily understood, its *Gross Output*. Gross output *minus* cost of materials (and services supplied by other firms) used up in production we shall call the *Net Output* of the firm; we may say, if we like, that net output is the part of the social output which is attributable to this firm itself. At the next step we want to deduct Depreciation. Since the terms 'gross' and 'net' mean nothing else but 'before and after deducting something', it will be inconvenient to 'net' again, and talk about 'net output net of depreciation'. We need something less clumsy. What I find the most convenient procedure (and one which fits in remarkably well with common usage) is to associate the term 'product' with the depreciation deduction. What we shall therefore do is to say that the *net output* of the firm is the same thing as its *Gross Product*.[3] Its *Net Product* is its gross product *minus* depreciation. The basic equation then tells us that net product equals wages *plus* profits.

[1] Depreciation is here used in the business man's sense, as depreciation of fixed capital only. See Appendix, Note C.

[2] From the accounting point of view, it is the trading account of the Firm. See Chapter XX below.

[3] It is in practice more common to use instead of 'Gross Product' (or 'Net Output') the term 'value added'.

The basic equation is thus broken up into three steps.

Gross Output = Cost of materials and services + Net Output
Net Output = Gross Product = Depreciation + Net Product
Net Product = Wages + Profits.

These equations are true for every individual firm taken separately.

If now we take all firms together, as we must do for the calculation of the social product, we find that the sum of the net outputs of all firms equals the sum of the gross outputs of all firms minus the cost of the materials and services used in production. But in interpreting this relation, we must take account of the services performed by one firm for another, and of the materials sold by one firm to another. The transport, insurance, etc., which figure among the expenses of production for most ordinary firms, are part of the gross output of such firms as the railways and insurance companies, and can be cancelled out against that output. Materials which are produced by one firm within the year, and used up by another firm within the year, are reckoned in the gross output of the first firm and in the cost of materials of the second; thus they also can be cancelled out when all firms are taken together. But some of the materials which are produced during the year will not be used during the year, but will be added to stocks; some of the materials used during the year will not have been produced during the year, but will be taken from stocks. Thus *all* materials will not necessarily cancel out. It should also be noticed that there are some goods which are sold by one firm to another which will not cancel out, because they are not such as to be used up in the production of this year's output; these are the durable-use goods, the fixed-capital goods, which go towards replacing or increasing industry's stock of fixed capital.

When we have performed these cancellations, the sum of the net outputs of all firms comes out as follows:

	Gross output of goods sold to consumers
plus	Gross output of fixed capital goods sold to other firms
plus	Value of materials added to stocks
less	Value of materials taken from stocks.

The first of these items is the output of consumption goods, plus fixed-capital goods (such as houses) sold to consumers; the second is the gross output of fixed-capital goods used in industry—gross investment in industrial fixed capital; the difference between the third and fourth items represents the net investment in materials. It is convenient to use the term *Gross Investment* to mean *gross* investment in fixed capital *plus net* investment in materials. Thus we have shown that the sum of the net outputs (or gross products) of all firms equals the gross output of all consumption goods plus investment goods produced by industry. In fact, if we neglect the complication about investment in materials, we may say that the distinction between gross output and gross product, which is so important for the individual firm, disappears when all firms are added together. This is precisely what happened when we were considering the giant Firm.

The net product of each firm is the difference between gross product and depreciation. Thus the sum of the net products of all firms is got by deducting the sum of depreciation from the sum of gross products (or net outputs). But the latter has been shown to equal the sum of the output of consumption goods plus gross investment. Deducting depreciation from this,

Net Product of industry = Output of consumption goods +Net Investment.

But the net product of industry is the sum of all the wages and profits earned in industry. Thus we have shown that the sum of the wages and profits earned in industry is equal to the output of consumption goods produced in industry plus the net investment produced in industry—just as was the case with the giant Firm.

6. So far we have been concerned with the wages and profits *earned* in industry; we must now proceed to follow them through until they (or the greater part of them) become personal incomes in the hands of individuals. The wages earned during the year are of necessity paid out directly to private persons—the wage-earners; thus at this round there is nothing to be considered on the side of wages. Profits, on the other hand, are not so simple, for a part of profits may be held back in undistributed profits, and part may be paid out to other firms. But if we are to take notice of the possibility that firm *A* distributes dividends to firm *B* (which holds shares in firm *A*), we must also take account of the possibility that firm *A* itself may hold shares in firm *C*, and receive dividends from firm *C*. These dividends, like the profits made by firm *A* itself, are available for distribution to the shareholders of *A*.

Thus, in considering the distribution of a firm's profits,[1] we have the equation:

Profits earned in production
+Interest and dividends received from other firms
= Interest and dividends paid out to private persons
+Interest and dividends paid out to other firms
+Undistributed profits.

When all firms are taken together, the interest and dividends received from other firms and the interest and dividends paid to other firms must be equal; they can therefore be cancelled out. Thus, for all firms taken together,

Profits earned in production
= Interest and dividends paid out to private persons
+Undistributed profits.

Now we have seen that the net product of industry equals the sum of wages plus profits earned in industry; it therefore follows that the net product of industry equals the wages and profits paid out to wage-earners and shareholders (or property-owners) *plus* undistributed profits. This is just as it was in the case of the giant Firm, so that the validity of our table showing equality of net social product and social income, on the earning side, is fully checked up.[2]

[1] Taxation, in accordance with the general practice followed in this chapter, is of course still left out.

[2] This account of the distribution of a firms' profits has been put in terms of the joint-stock company (see Chapter IX above); for that is nowadays the most important type of firm. Other types can be fitted in, however, without much difficulty. A man who is in business by himself does not distinguish between profits paid out to himself (as sole shareholder) and undistributed profits—in effect all his profits are distributed; but he may still have to pay interest to other firms, as, for instance, on a loan from his bank. A farmer who rents his land from a landlord is best regarded as paying rent in place of interest (for he might have borrowed money and purchased the land out-

7. When we turn to the spending side, things can easily become a bit tricky; this is indeed a field where some quite classic muddles have been known to occur. One is tempted to say (as eminent economists have in fact said on occasion) that the equality of social income and net social product has already been established along one route, so that it must hold along the other also—which makes further discussion unnecessary. But the reader would be justified in feeling that a short cut of this sort is a bit unsatisfactory. There is nowadays no reason why we should not follow the thing through, and satisfy ourselves that the equality holds along this other channel also. If we go step by step, and watch our steps carefully, we shall come out all right.

The chief thing which has caused difficulty, and about which we have to be careful, is the role of money. When a private person saves, he may use his savings to buy consumers' capital goods, such as a house (we have taken account of that); or he may use them to buy shares or bonds (we have taken account of that too); or finally he may use them to add to his holding of cash, such as his bank balance. It is over this last form of saving that trouble so frequently arises. We can, however, avoid all this trouble, once we remember the principle which was established on pp. 130–1 of the preceding chapter, when we were discussing the national capital. Apart from the gold reserves held for purposes of international trade (which can here be left out of account, as we are neglecting questions of external relations), modern money consists of nothing but a debt from a bank to the holder of the money; thus if a person increases his holding of money, he is simply increasing the debt owed to him by the bank—that is to say, he is lending to the bank. Now though there are important ways in which lending to a bank is different from lending to other firms, nevertheless from our point of view banks are firms; lending to a bank

right). The real difficulty about these latter cases is the absence of a clear distinction between wages and profits; income derived from the man's own labour and that derived from the capital equipment in his possession is not clearly divided up. This lack of distinction will cause us a good deal of trouble later; but since the total of wages *plus* profits earned in such activities is quite clearly defined, it obviously does not affect the principle with which we are here concerned.

must be reckoned as lending to firms, like other lending to industry and commerce.

It follows that all saving, which is not employed in purchasing consumers' capital goods, must be lent. Since lending by one private person to another will evidently cancel out, when all private persons are taken together, we must have, for all private persons taken together

Personal income
  = Consumption
    +Saving
  = Purchase of consumption goods and services
    +Purchase of consumer's capital goods
    +Savings lent to firms.

In order to show that social income equals social output, by the spending route, we have to show that this saving lent to firms by private persons, *plus* the saving provided by the firms themselves out of undistributed profits, equals net investment by firms.

In order to see that this is so, we must look back at the typical balance-sheet of a firm, as shown in the table on p. 121 above. The balance-sheet must balance, at the end of the year as at the beginning; therefore the sum total of the increases in assets (on one side of the account) must equal the sum total of the increases in 'liabilities' (on the other).[1] Now the changes which occur over the year in the various balance-sheet items can be identified with sums which fit into the yearly account, on which we are now working. The increase in equipment equals gross investment *minus* depreciation, or *net investment*. An increase in 'trade debtors' is equivalent to *new lending* by the firm. Increases in shares issued, in bonds, in bank debt, or in trade creditors, can all be regarded as *new borrowing*, of one kind or another. An increase in the reserve balance can only come from undistributed profits. Thus the balancing of the balance-sheet, at the end of the year as at the beginning, tells us that

New borrowing + Undistributed profits = New lending + Net investment

[1] Some (or all) of these increases may of course be negative (decreases).

This equation is true for every firm,[1] and the corresponding totals will therefore still be equal when all firms are taken together. But when we add up, lendings and borrowings from one firm to another will cancel out; lendings by firms to the public must be deducted from the borrowings from the public. Thus, for all firms taken together,

Net new borrowing from private persons + Undistributed profits = Net investment by firms

This is what we had to show. For the net borrowing from private persons equals the personal savings lent to firms. Subject to the assumptions which we made at the beginning of this chapter, the equality between social income and net social product is fully checked up. It is valid whether we look at it on the side of earning, or on the spending side.

8. The methods which are commonly used by statisticians for the calculation of the national product (or national income) now suggest themselves at once. Although there are certain corrections which have to be introduced when the simplifying assumptions are dropped (we are going to discuss these corrections in the following chapters), the connection between net national product and the sum of incomes remains close enough for it to be possible to approach the same problem from either side, from the side of output or from the side of income.

Let us begin by considering the *income* method, which proceeds along the route of adding up the incomes of all members of the community. This was the method that was originally used for the calculation of the national income of the United Kingdom. Even before 1939, when the proportion of the population paying income tax was much smaller than it is today, the income method was quite usable; for the incomes of most people who were not wage-earners were classified

[1] It is useful to notice that it is just as true for a financial business, such as a bank, as it is for an industrial concern. In the case of a bank, net investment in equipment will almost certainly be tiny; even if the banker is building new branches, the cost of the new buildings will be small relatively to the general scale of its operations. It is the new borrowing and lending which matter to the bank; but we see from above that these fit into their place.

in the accounts of the Income Tax, and the incomes of the wage-earning population could be assessed from the statistics of earnings collected by the Ministry of Labour. The gap which was left to be covered by indirect estimates was therefore quite narrow. With the great extension of liability to income tax which took place during the war, and which has been maintained subsequently, the use of the income method has become still easier. There are, however, not many other countries which are so well placed as Britain for the use of the income method; though since the extension of income tax to wider sections of the population has been a fairly common experience, quite a number of countries are better placed for use of the income method than they were before 1939.

The second method is the *production method*, which approaches the problem from the output side. If there exists a census of production for the year in question,[1] the net products of most firms can be calculated from it, and have only to be added together. Estimates have to be made for the sorts of production not included (or not satisfactorily included) in the census, and these are inevitably less reliable; nevertheless, there exists a variety of indirect methods by which quite good estimates can be made. Once the production method has been applied to a year for which there is a census, the indirect methods allow it to be extended to neighbouring years; this can give quite good results, and is a very different matter from a production estimate that is entirely based upon indirect evidence, without any census of production to serve as a check. In such countries as the United States and Sweden the first estimates of the national income were based upon the production method; but though the production method continues to be employed, the income method is more usable in such countries than it used to be.

With greater experience, and the increasing abundance of economic statistics, the accuracy of both methods has been very generally improved; but perhaps the most important development in this field which has occurred since 1940 has been the general practice of checking the results got by the one method against those got by the other. As the theory of

[1] See above, p. 6.

the national income has become better understood, it has been realized not merely that the totals need to square, but that several of the component parts can be checked against one another as well. A good modern estimate of the national income of a country is based upon both methods, and is thereby both better and more informative than it would be if it were based upon one of them alone. A very ample supply of economic statistics is, however, needed before it is possible to satisfy these rather exacting requirements; a country whose general sources of economic information are poor cannot hope to have its national income estimated in a manner which is at all trustworthy.[1]

The double method, of estimating from the income *and* from the production side, can sometimes be supplemented by a third approach, from expenditure. The social income, on the side of spending, is equal to the value of consumption *plus* saving. An estimate of the value of consumption can sometimes be made by using statistics of retail trade; information can sometimes be got about some, at least, of the channels of saving. If these figures are available, a rough estimate of the national income can be made from them. The expenditure method is less reliable than the other methods, but since its results ought to square with those got by the other methods, it is useful as a check. And estimates of the value of consumption and saving are of course exceedingly interesting in themselves.

We shall examine the results of some of these investigations later; but before we can do so, we must discuss the qualifications to the statement that net national product equals the sum of the incomes of members of the nation. We shall begin with the question of external relations.

[1] This is only too true of quite a number of countries, for which one will find statistics of national income (or Gross National Product) in United Nations' publications.

CHAPTER XII Foreign Payments and the National Income

1. So long as we are concerned with a self-contained (or 'closed') community, the theory of the social income is quite a tidy matter. It has plenty of complications, which have caused us some trouble in the preceding chapter, but in every case the complications come out in the wash, and we are reduced to the fundamental equations of earning and spending:

Net Social Product = Wages+Profits = Social Income
Social Income = Consumption+Saving
= Consumption+Net Investment = Net Social Product.

The snake always eats its own tail.

When, however, we proceed to apply the same arguments to the case of an 'open' economy, such as a nation ('open' because it has economic relations with foreigners, people outside it) we cannot expect to get the same tidiness. Every sort of economic relation with foreigners leads to a particular kind of lose end. There is a sense in which the loose ends can get tied up, after a fashion. But before we attempt to tie them up, we must begin by identifying them, and finding places for them. They can in fact be reduced to six types.

i. The first kind of economic relation with foreigners which has to be considered is the selling of goods and services to foreigners—exports.[1] From our point of view, the existence

[1] Throughout this chapter I use the words *imports* and *exports* to mean *all* goods and services sold by members of the nation to outsiders or bought by

of exports means that not all the goods which enter into the national product are purchased out of the national income. Some of the national product is purchased by foreigners, whose incomes are not part of the national income.

ii. The second kind is the purchasing of goods and services from foreigners—imports. It is no longer true that the whole of the national income is spent upon buying the national product; some of it is spent upon goods produced by foreigners. These two points are relatively obvious.

iii. We next come to a point which we have already encountered, in another form, when we were dealing with the national capital. The social capital of a closed community consists of the goods possessed by its members; the social income of a closed community is derived from the output of labour working on those capital goods. That is why, for a closed community, social income equals net social product. But the national capital of a nation may include not only goods but also obligations due from foreigners; in this case, there will be members of the national community who derive incomes from interest or dividends on these foreign assets, as well as from the product of the capital and labour that is employed at home—what is usually called the domestic product. Or, on the other hand, it may be that members of the nation have obligations owing to outsiders, on which they have to pay interest or dividends; if so, a part of the domestic product has to be paid to foreigners, and only what is left over after these payments have been made remains to form the incomes of the nation's own members. Thus it is no longer true that the total of interest and dividends paid out to private

them from outsiders. This is the natural economic meaning. But before we can apply our reasoning to the published statistics of imports and exports, a warning is necessary. The imports and exports recorded in the statistics are only those which pass under the noses of customs officials at ports or customs houses; but not all the things which are imports or exports in the economic sense do so. The imports and exports which are recorded by the customs officials are called *visible*; the others are called *invisible*. A very important invisible export of Great Britain is the transport by shipping which British sailors perform for outsiders; another is the insurance done for foreigners by British insurance companies; neither of these get included in the official statistics of exports. Another invisible export is the services performed for foreign tourists. When Americans travel in England, England is (invisibly) exporting; when Englishmen travel on the Continent, England is (invisibly) importing.

people within the nation, *plus* undistributed profits accruing within the nation, equals profits earned within the nation. Some part of the profits may be paid out to foreign creditors; and some of the interest and dividends received may come from foreign debtors.

iv. Before interest can be received and paid on foreign loans, the loans themselves must have been made. Thus the fourth kind of economic relation which has to be taken into account is foreign lending and borrowing. It is no longer true that net lending by private people within the nation (after lending by one person to another has been cancelled out) equals net borrowing by firms within the nation (after lending by one firm to another has been cancelled out). For it is now possible that private persons may lend abroad; and that firms may borrow (or lend) abroad. Thus in the open economy it is no longer true that saving equals net investment; we have to say that saving equals net investment plus net foreign lending.

These are the main sorts of economic relation with foreigners which have to be allowed for when we are considering the national income of an open economy. But there are two minor modifications which need to be added for the sake of completeness.

v. The first of these is the matter of gifts. In a closed community gifts do not require any special attention, since gifts from one person to another are bound to cancel out when all private incomes are taken together. But in an open community, it is possible that there may be gifts which are made from outsiders, or to outsiders, so that they will not cancel out. It might be thought that gifts across national frontiers would not be very important. But there are cases in which they have been quite important. The Irish economy, for instance, was at one time very dependent on remittances from emigrants to their relatives who stayed at home; the Israeli economy is very dependent upon gifts from co-religionists in other countries. There are also the government gifts, such as the Marshall aid from the United States which played so important a part in the post-war recovery of Europe; and the 'aid to underdeveloped countries' which continues, on a more modest scale, to this day. Thus gifts are altogether too important to be neglected.

What is the best way of dealing with such gifts? The natural thing is to regard them as an exception to the rule that income equals consumption plus saving. We then say that if a man receives a gift, he is enabled to consume and save in excess of his income by the amount of the gift; if he makes a gift, it comes out of his income, but does not reckon into his consumption or his saving. That is how we shall deal with international gifts, whether they are made between private people (migrants' remittances) or between governments.

vi. Finally, it will be remembered that when we were dealing with the place of money in a closed economy, we found that it required no particular attention in our equations, because an increase in the holding of money by a person or business could always be regarded as a special type of lending—lending to a bank. But it was already pointed out there that this might not be the case when we were dealing with an open economy. For it now becomes possible that a bank may use some part of the funds entrusted to it (or which it has saved) to acquire international money, money, that is, which is acceptable to foreigners. Such money may itself be 'debt' money, taking the form of a loan to (or deposit in) a bank in some other country. In that case we should have no trouble which we have not already faced. But it is possible that the international money acquired may be Gold, the old-fashioned metallic money which has not lost its international acceptability.[1] We have therefore to take into account the possibility that some part of the net saving and borrowing by business (in the widest sense, which includes the bank) may result, not in net investment, in the usual sense, but in the acquisition of gold.

2. The next thing to be done is to rework our tables of the earning and spending of the social income, in order to fit the loose ends into their places. For this purpose we do not need to raise again all the complications which bothered us in the preceding chapter. It will be sufficient if we go back to the giant Firm. We have shown that the splitting-up of the giant Firm into numerous individual firms makes no essential

[1] In practice, it is only central banks and governments which acquire gold to an important extent.

difference to the argument; the same will evidently hold for the open national economy as held for the closed economy which we considered previously. Let us therefore suppose that all the industry and trade of the country—all its economic activities—are carried on in a giant Firm; this will mean that all the foreign trade goes on through the Firm. Thus all the exported goods are sold by the Firm; and all the imports are bought by the Firm in the first place, being either resold directly on the home market (the Firm merely acting as agent) or used as materials for further production. By this device we can reckon all the goods purchased by home consumers as part of the Firm's output; the imports will all reckon as purchases by the Firm, that is to say, as materials used by the Firm.

With these understandings we can proceed at once to adapt the notions which we used in the last chapter for the case of the Firm,[1] so as to work out the earning and spending of the *national income*. It will be convenient to have a name for that part of the gross output of the 'nation-firm' which is not exported; let us call it Gross Retained Output.[2] In accordance with what has just been said, gross retained output will include the whole output of consumers' goods and service enjoyed by home consumers. It will also include the whole output of fixed capital goods used for extending or replacing the equipment employed in home industry; this latter is not quite the same thing as Gross Home Investment,[3] but it will be convenient to stretch the definition of gross retained output so as to include the whole of gross home investment. Thus

Gross Retained Output
= Home Consumption + Gross Home Investment, while
Gross Output of the Nation-Firm
= Gross Retained Output + Exports.

[1] See above, p. 147.

[2] It is odd that no one has coined a generally accepted name for this item, which actually figures to a large extent in many economic discussions.

[3] The difference, which we are here allowing for, will be recognized by the reader of the preceding chapter as being equal to net investment in materials. Since we are going to reckon this into gross output (for present purposes), the cost of materials and services which has to be deducted before arriving at net output will have to *include* net investment in imported materials. That is to say, we have to deduct the *whole* amount of materials and services imported from outside, which is the whole amount of imports.

The Net Output (or Gross Product) of the nation-firm is the difference between its gross output and the cost of materials and services acquired from outside.[1] Thus the *Gross Domestic Product* (which is the name which it is customary to give to the Gross Product of the 'nation-firm') equals

Gross Retained Output + Exports − Imports.

The Net Domestic Product (once again, just as in the case of the firm) equals Gross Domestic Product *minus* depreciation. Now since gross retained output includes gross home investment, and depreciation is an offset against gross home investment, it will be convenient to set off depreciation against gross retained output, calling the difference Net Retained Output. Net retained output is therefore the sum of home consumption and net home investment. We can accordingly sum up the whole of this part of our argument in the equation:

(*A*) Net Domestic Product
 = Net Retained Output + Exports − Imports.

In this equation the first two of the ways in which the nation differs from a closed economy are already allowed for.

We now pass on to the third complication. Just as in the closed economy, it is still true that net domestic product equals the sum of wages and profits earned at home, for these are all that remain to be allowed for in the account of the 'nation-firm'. But it is not true, as in the closed economy, that this sum of wages and profits equals the national income. Income from foreign assets (positive or negative) has also to be considered. The national income equals this sum of wages and profits *plus* net income from foreign assets. Thus:

(*B*) National Income
 = Net Domestic Product + Net Income from Foreign Assets.

In equations (*A*) and (*B*) the earning side of the national income is fully set out.

We now turn to the spending side, where we have to face the three remaining complications. First of all, there is the question of gifts. It is now no longer true that income is

[1] See preceding note.

necessarily equal to consumption plus saving; as we decided, we must write

Income = Consumption+Saving+Net Gifts to Foreigners.

And it is no longer true, as it was in the closed economy, that all saving (which is not spent on durable-use consumers' goods) must be lent to the 'nation-firm'; so that saving is necessarily equal to net home investment. Saving may be invested at home, or it may be lent abroad, or it may be used for acquiring gold. Thus

Saving = Net Home Investment+Net Foreign Lending +Net Acquisition of Gold

It then follows, since

National Income = Home Consumption+Saving +Net Gifts Abroad

and

Home Consumption+Net Home Investment = Net Retained Output

that

(*C*) National Income = Net Retained Output+Net Foreign Lending+Net Gifts Abroad+Net Acquisition of Gold.

In this equation (*C*) the spending side of the national income is summed up; in equation (*A*), (*B*), and (*C*) all the loose ends have been fitted into their places.

3. But now we come to the most important difference between the theory of the national income in an open economy and the corresponding theory in a closed economy. In the case of a closed economy we were able to establish the identity between social income and net social product on the earning side *and* on the spending side. Thus it was not really necessary to work the whole thing out on both sides (though it was instructive to do so) since we got the same result either way. In the case of the open economy we do not get the same result either way. The two ways of reckoning give us different results. But it is still true that the two ways of reckoning must be consistent with one another. That can only happen if

there is a relation between the loose ends which figure in the equations (*A*), (*B*), and (*C*). Now (*A*) and (*B*) have shown us that the difference between national income and net retained output equals

Exports—Imports+Income from Foreign Assets;

(*C*) has shown us that the same difference equals

Foreign Lending+Acquisition of Gold+Gifts to Foreigners.

These two must be equal. Now this difference, which can be expressed in either of these ways, is a very important magnitude. It is called the Balance of Payments.

Thus what we have shown is that the balance of payments is the difference between national income and net retained output; and that it can be expressed in either of the ways we have just written. These statements about the balance of payments sum up all that need be said about the special problems of the national income of an open economy.

It will be noticed that there is no reason why the balance of payments should necessarily be positive (or 'favourable'). In fact, it appears at once that if one country has a favourable balance, some other countries must have an unfavourable balance. For consider a world in which there are only two countries. The exports of one country would be the imports of the other; if one country had a positive income from foreign assets, the other must have a negative income from foreign debts. Thus a favourable balance for one country *means* an unfavourable balance for the other. The same reversibility obviously holds when the balance of payments is expressed the other way.

4. The identity between the two ways of expressing the balance of payments can also be shown in a more direct, but perhaps at bottom less instructive, manner. As we have seen, the money possessed by a particular person (or firm) at a particular time consists of nothing else but a debt to the holder from his bank (or, in the case of bank notes, from the bank which has issued the notes). Therefore, if an English firm buys machinery from the United States, the only way in which the import can be paid for in the first place is by giving the American seller a claim on an English bank; the

transferring of this claim may take various forms,[1] but the simplest is to hand over a cheque. The cheque is an instruction to the English bank to transfer part of the money which stands to the credit of the English buyer and put it to the credit of the American seller. The result of the transaction is that the English buyer acquires the machine, and the American seller acquires a claim on the English bank—a debt due to him by the English bank. If the American seller now pays the cheque into his own bank in America, the American bank acquires the claim on the English bank, but has a debt owing to the American seller to set on the other side of its account.

There are thus at least four parties to the transaction—the English buyer, the American seller, the English bank, the American bank. The transactions between the English buyer and the English bank, and between the American seller and the American bank, are internal to their respective countries, so they do not affect the balance of payments. As between England and America, there is the English import of American machinery, and the debt from the English bank to the American bank which offsets it. And that is all. England has imported the machine, and an English bank has borrowed from an American bank to 'finance' the import.

The same thing happens when anything is imported into Great Britain; it also happens when British people pay interest on foreign liabilities; and it also happens when they lend directly to foreigners (for example, by buying shares in foreign companies). All these things involve loans from foreign banks to British banks.

Most of these loans, however, are speedily cancelled out. For when anything is exported from Great Britain, or when members of the British community receive interest or dividends on foreign assets, or when foreigners buy shares or bonds from British people or from British companies, debts between banks are set up which go in the opposite direction. All these things involve loans from British banks to foreign banks, and they go a long way towards cancelling out the first set.

[1] The other forms (bills of exchange, etc.) are described in all textbooks on money.

It is usual for the two sets of bank debts to cancel one another out almost completely. If so, the balance of payments balances, or nearly balances, without the bank lending being taken into account. But the balance still formally balances, even if a net lending by banks (British banks to foreign banks, or foreign banks to British banks) is necessary to settle a difference; for the bank lending *is* lending, so that when *all* lending is included, the two sides must add up to the same figure.

Nevertheless, bank lending or borrowing, necessary to settle differences, is not like other lending or borrowing; when it increases beyond a certain point, trouble arises. For the amounts which the banks of any nation can borrow from the banks of other nations in this way are limited; the limit may vary in different circumstances, but it is always there. As the limit is approached, the government (or central bank) may sell gold, a reserve of which is kept for such emergencies. But most countries (including Britain) do not possess so much gold that they can protect themselves very far by such means. So when they are unable to pay for their imports excepting by a large amount of bank borrowing, they are in an awkward predicament. It was this position which Britain reached in 1949, on the occasion of the first post-war devaluation, and again at the time of the second devaluation in 1967. We shall have something further to say about such 'balance of payments crises' in Chapter XVI.

5. The balance of payments equation throws a great amount of light upon another range of problems also. When we are concerned with the broad movements of economic history, we need not pay much attention to the balancing loans of the banks, nor to gold movements, which are only important at moments of crisis. Nor need we worry about international gifts. We can write the balance equation.

Net Foreign Lending

= Exports − Imports + Net Income from Foreign Assets

and not worry much about the other items.

Now consider the position of a country, such as Great Britain must have been at some time in the late eighteenth century, which is neither a creditor nor a debtor country to any considerable extent. If such a country lends abroad, it can only do so by exporting more than it imports. This is the first phase of lending. After it has lent abroad for a number of years, the interest on its past loans will begin to amount to a considerable sum, so that if it is to retain a surplus of exports over imports, it must lend abroad more than ever. Even if it goes on lending abroad, but lends less than the amount of the interest on its past loans, imports will become greater than exports. This seems to have been the usual situation of Britain after 1850; she was still lending abroad, still adding to her foreign assets; but her new lending was usually rather less than the interest on her old loans, so she had a surplus of imports over exports.

Now suppose that as a result of some emergency, such as a war, the country which had been lending abroad begins to borrow abroad, or to sell off its foreign assets. During the war, since net foreign lending is negative, and net income from foreign assets is still positive, the excess of imports over exports becomes much larger than usual. But this excess of imports is paid for by giving up foreign assets; if the loss of foreign assets is large, net income from foreign assets will be much reduced when the war is over; consequently the country will be unable to lend abroad and build up its foreign assets at the old rate, unless it manages with a smaller excess of imports over exports than it did in the past. Something like this seems to have been the situation of Great Britain between 1919 and 1939; during these years her net foreign lending was very small indeed. It will be observed that if the loss of foreign assets goes still further, so that there is no net income from foreign assets any longer, the country will only be able to lend abroad, and so build up its foreign assets again, if it can secure an excess of exports over imports, as in the first phase. That, roughly speaking, is the situation to which Britain came for a while after 1945.

So far we have considered the position of a lending country, which only borrows in an extraordinary emergency; but for every lender there must be a borrower—where could the normal lending of the earlier phases go to? It is perfectly reasonable and sensible for a country to borrow abroad as a normal policy if the borrowing is used productively—if it enables the borrowing country to make net additions to its national capital. The national capital of a borrowing country, let us remember, consists of the capital equipment it possesses at home *minus* its foreign debts. If foreign borrowing is spent wastefully, it involves a net loss of national capital, just because debts mount up; but if the borrowing is employed to make additions to home equipment, which are more valuable than the debt outstanding against them, then national capital is actually increased as a result of the borrowing. There can be little doubt that most of the foreign borrowing carried out by overseas countries has been of this type; the British Dominions and even the United States could not have grown as they have done (they could not even have drawn the populations they have done) if they had not borrowed on a vast scale during their period of growth.

The phases of borrowing can be followed through in the same way as the phases of lending. Suppose that a country (which is initially neither a creditor nor a debtor) begins to borrow abroad; then in the first phase its imports will exceed its exports. The additional imports may consist of capital goods or of consumption goods; it should be noticed that the import of large quantities of consumption goods, financed by borrowing, does not necessarily mean that the borrowing is being used unproductively. For the import of consumption goods may enable the country's own labour force to be turned over to the production of new capital equipment; if the consumption goods had not been imported, they would have to have been produced at home; if they do not need to be produced at home, the factors of production which might have produced them can be used to make additions to equipment. In a practical case, when a country borrows to build a railway, the additional imports consist partly of railway equipment produced abroad, partly of consumption goods supplied to the workers who are installing the equipment or doing the other parts of the construction which have to be done on the spot. Or perhaps the rearrangement of production is even more complicated; but the principle remains the same.

The second phase on the borrowing side comes when the interest on past borrowings mounts up; then (exactly as in the lending case) the country will have to borrow even more rapidly than before if it is to retain a surplus of imports over exports. If the rate of borrowing falls off, or fails to expand, sooner or later a point must be reached when exports must exceed imports. In practice, this point always is reached after a certain time.

If the borrowing has been used productively, the excess of exports over imports can generally be brought about with very little trouble. For the increase in capital equipment will have increased the nation's productive power; the production of goods is increased, and out of this increased production, extra goods can be spared for export without any great sacrifice. We do in fact observe that in the latter years of the nineteenth century, when the second phase was reached by a large number of debtor countries, their exports (particularly their exports of raw materials and foodstuffs) expanded notably. Out of these exports they paid the interest on their debts, but they were able to pay and still to enjoy a mounting prosperity.

6. Productive lending and borrowing, as we have been describing it, is a profoundly beneficent process. Without the international lending of the nineteenth century the productive powers of the borrowing countries could hardly have been developed at more than a snail's pace; and without the development of production in new lands the older countries would have lacked the foodstuffs and raw materials which have enabled them to support rising populations at rising standards of living. It is highly probable that the economic opportunities for such productive lending are far from exhausted; the mass of poverty in Asia and Africa still needs a vast increase of capital equipment if it is to be remedied; it is unlikely that the peoples of the poorer 'underdeveloped' countries will be able to provide what they need from their own savings within any measurable period.

We should never forget, however, that international lending leads to political difficulties which do not arise from internal lending. The fact that borrower and lender live under different governments and different legal systems makes the obligation from borrower to lender harder to enforce; thus international lending will often proceed more smoothly (lenders will be more willing to lend) if the government of the lending country can influence the government of the borrowing country to see that the debts due to its citizens are respected. But such pressure is widely resented, partly on grounds of national self-respect, partly because it weakens the authority of a government that submits to it. It is therefore easy to work up strong feelings against 'capitalist imperialism', feelings which have had so clear a run during the last twenty years as to make the development by international lending of the old type nearly impossible, at least for the time being. It is probable that these feelings have derived some of their strength from the belief that there are alternatives. It may be worth while to say a word about these alternatives from our present point of view.

One of the alternatives is Communism. Russian Communism itself was originally, in one of its aspects, a revolt against the 'tyranny of international capital'. Chinese Communism is even more clearly a movement of this kind. The Russian example has shown that it is possible, under favourable circumstances, for a country to develop itself with great rapidity out of its own savings—though the sacrifices that must be imposed upon a poor people, in the course of such development, are exceedingly severe. That the same thing can be done by countries with fewer natural resources, and with less skill and stamina, looks improbable. Nevertheless, there are many people, in many countries, who would like to try the experiment, whether they call it Communism or something else. They may or may not be successful; what is certain is that a poor country can only develop itself by this route at the cost of much privation, which is not a good thing in itself, and which it takes much determination to stand. Development through international lending is a much easier and less painful process. It would be preferable (as a second view would admit) if only its political consequences could be avoided.

This second line of thought leads to the idea of canalizing international lending through international institutions (such as the World Bank) of which a variety already exist. On such institutions the borrowing country, and other borrowing countries, will be represented; the lenders will not have it all their own way, so that the borrowers will be protected against 'imperialist' pressure. The lender will be able to get his rights, as assessed by an international body, but no more. So far, although much has been done in the way of setting up such institutions, it must be admitted that they have not achieved a great deal. The private investor may well have some doubts about the security offered; governments (the alternative source of funds) are almost obliged to look upon any international lending for which they are responsible as an instrument of foreign policy. So the way is not so clear after all. It remains to be seen whether either of the 'modern' methods of financing development is as effective as the old-fashioned lending by private investors, which worked remarkably well in those cases where the people of the borrowing country kept their word and adhered to the contracts they had made.

CHAPTER XIII

The State and the National Income

1. The second set of qualifications to the fundamental equations of earning and spending relates to the economic activities of the State. The government of a nation is a particular part of the nation's organization; its primary function is to protect the community against internal disorder and external aggression. To this primary function many other functions have in the course of time been added; but it is in the field of 'Justice, Police and Arms' (to use the language of Adam Smith) that a government's main responsibility still resides. Let us begin by considering some of the economic aspects of these central activities of government, and then pass on to deal with the other functions.

For the purpose of maintaining law, order, and defence, the State has to employ a large number of people (soldiers and sailors, policemen, judges, civil servants) and to purchase goods for them to use, goods which range from military aircraft to writing-paper. In order to cover its expenditure in these directions it raises taxes—that is to say, it levies compulsory contributions upon its citizens or subjects. How do we fit this revenue and expenditure of the government into our account of the earning and spending of the national income? The usual way of doing so is to say that the people who work for the government in these ways are working, like others, to satisfy the wants of the community; that when the government pays them their wages, it is acting as agent for its citizens, who are the ultimate employers, and whose contributions to taxation are therefore essentially similar to their ordinary spending. The suggested analogy is that of a voluntary association. When the secretary of a golf-course employs greensmen to keep the turf in order, he is acting on behalf of his members; the funds are provided by the members' subscriptions, and there can be no doubt that the subscriptions paid by members are part of their ordinary spending. It is perhaps a little dangerous to use this analogy for the case of the State and its taxes, since the State is a compulsory association, not a voluntary one. People have to pay taxes whether they like it or not, and cannot easily protect themselves against what they consider unjust treatment by the State, simply by joining another club instead. The problem of achieving some degree of fairness in the distribution of taxation among different people is much more urgent in the case of the State than the parallel problem is in a voluntary association. But the existence of this problem does not prevent us from regarding the taxes, which are levied to pay for the public services, as being economically analogous to club subscriptions.

There is, however, the further question: are the services which maintain order and defence to be regarded as services which satisfy the wants of consumers directly, or are they to be regarded as facilitating the production of other sorts of goods and services? If we accept the first alternative, then we must say that the public services are an additional part of the national product, which we have not reckoned previously; but if we adopt the second, then they are merely a part of the process of producing those same goods which we have previously taken into account. Now there would seem to be good reasons for supposing that the public services are partly one and partly the other.

The wicked millionaire, whose well-deserved murder has served as the theme of so many detective stories, often employs a private bodyguard; if we met such a case in real life, we should have no hesitation in saying that the wages paid to the bodyguard are part of the millionaire's consumption expenditure, just as much as the wages paid to his butler. Most of us are contented to satisfy our more modest wants for personal protection by relying upon the police and other governmental defence forces; it seems reasonable that our expenditure on this protection, through the taxes we pay, should be reckoned as a part of our consumption expenditure in a similar manner. But now consider the case of a firm, which (instead of trusting to the police to see that its goods are not stolen) employs a night-watchman; in this case the wages of the night-watchman are included as part of the cost of the firm's output. The services of the night-watchman are not treated as an independent part of the national product; they are included in the goods which the labour of the night-watchman helps to produce (by ensuring that the process of producing them continues without interruption). One would suppose that when the public services perform similar functions to this they ought to be similarly reckoned; and there can be no doubt that to do so would be the ideal arrangement. If, as the result of an epidemic of shopbreaking, a local authority decides to pay its policemen to stay on duty for longer hours, are we to say that the social product has increased, because of the additional output of policemen's services? Surely it would be much more sensible to put it that the additional labour is needed to produce the same net output of useful goods. It would be much more sensible to put it like that; but it is unfortunately quite impossible to say how much of the work of the police and defence forces is directed towards the protection of life and liberty and personal possessions, and how much is concerned with the protection of the productive process. Being unable to draw a line, British statisticians have invariably decided to neglect the assistance given by the public services to the production of other goods; they treat the whole of the public services as direct services, ministering to consumers' wants in the same way as consumption goods do.

In practice there may be nothing else for it; but we ought to be aware that the solution is unsatisfactory, and to be prepared for some awkwardness in its consequences. The most notable awkwardness concerns the calculation of the national income in time of war. The expansion of the armed forces which takes place in war-time is an expansion of the public services; if we regard the public services as satisfying consumers' wants directly, we are obliged to regard the men who are in the armed forces or the munition industries as producing things which consumers are willing to accept as substitutes for the ordinary goods and services of peace-time. Thus, in spite of the reduced supply of peace-time goods, the nation is not shown to be appreciably worse off. The national income is not diminished. This way of looking at the situation might have some plausibility if it was applied to an aggressor nation, which willingly accepted guns for butter, and glory for cakes and ale; but the position of a nation engaged in a defensive war would surely be described better in another manner. If we were allowed to say that the import of goods from overseas is rendered more costly, not only because of the loss of ships from enemy action, and because of the extra time spent in dodging submarines, but also because of the need for a large navy to ensure that these losses are not even greater; if we were allowed to say that the production of goods at home is rendered more costly, not only by the actual losses from air raids, but also because of the need for guns and aeroplanes to repel air attack; if we calculated the national income in war-time on this basis, we should find that the nation is much poorer in war than it is in peace, which surely corresponds much better with the facts. But we are not allowed to say these things, once we have agreed to treat the public services as a direct part of consumption; and so we must be prepared for the results we get.

2. The expenditure of the State on goods and services needed for the performance of the primary functions of government is therefore to be regarded as consumption expenditure; but it is so different from the ordinary consumption of private persons that we should always show it as a separate item. We may call it Public Consumption. The wants satisfied by such public consumption are collective wants, not individual wants; it is impossible to say how much advantage any particular individual gets out of it.[1] But the taxes which are raised by the government to meet this expenditure have to be divided up among individuals, and must be divided on some plan. There is no reason to suppose that

[1] See above, pp. 22–4.

individual contributions to taxation have ever had any relation to the advantage which public consumption confers on the individual—not even the very loose relation which exists between subscriptions to a club and advantages derived. The taxes paid by the individual cannot therefore be regarded as a part of *his* consumption expenditure, even when they are used to finance public consumption by the nation as a whole. We have to reckon taxation as an additional call on income. Instead of saying that income equals consumption plus saving, we must say that the individual's income equals

Private Consumption+Saving+Taxation

as is agreeable to common sense. Nevertheless, if all the taxes were used to pay for public consumption, we could regard the taxation as being transmuted (at the next stage) into public consumption, just as saving is transmuted (in a closed economy) into net investment; so that the national income would still be spent, at the last round, on consumption and net investment—though the consumption would include public consumption as well as private.

3. In fact things are by no means as simple as this. We have quite a number of other State activities to fit into the picture, and they have to be treated in several different ways. Let us go through them in order, beginning with what are commonly called the 'social' activities.

Taxation itself is widely used at the present time for 'social' purposes—the rich being taxed at higher rates than the poor—but this does not affect the scheme set out in the preceding paragraph. The existence of progressive taxation reminds us that the tax system makes no attempt to allocate taxes in proportion to benefits derived from public consumption; but that is all there is to it. When, however, 'social' policy goes one stage further (as it has done in Britain on an increasing scale during the last fifty years), when it uses the proceeds of taxation as a means of supplying consumers with things which they might have bought out of their incomes, but which some of them would have been unable to afford, then we do have to take notice. 'Social' expenditure is a new complication which has to find a place in our tables.

But it is not a simple item, all of which can go into one place. It has to be divided, for our purposes, into no less than three separate headings. The first head, of which government expenditure on education is a good example, involves the purchase of goods and services by the government, just like the public consumption on our first list. The teachers are public servants, just like soldiers and policemen; the government (or local authority) buys paper for school-books just as it does for files. The only distinction is that the services of teachers are more identifiably for the benefit of individuals; they are similar in kind to the services of teachers at private schools, which some people still pay for, so that they are included in the personal consumption of those people. Thus it is not nonsensical to ask how the benefits from social expenditure of this first sort are divided up, as it really is nonsensical to ask how the benefits from public consumption proper are divided. Social expenditure of this type is like personal consumption in some ways, but like public consumption in others. We might call it Semi-Public Consumption.

The other sorts of social expenditure cannot be treated in that way. Take the case of family allowances. The government pays out fixed sums every week in family allowances; this money is not paid in return for services provided; it has no relation to any contribution which the recipient may or may not be making to the social product, as we are reckoning it. Family allowances are an outpayment by the government which has no relation to services performed for the government; just as taxes are an inpayment to the government which has no relation to the services the individual taxpayer receives. Family allowances (and all other payments of a like kind, such as unemployment benefit) must therefore be treated as being, for our purposes, just like taxes—excepting that they go the other way. These 'transfer incomes', as it is customary to call them, are to be reckoned as *negative* taxes.

Transfer incomes are incomes, in a sense, but they are not part of the total of wages and profits. We therefore need, if we are to manage them comfortably, a further distinction. We must distinguish between 'incomes before tax and transfer' and 'incomes after tax and transfer'—or *Disposable incomes*, as the latter are called for short. In order to get disposable income from pre-tax income, we have to subtract taxes and add transfers. Thus the rich man, whose transfer income is negligible, has a disposable income which is less than his income in the ordinary sense by the taxes he pays. At the other end of the scale comes the unemployed family, which may have no income at all 'before tax and transfer', but which has a disposable income, since the transfers it receives are greater than the taxes it pays. The rule that income equals consumption plus saving holds without qualification as soon as we take income to mean disposable income.

The third sort of social expenditure is expenditure on subsidies, including both the housing subsidies which have been with us since 1920, and the subsidies on foodstuffs which were a legacy of the Second World War. Subsidies also are a negative tax; they lower the prices of articles which are such that the government desires to encourage their consumption (or their production), just as taxation raises the price of other articles, which the government desires (or is not unwilling) to discourage. The fitting of these 'indirect' taxes into the accounts of the national income is rather a ticklish matter; it will be easier to explain it when we are dealing with a concrete case in the next chapter. Subsidies raise precisely the same difficulty as indirect taxes.

4. We have now provided pigeon-holes into which we can fit the greater part of government expenditure; but there are still some special sorts of expenditure which remain unaccounted for. Let us begin with the question of interest on the National Debt.

A large part of the extra expenditure which falls on governments in war-time is financed out of borrowing, not out of taxation; once we have decided to regard war expenditure as a part of public consumption, we are obliged to treat war borrowing as being analogous to a spendthrift's borrowing for consumption purposes. When the war is over, the government will find that it is left with a national debt on which it has to pay interest (most national debts are legacies of past wars); but no capital goods have been acquired by means of the war borrowing, so that there are no profits out of which the interest on the national debt can be paid, as is the case

8281730 N

with the debts of firms. Extra taxation has to be raised each year to meet the interest on the national debt; and this extra taxation cannot be regarded, like the taxation raised to pay for the public services of the year, as a form of consumption expenditure, for which the State acts as the taxpayers' agent. Nor is it quite satisfactory to treat interest on national debt as a transfer income. This is how it used at one time to be treated; if we compare the case of war pensions, another hang-over from war, which are treated as transfer incomes (no *current* service being provided against them), it will be seen that the line between income from national debt interest and transfer income is a very thin one. Nevertheless, this is not the best way of reckoning it. To the recipient of national debt interest (who may be a private person, or a firm, or a foreigner) it looks exactly like the interest on a commercial debt; he can, after all, sell his war loan and buy shares in a company at any time he likes. Thus it is tidier to treat it as nearly as possible in the way other interest payments are treated. Let us recall how we treated the interest payments of firms, in order that we may find a way of fitting national debt interest in on the same plan.

Before we began to consider these 'State' complications, we said that the net social product of a closed economy was equal to wages plus profits; that profits were partly paid out in interest and dividends, partly undistributed; and that the social income was therefore equal to the sum of personal incomes (wages plus interest and dividends) plus undistributed profits. Net social product equals social income. Now if we want to retain the equality between net social product and social income (as we certainly must do if we can), but have to find a place for the receipt of national debt interest in private incomes, we shall have to say that the national income equals

All personal incomes
(including national debt interest received by persons) + Undistributed profits – National Debt interest paid out.

That is to say, while companies are left with a positive remainder (of undistributed profits) after paying out interest and dividends, the government has a negative remainder, which it subsequently covers by taxation. This is the arrangement to which we have to come. It looks curious, but it is consistent with what we have said before. It fits in with the picture shown on our national balance-sheet;[1] and it also fits in with the picture we got in the last chapter, when we had to allow for the way in which national debt interest may be paid *abroad*.[2]

5. All of the economic functions of government so far considered are related to the *spending* of the national income; we come finally to a group of activities which belong on the *earning* side. Even before the days of nationalization, the State (in the wide sense of the term, which includes the local authorities) had taken over responsibility for certain productive processes—the Post Office, much of the 'public utilities' of water, gas, and electricity, as well as (from 1920) a share in the provision of housing. To these the Attlee government, in accordance with its socialist principles, added coal and railways; eliminated private (and local) elements in the control of gas and electricity; nationalized a section of road transport; and encouraged the development of civil air transport, which had always been very largely a public undertaking. Then the Wilson government (in 1967) added iron and steel. Something must now be said about the way in which these activities are to be fitted in.

The industries which were nationalized by the Labour Governments were organized as 'corporations' which are formally similar to companies. Though the government 'owns' them, and has a responsibility to come to their help if they get into difficulties, the normal relation between their finances and those of the government is much the same as that between an ordinary (non-nationalized) company and its shareholders. The profits which they make are not supposed to be greater—in the long run—than the sum needed to pay interest on their debts; but in a particular year they may earn more or less than what is needed to cover this interest (together with the taxation which they pay, just like other companies). Accordingly they may show a (positive or

[1] See p. 133 above.
[2] See p. 157 above.

negative) undistributed profit. Nationalized industries of this sort can therefore be dealt with, sufficiently for our purposes, by the methods which we employed for other 'firms' in Chapter XI. Their accounting is just like that of other companies; they can be lumped in with other companies, if we care to do so.

The accounting arrangements of these public corporations are quite orderly; and there have been praiseworthy efforts to get as much as possible, of the productive activities for which public authorities are responsible, 'organized' in this public corporation form. It was long the case that there was one most important activity of the Central Government which remained in this sense 'unorganized'—the Post Office. The Post Office was unorganized because it was nationalized long before the day when the public corporation was thought of; but now (since 1969) it has become a public corporation, and its accounts were in fact available in public corporation form some years before that date. Thus it is no longer necessary (as it was for previous editions of this book) to pay special attention to the affairs of the Post Office.

Something must nevertheless be said about such 'unorganized' public undertakings; partly in order to bring out the point of the 'organization', and partly because there remains one important activity which is still 'unorganized'—the housing activity of local authorities. What the national income statisticians do, when they come to deal with these 'unorganized' undertakings, is to fit them, as nearly as possible, into the 'organized' public corporation form. It is necessary, for that purpose, first to distinguish the revenues which are derived from the sale of the services produced (there is usually not much difficulty about that); and then to set against them the current costs which have been incurred in the provision of these services. It is this last which is the tricky point, for an 'unorganized' undertaking is unlikely to take the trouble of distinguishing between current and investment expenditures—the expenses that *belong* to this year's output and those that belong to the output of future years—so that it is unable to tell whether its revenues exceed its current expenditures, whether (that is) it has made a profit. By examination of the accounts, a rough division can nevertheless, in most cases, be made, so that an estimate of the profit which is earned can (very broadly) be reached.

In order to ascertain the *net* profit of a public undertaking, it is not only necessary to divide this year's expenditure between current and investment; it is also necessary to consider what part has been played in the production of this year's output by the using-up of initial equipment: to make an allowance, that is, for depreciation. An 'unorganized' undertaking is unlikely to bother about depreciation. Estimates of the depreciation which ought to be allowed can, however, be made; when they are made it is frequently revealed that the undertaking is running at a loss. A private business cannot continue in existence if it goes on running at a loss; but a public undertaking can, since its losses can be subsidized out of the general budget. It is not necessarily wrong for a public undertaking to be run at a loss; it is nevertheless a good thing that the losses which have to be subsidized, the bills which have to be met, should be made plain, so that those who are responsible know what they are doing.[1]

6. One final point. As has already been indicated, the government expenditure which has been considered in this chapter is not that of the central government alone. All public authorities, for instance local authorities, must be

[1] It will probably occur to the reader that the distinction between current and investment expenditure, which is made in the accounts of the public corporations, and needs to be made for the 'unorganized' undertakings, has a bearing on other parts of the government's expenditure, even on that which we listed as 'public consumption' in the first place. We agreed to call expenditure on the services of teachers public consumption; but what about expenditure on building new schools? What about expenditure on building bombers? In all these cases, something is left behind at the end of the year; there is a case for classifying a distinctly large part of the government's expenditure as public investment, and for depreciating it like the investment expenditure of private industry.

On present practice, quite a lot of government expenditure is in fact so classified (not indeed in the Chancellor's budget, but by the time the national income statisticians get their hands on to it). They do not quite bring themselves to the reckoning of expenditure on bombers as public investment (with a corresponding depreciation charge for the services of bombers left over from past years); but, short of that, they go very far. Though military installations are not regarded as investment, civil defence installations (apparently) are. All the schools and hospitals and suchlike public buildings go, of course, on to the investment side. We shall follow them in this classification, though with (I hope) some reservations about it. We must recognize that the lines which are drawn in this field are pretty thin.

included. Local authorities raise taxes (local rates) just as the central government does, spending the proceeds in ways which can be classified under the various heads which we have been setting out. But local authorities do not depend on rates in the way that the central government depends on taxes. An even larger part of their revenue is derived from *grants*. These grants are transfers *from* the central government *to* the local authorities, so that when the two are taken together, as we have to take them for national income purposes, the grants cancel out. Grants from Whitehall to the Birmingham City Council are treated in the same way as payments from the Treasury to the Ministry of Labour. But in doing this we beg no questions about the independence of local authorities; the cancellation is performed in the same way, and for the same purposes, as we have agreed to cancel payments of interest from one company to another.

Another set of public bodies which receive large grants from the central government are the national insurance funds. The benefits provided by social insurance (pensions, sickness, and unemployment benefit) are financed chiefly by contributions, made in approximately equal amounts by all contributors,[1] but to a significant extent by grants out of general taxation. The cynical comment on these insurance schemes is that they are a means of making it appear that there is more social expenditure for the benefit of the less wealthy than there really is; it may be argued on the other side that the insurance device has a real social advantage, for it enables the beneficiary to receive his benefits as a right, and not as 'charity'. Psychologically this is important; but in a scheme where contributions are compulsory, and benefits may be varied at any time by government decision, the insurance element is in practice largely bogus. The realistic thing to do is to fit national insurance into the ordinary classification of government revenue and expenditure. We shall therefore regard the national insurance benefits as transfer incomes (or, in a few cases, as semi-public consumption); and shall treat national insurance contributions as a particular sort of tax.

[1] Rates of contribution are distinguished by age and sex, and by employment or non-employment, but not by income.

CHAPTER XIV The British National Income in 1969

1. We have now reached a point where it will be useful to look at some figures, so as to see how the calculation of the national income comes out in a particular case. In earlier editions of this book the figures chosen for this purpose were those of the British National Income in 1938, then in 1949, and then in 1957; but time rolls on, and 1957 is now becoming too distant a date to be very interesting to the modern reader. He will want to do the exercise on something more recent. Yet it is not easy to find a set of *annual* figures which represent the state of the economy, as it was in the late sixties, at all fairly. One can now see, from the present distance, that my former choice of 1957 was a good one for its purpose; though that could not have been seen at the time, and it was only by luck that I chose it. The fact is that 1957 was the climax of Britain's post-war recovery, the best year in the fifties, a year that can stand, for the performance of economy in the middle fifties, very well indeed. There is no recent year which will do this job for us. There is no recent year that has not been marked by some kind of economic crisis—either a crisis which has actually broken out (like the devaluation of 1967 or the inflation of 1970) or one which can be seen, when the social accounting figures of the year are analysed, to have been brewing. Let us hope that a 'normal' year, of the 1957 type, is somewhere ahead of us; but it seems hardly likely that it is just round the corner. I have therefore decided that I must take one of these years of the late sixties, disturbed as they have been. It is only because it is the last year for which figures are complete (as I write) that I have chosen 1969.

The figures which we shall use are derived from the 'Blue Book' on *National Income and Expenditure*, an official publication which appears annually, and in which the statistics of national income are set out in considerable detail. These official statistics began in the nineteen-forties. Before that time, all the work which had been done on the British national income had been done by unofficial investigators. The first estimate which attained a modern standard of accuracy was made by A. L. Bowley for the year 1911; it was followed by a further estimate, for the year 1924, by Bowley and Josiah Stamp. These classic investigations[1] were entirely based upon the income method;[2] and the series of estimates for the years 1924–38, which Bowley published in his *Studies in the National Income* (1942), and which long remained one of the main sources of information about national income during the inter-war years, still used the income method alone.

Meanwhile, however, in 1937 Colin Clark had published his *National Income and Outlay*, which gave a series of estimates for 1924–35, using both the income and the production methods. In this work the difficulties inherent in the double approach were not wholly overcome, but Clark's investigations nevertheless did much to point the way for what followed.

Only when the way had been prepared in this manner could the government take a hand. It was in connection with the budget of 1941 that the first official estimate appeared. This gave estimates for 1938 and 1940; estimates for each of the succeeding years have been published in relation to subsequent budgets.[3] The 'hole' of 1939 was later filled in, so that we now possess a complete series of official estimates

[1] They have been reprinted in Bowley and Stamp, *Three Studies in the National Income* (London School of Economics reprints).

[2] See above, p. 153.

[3] The modern practice is for preliminary estimates to be published quarterly (in *Economic Trends*). The Blue Book, which contains the revised figures for the whole of the preceding year, appears (usually) in August. Our 1969 figures are taken from the 1970 Blue Book.

from 1938 to the present. These official figures are the basis for all contemporary discussion on the subject in Britain.

It must be emphasized that an official estimate of the national income is only an estimate like other estimates. Its authors have advantages in the means of information open to them, but that is all. The official estimates are, however, important, not merely because they are official, but because their appearance marked a change of purpose. All that the unofficial estimators had sought to do was to get a global figure for the national income, and to show how it was divided up into incomes of various sizes and various sorts. Such information is very interesting in itself, and it still emerges out of the Blue Book figures, but almost as a by-product. For the purpose of the Blue Book is more ambitious; it is the preparation of figures which can serve as a guide, to the government and to Parliament, in the preparation of economic policy. For this wider purpose something more than a mere total, or a divided-up total, is needed; the object in view can only be attained by the provision of a set of accounts.

The basic figures which appear in a modern Blue Book are indeed best regarded as a set of accounts—accounts for the nation as a whole, which are exactly parallel to the accounts which a business organization gets out for its own purposes. The Blue Book cannot be fully understood until it is looked at from the accounting point of view. The reader of this book will, however, find it convenient to start his studies of the subject in a simpler manner. The main results which can be got from a study of the national income in 1969 will be explained in this chapter in the simplest terms possible. In order to simplify it will be necessary to leave out some complications; thus anyone who tries to check this chapter against the official publication will not always find the check to be very easy going. If he wants to do a check, he had better begin with the additional Chapters XX and XXI, which explain the social accounting approach on a less elementary level.

In these chapters I give the figures in £ millions; but here, so as to avoid distracting the reader with digits that do not matter, I have rounded all figures into hundreds of millions of pounds. As in Chapter X, I shall denote this unit by £H. Thus 15£H means £1,500,000,000.

2. According to the official figures, the gross domestic product[1] of the United Kingdom is estimated for the year 1969 at 385£H. There is a good deal of controversy about the right figure to deduct from this for depreciation;[2] the official figure is 37£H, and in this place we have no choice but to accept it. Net domestic product (gross product *minus* depreciation) was therefore 348£H. In order to get the national income from this,[3] we have to add the difference between income received from foreign assets and that paid out as interest on foreign debts. Now, in spite of all the borrowing from banks in other countries, which had marked the period before (and after) the devaluation of 1967, it was still the case in 1969 that Britain had a small surplus, of net income from abroad, between 4 and 5£H. So the National Income, after allowance for this income from foreign assets, comes out as 353£H.

As we know, the net domestic product is the sum of wages and profits earned at home, each of these terms being understood in a suitably wide sense. In this wide sense, where wages means the whole earnings of labour, it will include what are reckoned in the official tables as wages, salaries, and the pay and allowances of the armed forces. Profits will include the trading profits of companies, and the rents of land and buildings. These headings are easily classified, but there are others which create more trouble. There are the profits of public undertakings, both the nationalized industries (organized as public corporations) and the 'unorganized' undertakings, which were discussed in the

[1] What the Blue Book calls 'gross domestic product at factor cost' (see below, p. 196). I have had to amend the Blue Book figure by adding back no less than 3£H of 'residual error'. This tiresome item arises because, through deficiencies of information, the totals that are calculated by the income method and by the production method do not come out quite right. The figure which the statisticians prefer to show as their 'correct' figure is that which they get by the production method; but there is really no reason why one should be better than the other. Since we are going to be mainly interested in the income figures, it is better to use the figure which belongs on that side; this is the figure above stated.

[2] See Appendix, Note C.

[3] See above, p. 161.

last chapter. Then there is an item which is nowadays described as 'income from self-employment'. This includes the earnings of farmers, the profits of small businesses not organized as companies, and the earnings of professional people (such as lawyers or authors) who work on their own account. We are going to have a certain amount of difficulty with this item; for though the earnings which come under this heading are largely labour earnings (even the 'profits' of the shopkeeper are largely labour earnings) they do contain an element of capital earnings as well. It was formerly customary to bring this out by calling the item 'mixed earnings'; since this term is rather convenient for our purposes I shall often employ it here.

The division of the net domestic product into earnings of labour and of capital may then be summarized as follows:

	£H
Earnings of labour	272
Mixed earnings	25
Earnings of capital (including rents):	
in private ownership	41
in public ownership	10
Net domestic product	348

In percentages these are approximately: labour 78 per cent, mixed earnings 7 per cent, capital in private ownership 12 per cent, in public ownership 3 per cent. Allowing for the fact that at least half of the mixed earnings must really be labour earnings, it seems safe to say that true labour earnings must have amounted to round about 82 per cent of the net domestic product in 1969.

3. This, it should be realized, tells us nothing more than the way in which the national product is divided between Labour and Capital on the *earning* side; in order to find out anything about the division on the *spending* side, in which most people are far more interested, we have to go a good deal further. We proceed, as before, by steps. In the first place, we must distinguish between those company profits which are distributed to private persons (as dividends or interest payments) and those which are held back by the firms which have made them (undistributed profits). But what about public profits? If we are allowing, at this stage, for interest payments by companies, it seems reasonable to allow for interest payments by government at the same time. This we shall do, even though (for reasons explained in the last chapter) interest payments by government swallow up a good deal more than the profits of capital in government ownership.

Our next table accordingly shows the *National Income* (including what we have shown as income from foreign assets) divided up into (1) personal incomes, (2) undistributed profits, (3) the *negative* 'income before tax' of the government. It should be understood that part of the national debt interest is paid directly to private persons,[1] while part is paid to businesses (such as the banks). National debt interest paid to firms will be added to their profits (as already reckoned) and the total will be divided up between the shareholders and the 'kitty' of undistributed profits. We cannot follow through this process in detail; all we know is the result, which is as follows:

National income before taxation

	£H
Personal incomes	
Incomes from labour earnings	272
Mixed incomes	25
Income from property (dividends, interest, and rents)	41
All personal income	338
Business income	
Undistributed profits	22
Public income	
Public income from property *less* national debt interest	−7
National income	353

It can at least be seen that the total comes out right.

The total of personal incomes, in this sense, was 338£H, or 15£H less than the National Income. Out of these personal

[1] Or to pension funds, the incomes of which are reckoned (for the purposes of these tables) as *personal incomes*.

incomes, 12 per cent were incomes from property. Let us, however, remember that there are included among these property incomes the 'incomes' which home-owners are reckoned to get from their houses[1]—perhaps one-third of the total; also the incomes of pension funds, from which all retired persons, not provided for by the State, get their pensions. These, between them, are the things of which this personal property income mainly consists.

4. But obviously we cannot stop at that point. It would really be nonsensical to do so, for we have left a yawning gap in the public revenue which must somehow be filled. And we know well enough how it is filled—by the imposition of taxes.

We now come to a difficult and awkward point.[2] The government imposes many sorts of taxes, and we cannot bring them into the accounts of the national income in precisely the same way. For this purpose, we have to distinguish three sorts of taxes. The first consists of the *direct taxes on income*, which have to be paid out of the incomes listed in the above table before it is possible for the taxpayer to reckon what is to be left to him for his own consumption or his own saving. Income tax (including corporation tax) is the most important of these direct taxes, but there are a number of others, particularly the contributions to social insurance, which have got to be reckoned somewhere, and are most conveniently reckoned here. The second sort of tax is the indirect tax, of which the tax on tobacco and the purchase tax are good examples. While direct taxes have to be paid out of income independently of consumption, indirect taxes are only paid as income is spent or consumed. Finally, there is a third class, taxes on capital, of which death duties are the most important instance. These taxes are only paid on exceptional occasions, and may be regarded as falling outside the ordinary earning and spending of the taxpayer's income.

It is best to take these three sorts of taxes into account one at a time. In the year 1969 92£H were due to be paid[3] to

[1] These 'incomes' are no longer assessed to income tax; they are nevertheless still reckoned as incomes in the Blue Book.

[2] Which was held over in the last chapter (p. 177).

[3] For a discussion of the difference between tax liability and actual payment, see below, p. 280.

government, by persons, and businesses, as direct taxes falling on income; a sum vastly more than sufficient, by itself, to cover the gap left by the payment of national debt interest. But when we are taking into account this direct *transfer* from persons and businesses to government, we ought to ask—are there not some similar transfers which go in the other direction, and which ought to be allowed for at the same time? It at once appears that there are. We are reckoning social insurance contributions among the direct taxes; what about social insurance benefits? They are nothing else but the other side of the same transaction. Social insurance benefits are, however, only one of a large class of payments from the State to individuals, payments which result in 'incomes' that are not earned, even in the sense that profit incomes are earned. They do not arise out of the production of the social output, but are transfers of income, which has been collected by taxation, from the State to the person benefited. These *transfer incomes* (which include studentships and war pensions, in addition to social security benefits) have not previously been reckoned into our tables; but when the subtraction of direct taxation from some incomes is taken into account, the addition of transfers to other incomes should naturally be reckoned in at the same time.

Our next table accordingly shows the effect of direct taxes on income and the effect of transfers. The first column (repeated from the previous table) shows income before tax or transfer. The second column shows the additions and subtractions by transfer and tax.[1] The third shows the resulting amounts which are actually available for consumption and saving—we call them Disposable Incomes.

It will be noticed, on going through this table, that the

[1] It may be noticed that the direct taxation shown in this table does not (nearly) add up to the 92£H that was previously mentioned. This is because the taxes (and transfers) in the table are shown *net*. Thus the total tax levied on the undistributed profits was no less than 17£H, which, if it had been a net tax, would have left very little over, It was, however, partly offset by 5–6£H of *investment grants*, a transfer from governments to firms which complicates the social accounts between 1967 and 1970 (see below, p. 272 n.). Another offset is the small amount of direct taxation that is levied on the personal transfer incomes, which again are shown *net*. Here the government is giving, and taking some back; while in the case of the undistributed profits it is taking and giving some back. So the income which *passes through* government hands is considerably larger than the *net* receipts and payments of the government.

TABLE VII

The effect of direct taxes and transfers (£H)

	Income before tax or transfer	Tax or transfer	Disposable income
Personal incomes:			
From labour earnings	272	−60	212
Mixed incomes	25	− 6	19
From property	41	− 8	33
Transfer incomes	..	+38	38
Total, personal incomes	338	−36	302
Other incomes:			
Undistributed profits	22	−11	11
Public income	−7	+47	40
Total income	353	0	353

proportions of labour incomes, mixed incomes, and property incomes that are paid in tax are not very different—all between 20 and 25 per cent. (Precise percentages, calculated from rounded figures such as these, would have no significance.)[1] This, at first sight, is surprising. Surely one would expect the recipients of property income—the 'capitalists'—to be richer, and so to be paying income tax at higher rates?; besides, there is the *earned income allowance*, which is purposely introduced so as to cause earned income to be taxed more lightly. But these things do not seem to show. One of the reasons, no doubt, is that it is no longer so clear that 'capitalists' are richer than workers; the difference, at least, is very much diminished. But the principal reason is different. There are large parts of what counts as income from property which are not taxed at all. One of these is the income of 'charities' (churches, schools, and universities); this is included in

[1] The distribution of direct taxation between incomes from work, from property and from self-employment is not (nowadays) shown in the Blue Book; so I have had to estimate it, with the aid of the tax figures from which the Blue Book figures which used to be given were derived. These are now published, quite fully, in *Inland Revenue Statistics*; we have income tax receipts from Schedule E (wages and salaries) and earned income under Schedule D (self-employment); these are almost all that is necessary. But they are not so up to date as the Blue Book figures; I have therefore been obliged to use the proportions in which the 1967 revenue was divided, applying these proportions to the revenue of 1969. There is doubtless some error in this; but it is unlikely that the error would be perceptible, to the degree of approximation we are using.

'personal' property income. Another, much more important, is the 'income' which the owner of a house who lives in it derives from it. This is income in the economic sense, as we have seen, and it is reckoned as income for the purpose of these calculations, as it should be. But (since 1962) it has not been taxed.

So it is that the share of disposable income from property in disposable income *from work and property* is much the same as the pre-tax proportion—about 12 per cent. But its share in total disposable income of persons (transfer incomes included) is significantly lower—about 11 per cent. (The share of incomes directly derived from labour is, of course, reduced in almost exactly the same way.)

5. Now, before examining the other sorts of taxes, it is time to say something about saving. The undistributed profits of businesses, which remain after taxation, are of necessity saved; the disposable income of persons is available for consumption or for saving. Just what proportion of the 302£H was actually saved it is not at all easy to say; personal savings can only be estimated indirectly, and no great reliance can be placed on the result. The official figure for personal saving is 15£H. Personal saving, according to this figure, was about 5 per cent of disposable personal income. This doubtless conceals very different proportions in different social classes and from incomes of different sorts. We have no means of knowing what proportion was saved out of disposable incomes from labour and property respectively. (It is safe to assume that hardly any of the transfer incomes would be saved.) Suppose that two-thirds of the saving came from labour incomes; since so much of labour's provisions for retirement are made otherwise than through private saving, it does not seem likely that the proportion from labour incomes can be greater than this. Consumption out of property incomes and mixed incomes (together) would then come out at 44£H, against the 287£H of total private consumption. This is approximately 15 per cent. It does not look likely that if we were able to put a figure on consumption out of property income, in the narrow sense, alone, its proportion would be very different from the previous 11 per cent.

We have now accounted for personal saving, and for business saving (undistributed profits). But what about public, or government, saving? We cannot fit this into our tables until we have faced up to the difficulties raised by the other forms of taxation.

6. We begin with the indirect taxes. A large part of the price of such goods as cigarettes is really tax; when a person buys cigarettes he is buying consumption goods and paying taxes at one and the same time. In the case of a taxed article, the price paid by the consumer is greater than the price received by the producer by the amount of the tax; the opposite phenomenon occurs in the case of a subsidized article, where the price paid by the consumer is less than the price received by the producer by the amount of the subsidy. In the calculations we have made up to the present, consumers' expenditure has been reckoned, as it is natural to reckon it, in terms of the prices the consumers actually pay; but the value of the social output has been reckoned, as it is natural to reckon it, in terms of the prices producers receive. Each of these ways of reckoning looks perfectly sensible in itself, but the presence of indirect taxes and subsidies means that the results we get from them do not square. No wonder that we have been unable to find a place for indirect taxes and subsidies in our tables. Until we have adopted a consistent system of reckoning they are bound to slip through our fingers.

There are, in principle, two alternative ways of dealing with the difficulty. One (which is the easier statistically) is to redefine the national product as the value of the goods and services produced during the year, *valued at the prices people actually pay for them.* Since the value of indirect taxes, as a whole, is greater than the value of subsidies, the net domestic product, measured in this way, will be greater than the earnings of the factors of production. There will be a corresponding measure of the national income, got by adding income from foreign assets, as before. It is called *National Income at Market Prices.*

In the year 1969 the total government revenue from indirect taxes was 78£H, while 8£H was spent on subsidies. Thus the national income at market prices was equal to the

353£H, previously reckoned, *plus* 70£H (the difference between indirect taxes and subsidies). Thus the national income at market prices was 423£H.

The national income at market prices can of course be divided up in exactly the same way as we have done in our earlier tables. The only difference which will be made to Table VII is that an additional 70£H of public income will have to be included throughout. Personal incomes and business incomes; as shown in that table, will be unaffected, but disposable public income will have to be marked up from 40 to 110£H.

Now just as we went on to divide up personal disposable income into consumption and saving, so we can at this point divide up the disposable income of the government into public consumption and public saving. Public consumption, as defined for this purpose, will include what we have called 'semi-public' consumption,[1] but not the other forms of public expenditure; the expenditure on subsidies, and that which goes to provide transfer incomes, which have already been taken into account. Nor, for the reasons explained in the preceding chapter, should it include such public expenditure as we decide to regard as *investment*. The value of the public expenditure which the authors of the Blue Book consider to be reckonable as public consumption,[2] after these deductions have been made from the total, amounted in 1969, to 83£H.

The following table brings these figures together, and shows how disposable income at market prices was divided between consumption and saving. Thus in this sense just 12½ per cent of the national income was saved.

What happened to these savings? We already know, from our previous discussion, what must have happened to them; all that remains is to identify the figures. Saving must either be devoted to net investment at home, or to building up net foreign assets (including the repayment of debt). In 1969 the amount that is stated to have been used in this latter way

[1] See above, p. 176.

[2] Net gifts made abroad (whether by persons or by government) are included, as seems appropriate for this purpose, in consumption. (In the tables of Chapter XXI, they are, however, shown separately. This accounts for a difference of 2£H in the public consumption figure, as shown here, and in those other tables.)

was 4£H. The balance of 48£H should therefore be equal to net home investment. If we add to this the 37£H of depreciation, we get 85£H of gross home investment—the value of the new fixed capital goods produced (including, let us not forget, those which belong in the public sector, such as local authority housing) *plus* the increase in working capital and stocks. In this way, along this route, the whole thing comes out.[1]

TABLE VIII

Consumption and saving (at market prices) (£H)

		Disposable income	Consumption	Saving
Personal income		302	287	15
Undistributed profits		10	..	10
Public income:				
Before tax and transfer	−7			
Direct taxes *less* transfers	47			
Indirect taxes *less* subsidies	70			
Total public income		110	83	27
Total		422	370	52

7. So far, so good. But this method, although it gives a tidy result, has only done so by what may quite properly appear to the reader as something of a trick. The government has been shown as receiving revenue from a source which admittedly comes out of the national income, in the sense in which that has been defined for the purpose of the foregoing calculation, but which does not appear to come out of the pocket of anyone in particular. It must be admitted that in doing this, the calculation 'at market prices' gives a misleading impression. When the government imposes a tax on (say) tobacco, it does not conjure revenue out of the air; it imposes a tax, which is paid, and which it intends should be paid, by the consumers of tobacco and cigarettes. Can we rearrange the tables so as to show the spending of the national income in this, as it seems, more sensible manner?

[1] The gross home investment is shown in the Blue Book as 79£H in fixed capital, and 3£H in working capital and stocks. These add to 82£H, not the 85£H just given. The difference is the 3£H of 'residual error' which I have added in. What this means is that direct calculation of gross fixed capital investment only shows up 79£H, against the 82£H which is implied in the figures which are taken from the income side, the figures on which we have been working.

The only way of doing so is to adopt the second alternative, which we put on one side a little while back. We must value the national product at the prices producers receive, just as we did to begin with. This value of the national product is called (to distinguish it from the other) *national product at factor cost*; the corresponding value of the national income is *national income at factor cost.* But if we use this measure, we must be consistent in our use of the factor cost valuation. We must, in particular, measure personal consumption expenditure, not at the prices consumers pay, but at the prices which producers (and traders) receive for the goods which are bought. We must (that is) reckon personal consumption at factor cost, while the difference between consumption at factor cost and consumption at market prices must be shown where it belongs, as an additional tax paid by consumers and passing from the disposable incomes of consumers to the disposable income of government.

The rearrangement which follows from this decision would be fairly simple, if it were not for one snag. Not all of the indirect taxes which are levied by government fall upon goods which are purchased by British consumers during the year; part falls on investment goods, part (rather unintentionally) on exports, and part (still more unintentionally) upon goods purchased by the government itself. (Petrol, for instance, used by automobiles in government employ pays petrol tax.) It is necessary to separate out the shares of the revenue from indirect taxes which come from these four sources. That can be done, at least roughly; an estimated division is shown in the Blue Book.

The share of indirect taxes (net of subsidies) which is estimated to have been paid by personal consumers in Britain amounted in 1969 to 55£H. Thus, *at factor cost,* the spending of personal incomes comes out as follows:

	£H
Personal consumption at factor cost	232
Indirect taxes (*less* subsidies)	55
Direct taxes (*less* transfers)	36
Saving	15
Personal incomes before tax or transfer	338

On this way of reckoning, which is a sounder way of

reckoning, the proportion of personal income paid in (net) taxation was not 10 per cent, as appeared when (net) direct taxes alone were taken into account, but 27 per cent. If we also leave out of account the subsidies and transfers, the gross taxation on personal incomes from work and property amounted to no less than 137£H, which is a little more than 40 per cent. A little reflection will show that it is arithmetically impossible for such heavy taxation to be raised by 'soaking the rich'; it cannot be done without laying a heavy burden on the incomes of wage-earners.

It is indeed impossible to say at all firmly how the payment of indirect taxes should be divided up among incomes from work and from property. But no reasonable guess would give a distribution of consumption at factor cost which was very different from the distribution of consumption at market prices previously calculated.

Public consumption at factor cost must also be written down (by 6£H) to allow for the taxes the government pays to itself. The spending of the national income at factor cost can thus be divided up as follows:

	£H
Personal consumption	232
Public consumption	77
Saving	44
National income at factor cost	353

The proportion of the national income that was saved comes out much the same when it is reckoned in this way as it did in the other.[1]

8. In all this discussion we have said nothing about the third sort of taxes—taxes on capital, such as death duties. The fact is that we have not needed to attend to them. Taxes on capital do not affect the earning and spending of the national income, which has been our concern. The only way in which our tables might have created a wrong impression, as a result of this neglect, would have occurred if the reader had

[1] The difference between the figure for saving which we get in this way and that which we got from the market price calculation is to be explained by the indirect taxes falling on investment (6£H) and on exports (3£H). For further discussion, and for more sophisticated figures (which differ from these because of a more careful treatment of external transfers) see Chapter XXI below.

drawn a conclusion from them, which we were careful not to draw. The division which we have made between personal and business savings on the one hand, and public savings on the other, does show what sums persons and businesses were setting aside out of their incomes in order to increase their assets or reduce their liabilities, and what sums the government was setting aside for the same purpose. But it does not necessarily show the effect of the savings on private and on public property respectively. For if the government imposes taxes on capital, it in effect takes away some of the private savings and adds them to its own savings (private savings are used up in the purchase of assets sold in order to pay the taxes). The government must save the proceeds of these taxes, since all government expenditure out of income has already been allowed for. Thus the total of saving is unaffected; only its effect on the growth of private and public property may be different from what appears.

The capital taxes imposed in 1969 yielded about 6£H. This was a transfer from private capital to public capital; but the net transfer was smaller than this, because of a transfer of nearly 2£H in the other direction.[1] A large part of this 2£H consisted in 'capital' grants to educational institutions, such as universities, which are (nominally) not part of the Public Sector, and since they are not companies are classified as belonging to the 'personal' sector. The net result is that the additions to private property were about 4£H less, and the additions to public property (or the reduction in the National Debt) about 4£H greater, than would appear from the figures that were given earlier, about saving.

9. The account of the national income which has been described in this chapter may well seem quite complicated enough, but even so it has left out quite a number of minor

[1] As shown in the Blue Book, the transfer from public to private appears much larger than 2£H—actually offsetting the whole of the capital taxes; but that is because the Blue Book reckons the investment grants as a capital transfer (see p. 272 below). I have preferred to treat them as if they were investment allowances (such as were given in much the same place before 1967 and will be again after 1970). For comparative purposes, at least, this seems to make more sense.

difficulties. What has been given is as much as the reader can be expected to swallow at this round. If he wants more, he can turn to the additional chapters at the end of the book. What he will there find is an attempt at a consistent plan, into which the difficult points can be systematically fitted.

CHAPTER XV

The National Income in Real Terms—Index-Numbers

1. The national income consists of a collection of goods and services, reduced to a common basis by being measured in terms of money. We have to use the money measure because there is no other way in which a miscellaneous collection of different articles can be added together; but when we are seeking to compare the production (or the consumption) of one year with that of another, the use of the money measure may lead us into difficulties. A change in the money value of the national income may be due to a real change in the amounts of goods and services at the disposal of the community; but it may be due to nothing more than a change in money values. If exactly the same quantities of goods were produced in one year as had been produced in another, but in the second year prices were all 25 per cent higher, the money value of the national product would be increased by 25 per cent—but this increase would have a very different significance from that of an actual increase of 25 per cent in the production of goods and services. An increase of 25 per cent in the *real* output of goods and services would be an economic gain of tremendous significance; an increase of 25 per cent in money values, without any increase in real output, would not represent any economic gain at all. Before we can proceed with our discussions, we must learn

something about the means which are available for separating these two sorts of changes from one another.

It must be emphasized, in the first place, that no perfectly satisfactory method of separation exists. If a change in prices meant a change of all prices in the same proportion, it would be easy to correct for the change in prices; we should simply adjust all prices by the same uniform percentage, and we should then be able to proceed as if no change in prices had occurred. Alternatively, if when the outputs of goods increased or diminished, the outputs of all goods and services increased or diminished in the same proportion, it would then be perfectly clear what the percentage change in real output had been; we should find it easy to avoid being entangled in changes of prices. In practice these conveniently simple cases never occur. Between one year and another the outputs of some goods increase, those of others diminish; the prices of some goods increase, those of others diminish; even if (as has of late so often been happening) the prices of nearly all goods increase together, they increase or diminish by very different percentages. We are therefore reduced to makeshifts. It is a very delicate matter (which lies far outside the scope of this book) to distinguish the respective merits of the different makeshifts which are commonly used. Here we can do no more than indicate their general character.

2. The simplest way of estimating the *real* change in output which takes place from one year to another is to take the different quantities of goods and services produced in the two years and to value each year's quantities at the *same* set of prices. The value of the output of 1969 is ordinarily got by valuing the goods produced in 1969 at the average prices ruling in 1969; the value of the output of 1970 is got by valuing the goods produced in 1970 at the prices of 1970. If we compare these *money* values, we are confronted with a change which is partly due to real changes in output, partly due to changes in prices; but if we use the 1969 prices throughout, the relation between the figures we shall then get will cease to be influenced by changes in prices, but will only reflect the changes in the quantities produced.

For the years 1969 and 1970

$$\text{Ratio between money values of output} = \frac{(\text{Quantities } 1970 \times \text{Prices } 1970)}{(\text{Quantities } 1969 \times \text{Prices } 1969)}$$

$$\text{Ratio between real value of output} = \frac{(\text{Quantities } 1970 \times \text{Prices } 1969)}{(\text{Quantities } 1969 \times \text{Prices } 1969)}.$$

The brackets mean that the quantity of each good produced is to be multiplied by the average price of that good during the year stated; and the values thus arrived at for the outputs of different goods are to be added together.

The formula thus given for the ratio between the real values is got by using the *prices* of 1969 in both the top and the bottom of the fraction; but there is no particular reason why we should have selected 1969 as our *base* (as it is called) rather than some other year; the important thing is that the prices (but not the quantities) should be the *same* in both top and bottom. If, instead of valuing both top and bottom at the prices of 1969, we had valued both at the prices of 1970, we should have got a different formula for the ratio between the real values; there is no obvious reason why one of these formulae should be better than the other. Fortunately, in nearly all cases where an experiment has been made, it is found that the two formulae do not differ very seriously.[1] Either can therefore be used as a measure of the change in real value; it does not matter very much which we use.

It is even permissible, provided sufficient care is taken, to use for valuation the prices of some third year, which is different from either of the two years being compared. Thus it may be convenient, when we want to trace the movement of the real national income over a period of years, to select some particular year as base, and to keep it as base throughout the whole of the calculation. When calculating the movement of the real national income between 1950 and 1970, we might select 1960 as base, and use the prices of 1960 for valuing all the goods and services produced in any of the twenty years. This sort of thing is often done, and there may be no harm in it; but it is rather dangerous. A great deal can happen in twenty years; the circumstances of one year may

[1] There are mathematical reasons why this should be so (cf. Bowley, *Elements of Statistics*, pp. 87–8).

differ so considerably from those of another year ten years later that the different measures of real income, which would be got by selecting different years (out of the set of twenty years) as bases, might easily differ very considerably. It would be obviously absurd (to take an extreme case) if we tried to compare the real national income of England in 1700 with that in 1800 by using the prices of 1900 as a basis of valuation; indeed, it is doubtful if there is any basis of valuation which would enable us to make a useful comparison between the real incomes of two years a century apart. Comparisons of the kind we are discussing are sound and sensible if the circumstances of the two years we are comparing, and the circumstances of the base year, are not too dissimilar; but when there has been a great change in circumstances, as may sometimes happen even with years which are close together (1938 and 1940 may be a case in point), any kind of comparison needs to be made with great circumspection.

3. This is the principle of the method which is used for comparing real income and real output between different years. Even in principle the method is rather a makeshift; in practice we cannot do even so well as this, at least as a general rule. For although we can acquire, in one way or another, the information which is necessary for calculating the national income valued at the prices of its own year, we do not usually possess the detailed information about the prices and quantities produced of different articles separately, which would be necessary in order to calculate the value of one year's output at the prices of another year. So we are obliged to have recourse to indirect methods. The principle of these indirect methods is the following.

Take the formulae for the ratios of money values of output and of real values of output (between 1969 and 1970) which were set out on a previous page and divide one by the other. The denominators of both fractions are the same and so they cancel out. Thus we get:

$$\frac{\text{Ratio between money values}}{\text{Ratio between real values}} = \frac{(\text{Quantities 1970} \times \text{Prices 1970})}{(\text{Quantities 1970} \times \text{Prices 1969})}.$$

The fraction on the right of this new equation has the same

quantities top and bottom, but different *prices*. It is therefore a measure of the ratio between the levels of *prices* in 1969 and 1970. So we may write:

$$\text{Ratio between real values} = \frac{\text{Ratio between money values}}{\text{Ratio between price-levels}}.$$

If we can find a way of measuring the ratio between the price-levels, the ratio between the real values can be easily calculated from this last formula.

A really satisfactory measure of the ratio between the price-levels would of course involve just that knowledge of actual quantities produced, and actual selling prices, which we do not possess. But a rough measure can be reached in other ways. What we need is a measure of the average change in prices which has taken place between the two years. Such measures are called index-numbers.

Index-numbers of prices are put together in what is substantially the following way. We take a particular collection (or 'basket') of goods, so many loaves of bread, so many pounds of sugar, so many pairs of socks, so many ounces of tobacco (and so on);[1] we inquire how much it would have cost to purchase this basket of goods in the year chosen as base, and how much it would have cost to purchase the same basket of goods in the other year. The ratio between these sums of money is a measure of the average change in prices between one year and the other.

Suppose the cost of the basket was £2·50 in the first year and £2·80 in the second. The ratio is then 28·0:25·0 = 1·12. It is convenient in practice to write this multiplied by 100 (in order to avoid unnecessary writing of decimal points); so we say that the index-number of prices in the second year (with the first as base) is 112. The index-number in the base year must of course be 100.

4. The method of calculating an index-number which is employed in practice is slightly different from that which we have described, though it comes to identically the same thing. The situation in the base year is first examined, and the pro-

[1] It is important that the *qualities* of these goods should be as similar as possible in the two years.

portions of the total cost of the basket which are due to each of the separate articles are first calculated. These proportions are called *weights*. A simple example is set out in the table that follows. The basket is supposed, for simplicity, to contain only three sorts of goods, in the stated quantities. If the prices in the base year are as stated, the total values of these amounts can be calculated by multiplication, and the total value of the whole basket by adding up the value column. Dividing each of the separate values by their total, and multiplying by 100, we have the weights.

	Quantities	Base year prices	Total values	Weights
Bread	9	4p	9×4p = 36p	100×36/90 = 40
Milk	6	3p	6×3p = 18p	100×18/90 = 20
Beef	3	12p	3×12p = 36p	100×36/90 = 40
			90p	100

Now pass on to the other year which is to be compared with the base year. Suppose that in this other year the prices of the three articles were as set out in the second table on this page. If we recalculated the total value of our basket at the new prices, we should find that it came out to 94·5p. The required index-number of price change could be calculated directly by dividing this sum by 90p. But when there are a large number of different articles in the basket, and particularly when it is desired to calculate a whole series of index-numbers for different years on the same base, it is usually more convenient to reach the same result in a different way. We reckon what is the proportionate change in the price of each of the articles between the two years, expressing this in the form of a separate index-number for each article. Then we multiply each of the separate index-numbers by its corresponding weight, add up, and divide by 100.

	Second year Prices	Separate index-numbers	Separate index-numbers × weights
Bread	3·5p	3·5/4×100 = 87·5	87·5×40 = 3,500
Milk	3·5p	3·5/3×100 = 116·7	116·7×20 = 2,333
Beef	14p	14/12×100 = 116·7	116·7×40 = 4,666
			100)10,500
			105

Whichever method of calculation we employ, the cost of purchasing the basket has risen by 5 per cent between one year and the other; so the index-number of the second year (on the first as base) is 105.

5. Every index-number of prices is based upon a particular *basket*; but, of course, if we take a different basket we get a rather different index-number—a rather different measure for the relative change in prices. Different index-numbers are suitable for different purposes; for the purpose of comparing real national incomes we should desire to have a basket containing all the goods and services contained in the national income, in much the same proportions as they are contained in the national income itself—quite a tall order! The national income statisticians have nevertheless succeeded in putting together an index-number which purports to satisfy these requirements; but it should be appreciated that some components of this index are pretty tricky. Take, for instance, those that relate to investment in fixed capital. The sorts of buildings and machines that are produced in one year will always differ to a considerable extent from those produced in the next, so that it is almost impossible to conceive of a standard basket. The 'general' index-number is doubtless better than any alternative, for the purpose of making comparisons of real income (and the comparisons which we shall make, in the following chapter, are in fact based upon it). Some of the other index-numbers, which are less ambitious, are nevertheless more securely based.

In older days, before these improvements, there was one British index-number that was more familiar than any other—the cost-of-living index that used to be published by the Ministry of Labour. The basket of goods on which this index was based was supposed to be that consumed in a week by a representative working-class family. It thus appeared to be of fundamental importance; the prices whose movement it claimed to summarize are the important prices for the well-being of the bulk of the population; it should have covered a large part of the field which would be covered by the general index for measuring the national income in real terms. But it was not, at least in its latter years, altogether what it seemed; so it had to be scrapped and replaced by another index.

The cost-of-living index had a very curious history. As long ago as 1904 the government began to prepare an index-number of food prices; investigations were made into the quantities of different foodstuffs consumed by a normal working-class family, and a standard basket was defined as a result of these investigations This basket, containing food only, was used for calculations between 1904 and 1914. But after the outbreak of war in 1914 it was decided that a wider index-number was needed. Estimates (not based on the same detailed inquiry into the facts) were made of the probable consumption of such things as clothes, house-room, entertainments, and so on; these things were then added to the 'basket'. The 'basket' thus put together went on being used until 1947. The cost of living, as published, was expressed as a percentage rise in prices since 1914, so the base appeared to be 1914; but the real base was information about 1904 for the food items, and less secure estimates about 1914 for the non-food items, It would not have been surprising if an index-number with this queer and remote base had been seriously out of date by the nineteen-thirties; the government therefore decided to have a new inquiry made into working-class expenditure, so that a new index could be constructed. The inquiry was made (in 1937–8) and its preliminary results were published;[1] but the appearance of the new index was postponed by the outbreak of war. Accordingly, during the war, the old index-number went on being used; but in war conditions it had results which can only be called preposterous. It is quite probable that it had not been seriously misleading up to 1939; in 1937–8 it stood at 157 (a rise of 57 per cent above 1914) while calculation showed[2] that an index based on the basket which emerged from the 1937 inquiry would have stood at 159. During the war things got far worse. Since the basket used in the official index had become quite inappropriate to present-day

[1] *Ministry of Labour Gazette*, December 1940 and January–February 1941.

[2] The calculation was made by Professor Bowley in the *Review of Economic Studies*, June 1941, p. 134. The small divergence is certainly remarkable. It is a tribute to the foolproof character of these index-numbers—when no one is monkeying with them.

consumption, the government discovered that it was much cheaper to stabilize (by subsidies) the prices of those things which were included in the official basket, than it would have been to stabilize the true cost of living as a whole. Being unable to control the temperature, they controlled the thermometer! For other than political purposes, that made the thermometer useless; we can here make no use of the official cost-of-living index after 1940 is passed.

There is no doubt at all that prices did rise very greatly during the nineteen-forties; but the exact extent of the rise, as it occurred, was not at all easy to measure. There were two special difficulties. One was the decline in the quality of goods which occurred during the war, and in some cases persisted long afterwards; the other was the rationing system, which made it rather nonsensical to inquire into the cost of purchasing a 1938 (or 1914) basket, since the quantities of some of the goods in that basket would be quantities people were not allowed to buy. For these reasons, when at last the 1938 basket came into official use (in 1947) statisticians had little faith in it; the new index was called an 'interim index' and it was intended that it should be replaced by a proper index with a post-war base as soon as things had settled down. In fact, they took longer to settle down than expected, so that a second interim index had to be introduced in 1952. It was not until 1956 that the proper index (based, initially, on the now ration-free budgets of 1953–4) could be brought into action. This is the official *Index of Retail prices* which is still in use.

It differs in two ways from the old 'cost-of-living' index. In the first place, it is not a *working-class* cost-of-living index; it is meant to represent the level of prices which confronts a representative, or 'average' family, out of the whole population. Thus the 'basket', changes in the money cost of which are registered by it, is not confined to necessaries; it includes a fair number of less necessary commodities as well. Secondly (and this is probably of greater importance) it is not a *fixed* basket; it has been revised every year (since 1962), so as to take account of new goods, and of changes of other sorts in the pattern of consumption. Thus the rise in the index between 1962 and 1963 measures the increase in cost, between

1962 and 1963, of the 1962 basket; the rise between 1963 and 1964 measures the increase between those years in the cost of the 1963 basket; and so on. If what we want to measure is the rise in prices *from one year to the next*, this is clearly the right way to do it.

6. As has been explained, index-number comparisons are much better (they have more meaning) when they are made like this, for years that are close together, than they can possibly be for years that are far apart. Even if the new *retail price index* had been in existence for the whole of the half-century, and had been properly kept up for the whole of that time, it would not have measured the increase from 1914 to 1970 very satisfactorily. When people ask 'how much have prices risen since 1914?' or 'how much of its value has the pound lost since 1914?' they are asking a question that can, at the best, be only very roughly answered. If one just splices the index-numbers together, multiplying

$$1{\cdot}57 \times 1{\cdot}60 \times 1{\cdot}53 \times 1{\cdot}52$$

(which are the best estimates for the rises in the four periods[1] which we have distinguished) the result is approximately 6, a six-fold rise. 'The pound has lost five-sixths of its value!' But what does this mean? There is not much point in inventing the story of a Rip van Winkle, going to sleep in 1914 with one of the new Treasury notes in his pocket, and waking up in 1970 to find that it will only buy one-sixth as much as he had expected.[2] Nor is it much more helpful to say that the 1914 man, who returned from his week's work with three gold sovereigns in his pocket, was in a situation that is comparable with that of his 1970 grandson, who earns £1,000 a year. The things that the grandson can buy, but the grandfather could not, are so extensive. No electrical gadgets, no radio, practically no canned foods; there is a great deal which matters, but which the index-number comparison does not take into account.

[1] 1914–38, 1938–47, 1947–56, 1956–70. The 1·60 rise is that in the unofficial index for 1938–47 (London and Cambridge Economic Service).

[2] He would have quite a job to change it for something which he could spend! If he had (illegally) hung on to sovereigns, he would have done better, but not all that better. Even his sovereigns would have 'lost' (about) half their value.

All the same, it is useful to look at the history—though it is as well to express it in a way which involves us as little as possible in these awkward questions. That is what I have tried to do in Chart III. Though the curve in this chart is spliced on, the four periods are marked out by being put into 'boxes'. I hope this leads the eye to look at the boxes separately, and to make comparisons between them. The comparisons are significant, unlike the general effect of the movement from 1914 to 1970, which has just been shown to mean rather little. Again, in order to assist the comparisons, I have drawn the chart on a ratio scale (or log scale)[1] which has the property that equal (vertical) distances measure rises (and falls) of equal *percentages*. If one does not do this, the comparisons are badly wrong. If one had drawn the chart on an ordinary scale, with base (at 1914) equal to 100, the rise from 1964 to 1969 would appear as a rise from 500 to 600 (or thereabouts); but this is not usefully regarded as a rise of 100 points. It is a rise of 20 per cent; just the same as occurred between 1914 and 1915, when the cost-of-living index shows a rise of 100 to 120. They ought to be shown as being the same rise; that is what the ratio scale does for us.

7. The first thing which must strike one, when one looks at the chart, is the extraordinary difference in the way the index behaves in the first period (1914–38) from the way it behaves in the later periods. This is indeed a most important difference; it is the reason why I have had to go back to what may now seem to be rather ancient history. The movement in the first period seems all over the place; later on, by contrast, it looks very steady—though it is steady about an almost continuous, and quite considerable, rise. But let us look at the story in a little more detail.

It begins (as the chart, in the way we have drawn it, makes very clear) with a very rapid rise in prices between 1914 and 1920—the most rapid rise that is registered in any of the years that are shown. Nothing was done about it while the war continued, but in 1920 it was stopped—with quite a

[1] Since it is constructed by plotting the logarithms of the index-numbers on the vertical axis, not the index-numbers themselves.

bang! The brake was put on so hard that prices actually fell, as sharply as they had risen, for a couple of years; to the accompaniment of unemployment, and strikes, and other upsets. After that there were a few years in which the index looks rather stable; but then there was a further fall (the World Depression of 1929–33). The last of the inter-war

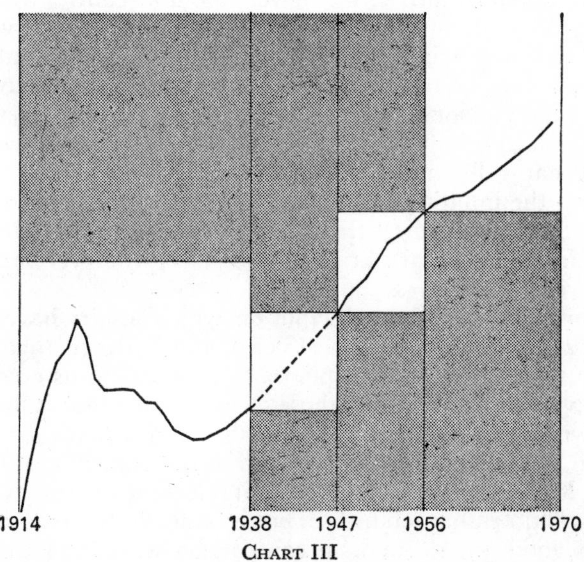

CHART III

years show a moderate rise; but even at the outbreak of the Second World War the 1929 level had not been again attained.

This was a dismal experience; but those who organized the British economy during the Second World War had learned from it, and were determined to do better. One of the results (as has been explained) is that we have no usable figures for 1938–47; the economy was so thoroughly 'managed'! So I have just drawn the rise during that period as a straight line on my chart. But it is not seriously misinforming; prices did rise more gradually in the Second World War than in the First—and when the war was over, there was no sudden check. Indeed, as may be seen, the rise continued, at very much the same rate; and has continued, at what appears no very different a rate, during the twenty years that have followed.

How has this happened? There are, of course, many cross-currents, which this is no place to explore; but the main part of the explanation is rather simple. The British economy, in the nineteen-forties, was never so out of control as it was in 1920; so there was never the same need to take violent action. It was true then, as it had been in 1920 (and as it is now) that inflation can always be stopped if you are prepared for the consequences; but with the earlier experience still fresh in mind, the idea of facing such consequences was (very naturally) abhorrent. All that seemed necessary was to stop the inflation 'running away'; and by this time there were milder remedies[1] that for that limited purpose seemed sufficient. Press on the brake; but be sure, whatever happens, that you do not press too hard.

This is in fact the principle on which affairs have been conducted in Britain, almost continuously, since 1950; and it is undoubtedly a principle that has much to its credit. It has avoided disasters like those of 1920 and 1930; it has had its own crises, but their impact has been, in almost every way, much less severe. Yet if one sticks to the principle of Never Too Much, it is practically inevitable that on the average one will do rather too little. That is basically the reason why these good times—and, in comparison with the past, they have been good times—have been times of inflation.

[1] That is where the 'Keynesian revolution' comes in.

CHAPTER XVI National Income and Economic Growth

1. One of the main purposes for which it is useful to put the national income into real terms (correcting for price changes in the manner described in the last chapter) is in order to use it as a measure of economic progress, or (as it is nowadays fashionable to say) economic growth. There is indeed no single index which is a perfect measure of economic growth; in order to see whether an economy is growing 'properly', we need to look at far more things than can possibly be expressed in a single figure. But income is a better measure than consumption, since consumption may rise (for a while) just because people have become less inclined to save—because, it may be, they have become less concerned about the future, without becoming fundamentally any better off. And income must certainly be taken in real terms; there is no gain if money incomes are higher, but no more can be bought out of the higher incomes, since prices have just risen to correspond.

What I shall be doing in this chapter is to illustrate the use of the national income[1] for this purpose by means of

[1] It is nowadays more usual to take as measure of growth, not the national income (which we shall here continue to employ) but the gross national product (G.N.P.), which is the gross domestic product+income from foreign assets, or the national income+depreciation. The reason for this is that the depreciation figure is rather conventional, and is considered unreliable. But there can be no doubt that the national income is in principle the better measure; the official statisticians have provided us with fairly good estimates of depreciation (or capital consumption), so there is no reason why we should not use the net figures. See Appendix, Note C.

British figures of the years 1955–69. In previous editions of this book I went much further back, to the twenties and thirties; but though (as we saw in the preceding chapter) it remains essential to go back to that old story when we are considering the movement of prices, we shall find that in this place (on all matters but one)[1] the quite recent history gives us plenty to discuss. There is the further advantage that 1955–69 is a period for which the National Income calculations are well established; so we do not need to use the rougher, and more fragmentary, information which is all we have for the time before the Blue Books began. We also exclude the war period, and the immediate post-war period, for which the figures (though they exist) are hard to interpret —for instance because of rationing. In both of these ways our fifteen years are much more straightforward.

We shall not be surprised, after what we have learned about prices, to find that the National Income, in money terms, has been rising, throughout these years, very rapidly. It has in fact risen from 155£H in 1955 to the 353£H of 1969 (where we found it in Chapter XIV).[2] But this is just a consequence of monetary inflation; when we measure the National Income in real terms, dividing the money figure by an index of prices[3] (as we have been learning to do) the appearance is very different. The result, called 'National Income at constant prices', should then represent what the value of the real goods and services, produced in each year, would have been, if they were valued throughout at the prices of the particular year that is chosen as base. But since there is nothing sacred about this particular year, it is better to divide the figures for the successive years, calculated in the way described, by the figure for the base year; showing the result (multiplied by 100) as an *index-number of real income.*

[1] See Chapter XVII, below.

[2] See above, p. 186. It is so chanced that in the year 1955 there was practically no 'residual error'.

[3] The index of prices that is here used is the *general* index, which is supposed to measure the cost of purchasing a 'basket' representative of all the goods and services which enter into the national product; it should in principle be distinguished from the retail index, previously discussed, for which the 'basket' consists of consumption goods only. But in fact, over our fifteen years, the movements of the two indexes are extremely similar. If one was substituted for the other, the effect would hardly be noticed.

The index that is got in this way is given in the Blue Book.[1] It comes out as follows (1963, which is taken as base year, is 100):

1955	1956	1957	1958	1959	1960	1961	1962
82·0	83·7	85·3	85·0	87·7	91·9	95·1	96·2
1963	1964	1965	1966	1967	1968	1969	
100·0	105·2	108·0	109·6	111·1	114·1	115·3	

These are very important figures; it is useful to look at them directly, but it is also useful to look at them another way.

I have drawn them out in Chart IV on a ratio scale (as previously described).[2] The point of this is not, as in the last chapter, to maintain comparability between movements that are far apart; for 82 and 115 are not so far apart. The point is to give a more exact representation of the movement from one year to another. We are very interested in that movement; for the percentage increase in this index, in any year over the preceding year, is what is called the *growth-rate*. On a ratio scale, we can see the growth-rate directly. The growth-rate for 1957 appears on the chart as the slope of the line that joins the 1956 point to the 1957 point. So we can see on the chart how the growth-rate has moved.

We can also see, on a chart of this kind, what is the average growth-rate over the whole period. It is shown (at once) as the slope of the straight line which joins the first observation (1955) to the last (1969). But this is not the line which I have drawn on the chart, for we can do rather better. The *average* line is too much influenced by the particular positions of the first and last observations; so a better representation of the whole movement is got by calculating the line which diverges to a minimum extent from all of the observations together. This is the line which I have drawn—the *trend* line, the statisticians call it.[3] As can be seen by eye (perhaps using a ruler) in our particular case the trend line differs very little from the *average* line.

[1] Table 14 of 1970 Blue Book. It is there described as an index of 'net national product at factor cost'.

[2] See above, p. 210.

[3] The calculation of the trend line (by minimizing squares of differences between the actual observations and the trend) is explained in any textbook of statistics.

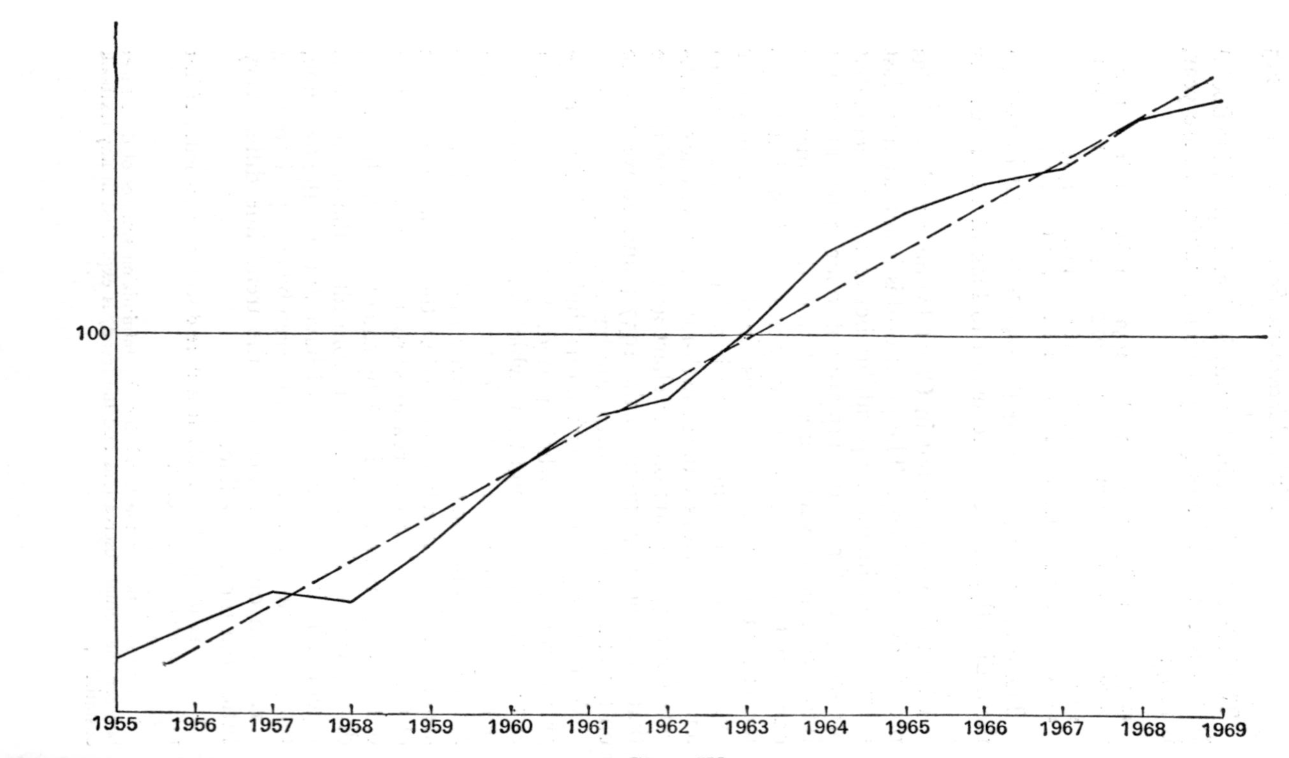
100
1955
1956
1957
1958
1959
1960
1961
1962
1963
1964
1965
1966
1967
1968
1969

One can see that the year-to-year growth-rate has varied a good deal. It was much faster in the middle years (1959–65) than in the early years, or in the latest years, that are shown. Nevertheless, the actual movement is fairly well represented by the trend line. The greatest divergences are in 1958, when the index is about 3 per cent below the trend line, and in 1964, when the index is about 4 per cent above it. Several of the actual figures, particularly in the middle, are very close to the trend. So it does look as if the trend is a fair representation of the 'long-term growth' of the British economy. Something very peculiar would have to happen between 1970 and 1975 if the trend, up to 1975, were to be very different from what it has been up to 1969.

Now the rate of growth that is represented by the trend line is almost exactly 2·5 per cent per annum. This is not very different from the 3 per cent growth-rate which historians believe to have been the typical growth rate of the British economy during the nineteenth century; but it is considerably below the growth-rates which appear to have been achieved by many other countries during the fifties and sixties. (For the years 1958–66, which—as will be noticed—were the years in which the British economy put on its best growth performance, the following figures are given[1] for some comparable countries:

U.K.	3·4	Germany	5·4
U.S.A.	4·9	Italy	5·4
France	5·2		

The difference is not so great as is sometimes supposed; but, all the same, it is quite striking.)

How do we explain these differences? What makes one country 'grow' faster than another? What makes the same country 'grow' faster at some times than at other times? These are large questions, some of the most difficult questions of economics, questions that have in fact been only very

[1] Source: OECD National Accounts 1957–66. The growth-rates there given (which I quote) are growth-rates of Gross Domestic Product (in real terms) not growth-rates of real national income. But the figure which is given for Britain differs very little from that which would be got, *for the years in question*, from the figures we have been using; so it is probable (or at least possible) that the growth-rates are comparable.

partially resolved. No more can be done here than to begin a study of them.

2. Remembering our general plan of the productive process, it would appear at first sight as if an increase in the real national income must be due to some combination of the following causes: (1) an increase in the supply of labour—in the widest sense, taking account not only of the number of workers, but also their ability (or skill) and of the effort they put into their work, (2) increases in the capital equipment worked, (3) improvements in technique—the utilization of more efficient methods of applying labour to capital. It will, however, be appreciated that since we are dealing with a *national* economy, there may be some other matters to be considered—matters which arise from its *external* economic relations. I shall come back to these later on, for they can be of great importance; but it does not appear that in the British case, during the years we are considering, they were of much importance, so we may hold them over to the following chapter.

There are several important (and fairly simple) things which can be said under the *labour* heading; *capital* and *technique* are much harder to deal with. For improvements due to increases in capital equipment and improvements due to advances in technique are hard to disentangle. In a period of advancing technique the effectiveness of new additions to capital is always greater than it appears to be, judging simply by the value of the additions. The increase of capital equipment does not merely consist of new capital goods being added to the old, new goods which are of the same sorts as the old; the additional capital goods are to a large extent goods of different sorts, more up-to-date sorts, which generally means more efficient sorts. The same thing applies indeed to the replacements of capital which take place during the period. Capital goods wear out and are replaced; but an old machine is not necessarily replaced by the same sort of machine as before. If there has been an improvement in technical methods in the interval since the old machine was acquired, the new machine is likely to be different from the old, more efficient than the old. The new machine may sometimes cost no more than the old machine which it replaces, so that the firm which uses it does not reckon that it has made any addition to its capital; but if it is more efficient than the old machine which it replaces, there is an increase in productivity, due (perhaps we may say) to an improvement in the quality of the capital equipment employed.

Improvements in technique do very commonly take the form of improvements in the quality of capital. The making of an invention—the discovery of a more efficient method of production—does not itself increase productivity; productivity is only increased when the new method is applied, and usually it cannot be applied until the new equipment with which to apply it has been constructed. Thus it frequently happens that increases in productivity which are ultimately due to a particular invention are not completed until several decades after the date when the invention was originally made. Probably the most potent of the inventions which increased productivity between 1924 and 1938 were the internal combustion engine and the electric dynamo; but neither of these was a new invention, each was inherited from the nineteenth century and had completed all the essential stages of its technical development before 1910. The great economic effects of these inventions belong to the later period, because the inventions had to be embodied in capital goods before they could be utilized, and the new capital goods took time to construct. It is well to remind ourselves of the variety of capital goods which are needed for the full utilization of a major invention like the internal combustion engine. Even in the field of terrestrial locomotion alone, it was not merely a question of making the motor-lorries and motor-buses, the motor-cars and motor-cycles; the plant for making these vehicles had first to be constructed, while garages to repair them were also necessary, metalled roads on which they could run, tankers to bring them their fuel, and petrol pumps from which to distribute it. And none of these things could function unless there were also available, at the ends of the earth, the oil-wells from which the essential fuel originally springs, and the tropical plantations to provide rubber for the tyres. When one remembers that only a limited proportion of the community's resources is available each year for new investment, and that there are other forms of new investment to be provided for as well, it is not surprising that a great invention should take some time to realize itself fully. But while it is realizing itself, it adds very greatly in the productivity of the additions to capital which are being made.

3. In view of these considerations, we shall hardly expect to find that there is a close connection between capital investment and the rate of growth of real income. We shall certainly not expect to find them keeping in step, from year to year; over longer periods (perhaps over five-year periods) a connection, one might think, should be more perceptible. Yet even this looser connection, on a summary view of the British figures, hardly shows up. The proportion of the National Income, at factor cost, which has been devoted to net investment (all kinds together) has, over our period, been rather steadily rising. It averaged 9·7 per cent in the first five of our fifteen years, 11·1 in the second, and 12·1 in the third. Yet (as we have seen) it was in the second five years that the growth-rate was highest. There is no obvious fit.[1]

We get a little more light if we look at the various kinds of investment separately. Table IX[2] shows the percentages of national income (at factor cost) which has been devoted to net investment under the four heads: (i) Fixed Capital investment in private industry, (ii) Fixed Capital investment in the public sector—central government, local government, and nationalized industries, (iii) net *real* increase in working capital and stocks,[3] (iv) the foreign balance—net increase in external assets, including international money. I have

[1] It is certainly true that the proportion of income invested has been higher in France and Germany than in Britain, and that their growth-rates have been higher. In Germany, in particular, the investment proportion has been remarkably high, nearly double the British figure. In France also it has been higher than in Britain, but the difference is mainly due to the very large French expenditure on (expensive) housing. As between France and Germany, investment expenditure has been much higher in Germany, but growth-rates have been much the same.

[2] Source: Tables 60, 66, and 46 in 1970 Blue Book.

[3] See below, p. 279.

thought it worth while to divide the Fixed Capital investment between private and public sectors[1]—for several reasons. One, which is obvious from the table, is that the figures in the first two columns (when they are separated) move in such a different way. A second is the difficulty, which we have already noticed, of knowing how far what is put down as public investment really is investment, and not consumption in disguise. (The contribution of new schools, or rebuilt railway stations, towards increasing the national product must inevitably be rather remote.) A third is that public investment is much more under the control of government—it responds much more to changes in government policy than private investment[2] is likely to do.

TABLE IX

The Forms of Investment (net investment at factor cost as percentage of national income)

	Fixed capital investment (private)	Fixed capital investment (public)	Working capital investment	Foreign balance
1955	3·3	3·9	1·9	−1·0
1956	3·4	3·3	1·5	1·2
1957	4·0	4·0	1·3	1·3
1958	4·2	3·4	1·8	0·6
1959	4·6	3·8	0·9	0·7
1960	5·6	3·7	2·8	−1·3
1961	6·1	4·1	1·4	0·0
1962	5·5	4·2	0·3	0·5
1963	5·0	4·3	0·5	0·8
1964	6·1	5·3	2·4	−1·5
1965	5·6	6·3	1·4	−0·3
1966	5·4	5·7	0·9	0·2
1967	5·3	6·7	0·7	−1·0
1968	5·9	6·2	0·6	−1·0
1969	5·3	5·0	0·8	1·2

[1] The division between these sectors *at factor cost* is not given in the Blue Book. I have therefore been obliged to assume the division would be the same as the division at market price, which is shown. This is not likely to introduce any perceptible error.

[2] Government has indeed endeavoured to accelerate private investment, and sometimes to restrain it, by taxation policy. But this effect is much slighter than the direct effect which can be exercised upon investment in the public sector.

So let us begin by looking at the first column—private investment. It starts at what, in terms of later experience, appears to be an extremely low level; then, all the way from 1955 to 1961, it steadily rises. It does not seem unreasonable to associate this rise with the more rapid increase in real income which we found to have occurred in the second of our five-year sub-periods. It is not surprising that the higher investment should have taken time to make its effect; so far, then, so good. But after 1961 this private investment figure remains fairly high; it goes up and down, it is true, but only a little; yet, as we have seen, the growth-rate soon falls off.

In the second column (public investment) there is quite a different story. There is no similar expansion in the fifties; up to 1963 the movement is very moderate. But then (from 1963 to 1965) there is a jump. (Two whole points, on a table like this, is quite a big rise; and it is very sudden.) There is a moderate fall in 1966, then a rise, in 1967, to the highest point that is reached in any year of the table. (At the end of 1967 the pound was devalued.) Afterwards, in 1968 and still more in 1969, there is a cut back—not yet to what would have been a normal level before the 'boom', but quite a long way towards it.

What is told in this column is, very evidently, a political story;[1] it is a matter of the economic impact of political decisions. One can see a good deal of the way it worked, by looking back at Chart IV. We can see that 1958 was a year of recession—nothing like the depressions, the periodical depressions, which had been so black a mark on the earlier history of industrialism,[2] but the biggest dip below the trend line which we find in any year among our fifteen. Then in

[1] But not a party political story. The decisions which led to the boom were taken, at the latest, in 1963, in the last days of the Macmillan (Conservative) government. When Labour took office, at the end of 1964, the boom was well established. It is true that for three years they let it rip; but the checks that were imposed in 1968 and 1969 (after the devaluation shock) were their work. Is it a rule that British parties should change their coats a year or so before they go out of office? It is what seems to have happened in 1963 and 1969, perhaps also in 1950. To the credit, one supposes, of the political efficiency of British democracy—but hardly of its economic efficiency.

[2] In 1958 (on the average) 2·2 per cent of the labour force was registered as unemployed; in 1932 22·1 per cent.

1962 the curve again begins to falter; one can understand that there were powerful pressures to take measures that would prevent a repetition of the former dip. It was undoubtedly wise to take such measures; but it would certainly appear that the measures which were taken were much too strong.

For let us look at the other columns. The third column (investment in working capital) does have a relation to the growth-rate—a relation which is well understood and which has often been illustrated. It does not show up well at the beginning of the column, where (presumably because post-war shortages were still not completely made up) the investment in working capital is larger than might have been expected; later on, however, it is very clear. The years in which the figures in this column are highest are 1958, 1960, and 1964; though these are not years in which real income was high (as we have seen, it was low in 1958, relatively to trend), they are years in which the growth-rate was increasing, or about to increase. Now it is rather obvious that an increase in output—especially an increase which is out of line with what has been happening previously—must be *preceded* by an increase in working capital. This is just because production takes time; before there can be an increase in output there must be an increase in the input of materials. At the stage when input has increased, but output has not yet increased, there must be an increase in working capital. That is what shows up, quite clearly, in the figures for 1960 and 1964.

But now look at the last column. The years 1960 and 1964, in which the figure in the third column is highest, are the very years in which the figure in the last column is lowest—minus 1·3 and minus 1·5 respectively. This again is not surprising; a big figure in column 3 marks a big input of materials, and in an economy such as Britain's, it is inevitable that a big input of materials should be largely imported. It is very difficult to step up the growth-rate without there being an adverse effect on the foreign balance.

Now there are circumstances (in the general experience the world they are not infrequent circumstances) in which this does not much matter. If a country's reserves of foreign exchange (gold, and substitutes for gold) are ample, it can stand a pressure of this sort, at least for a year or two; then, if the extra imports have been well used, the reserves will recover. But Britain, at no time since 1945, has possessed such ample reserves. At the best, they have been no more than just sufficient to meet the calls that are likely to be made upon them. It is therefore essential, when one looks at the changes which are recorded in our 'foreign balance' column, to look at a sequence of years, not at one year by itself. It should be remembered that our figures are percentages of a national income that, in money terms, was steadily rising; so they cannot simply be added up. Yet we can see from them the adverse balance of 1960 was not desperate, since it succeeded three years in which the balance had been favourable. The adverse balance of 1964 was more dangerous—and not only for the reason that it was rather larger. The adverse balance of 1967 was smaller, but it came at the end of a series of what, from this point of view, were bad years. That is why, as it turned out, it could not be borne.[1]

Now it will be noticed (and this is important for the present discussion) that since 1966 investment in working capital has not been high. That is what we should expect; for, as we have seen, these were years in which the growth-rate has been low. It is not a large investment in working capital which matches the adverse balance of 1967, nor is it a large investment in fixed capital by private industry. Neither of these were particularly large. It is the fixed capital investment in the public sector which is the thing that stands out. And it is the fall in public investment which is the principal counterpart to the balance-of-payments improvement in 1969.

4. All this can be said, looking only at the capital side; it takes us a good way, but it is not enough. It seems often to

[1] As will be seen, the adverse balance continued into 1968; the change in course, after devaluation (November 1967) could not be immediate. But the adverse balance was then less serious, for it became known that steps were being taken to remedy it. To any business, creditors will usually continue to lend, when they know that there has been a policy change which will remedy the trouble.

be supposed that it is enough; thus the low rate of growth between 1966 and 1969 is very commonly explained in balance-of-payments terms. If only (it is said) we were clear of that trouble—if additional reserves could, somehow or other, be conjured up—then all would be well. The growth-rate could increase, for the extra working capital that is needed to support an increased growth-rate could then be afforded. And (perhaps) at the end of our table that is actually happening, for in 1969 the balance of payments improves.[1] It will clearly be necessary (on this view) for the improvement to go on for some time, before it is possible to 'open out'; the reserves have been so much depleted. But the time should come when the corner will have been turned.

There is much in this; but it is not the whole story. Production needs labour, as well as capital. What had been happening, in the meantime, on the side of labour?

We have already discovered (Chapters IV–VII above) that the supply of labour is not a simple matter. We have to consider (1) the movement of population—not total population, but population which is of an age to be working—*potential working population*, we may call it; (2) the proportion which actual *working population* (which includes those who are seeking work, but are unemployed at the date the count is taken) bears to *potential* working population; (3) the proportion of the actual working population who are unemployed; (4) the effort of labour, of which the length of the working week is the most obvious index; (5) ability and skill. Something has already been said on most of these matters; but we need to look at them again, from the point of view of growth.

What happened, in the first place, to the potential working population (men and women together) between 1955 and 1968? As we have already seen,[2] it increased, but only very slowly, at an average rate of 0·3 per cent per annum.[3] The increase, however, was by no means uniform. It took place, almost entirely, between 1959 and 1965 (these would be the

[1] In 1970 (not shown in our table) the improvement continued.

[2] p. 72 above.

[3] So if we had calculated the growth-rate of real income per head of population (in this sense of population) it would have come out (over 1955–69) at $2\frac{1}{4}$, instead of $2\frac{1}{2}$.

years, it will be remembered, when the post-war bulge in births would be passing the 15 mark). Between 1955 and 1958 there was almost perfect stationariness (at 33·7 million); from 1965–9 there was again stationariness (at 35·3 million). But in the middle years, if they are taken alone, there was a rise at a rate of 0·6 per cent per annum.

It will, of course, be remembered that these were in fact the years (in our period) in which the index of real national income was rising most rapidly. So it already appears that a part (though not a large part) of the *extra* growth which we found in those years is a matter of population movement.[1]

It is more important that from 1965 to 1969 (when the growth performance was so disappointing) the *potential working population* was practically constant. It will rise again, later on, when the extra births about 1960 will come to increase it; but in the late sixties it was not rising at all.

While the potential working population (after 1965) was constant, the actual working population appears to have been falling. In the case of male workers the fall that is given is quite appreciable—from nearly 17·0 to less than 16·7 million. From 1965 to 1966 the fall in males is masked by a nearly equal rise in females; but after that the female working population is also falling.

Now it is possible that this fall in working population may itself have been a consequence of balance-of-payments trouble; people find it harder to get employment and do not bother to report. Yet it is hard to believe that the moderate rise in unemployment, which did indeed occur,[2] can have had a sufficient effect. The rise in unemployment, from 1965 to 1968, is actually less than the fall in the working population. Those actually at work in 1968 were about half a million less than in 1965; some of the fall was certainly due

[1] Even if we had deducted the 0·6 from the growth-rate of these years, and nothing from the others, the growth-rate in the middle years would still have been higher.

[2] The numbers unemployed (in the U.K.) in our years were as follows (annual averages—in *thousands*)

1955	265	1960	393	1965	360
1956	287	1961	377	1966	391
1957	347	1962	490	1967	600
1958	501	1963	612	1968	601
1959	512	1964	414	1969	597

to the measures which (deliberately, for balance-of-payments reasons) kept down the growth-rate; but it does not look as if they can be the only explanation.

Much the same as what has been said about working population applies to hours of labour. There has been a general fall over our whole period (1955 to 1969) in the number of hours per week *actually worked*[1] by manual labour (49 to 46½). This is undoubtedly in part a reflection of change in activity; for when unemployment is low, the number of hours worked tends to be high. But, here again, it does not readily appear that this will explain the whole of what has happened.

The general impression, when we put these things together, is that the 'quantity' of labour applied, after increasing very moderately in our middle years, must thereafter have tended to fall. In so far as the fall is due to unemployment (people seeking work but unable to get it) it is, of course, to be regretted; but in so far as it is due to other causes it may not be regrettable. If people take more leisure, because they want more leisure, that is economically desirable. It is a real gain, though it does not show up in the real national product in the way we measure it.

In a prosperous society, the number of man- (and woman-) hours worked per week might well be falling; but the fall should be offset by an improvement in the ability, or skill, with which the work was done. Something of that there must surely have been in the present case. Education, of a kind which significantly affects the productive capacity of the person educated, has been continually extended during the present century; but it should be noticed that its effects on the average skill of the labour force are extremely gradual. The proportion of the labour force who have had any experience (in their school years) of the educational improvements after 1945 cannot have reached 50 per cent until the late

[1] It is important to distinguish between 'normal hours'—the hours that are fixed in the agreements between employers' associations and Trade Unions—and the hours that are actually worked. The 'normal' week was generally reduced (in manufacturing industry) by new agreements made between 1960 and 1965, from 45 to 40 hours; but actual hours have remained much above, being paid for at premium rates (overtime). Actual hours are fairly sensitive to the state of trade, but over our years have shown this declining tendency.

sixties; there was, of course, a similar lag with earlier improvements. And it should not be assumed that education, as such, is bound to have an important effect on the skill of labour, in the sense that is here required. It is undoubtedly important that during the whole of the century, the proportion of workers who are capable of doing nothing better than quite unskilled manual work has been continually falling. But the *general* education, on which (during our period) so much was being spent, though it does this, does not necessarily do much more than this, in the way of producing a labour force which is economically more efficient. Much may be expected from it in other ways; but as a means of increasing the real national product (in the way we measure it) not, one would think, so very much.

5. We may nevertheless conclude, when all these things are taken together, that if it had not been for the balance-of-payments troubles, the growth-rate of the British economy could have been rather higher; even the trend growth-rate, over the whole period, could have been higher. But it does not look as if it could have been very much higher—3 per cent, perhaps, instead of $2\frac{1}{2}$ per cent—but not, easily, much more than that. This still leaves a wide gap between the British performance and that which appears to have been achieved elsewhere.

One must be careful, when making international comparisons, to be sure that in different countries it is the same question that is being asked. Anything, population, number of cars, or number of telephones, has a growth-rate; we should see that the growth-rates that are under comparison are growth-rates of (at least more or less) the same thing. Some of the growth-rates that are commonly quoted are quite clearly not of the same thing. The Communist countries, in particular, do not measure real income in anything like the way that has been described in this book; so to make a fair comparison between their growth-rates and those of Western countries is a very arduous task, perhaps an impossible task; for we do not have the information to perform it at all satisfactorily. To assume that their growth-rates, as published, are comparable with those of Western countries is just a mistake.

The growth-rates that are recorded for Western countries, however, are usually fairly comparable; even among them, the lowness of the British growth-rate stands out. How do we explain the difference? This is a burning question, but it is a very large question; it is impossible, in this place, even to begin to discuss it properly. There is, however, one rather simple point which can be made.

It does not appear that most of these countries have been so constricted by labour supply, in total, as Britain has been; but this, in itself, does not nearly account for the difference in growth. Much more important is the fact[1] that they have frequently been able to increase their manufacturing populations (as well as the labour engaged in 'service' trades) as a result of a massive movement of labour out of agriculture. Technical improvements have enabled agricultural output to be maintained, with very little new capital investment, but with very much less labour. The whole of the displaced labour force has thus been available to increase the output of other things. In the manufacturing sector, much more capital was required to employ the extra labour; it could not have been employed in these new ways if there had not been the extra capital; but the availability of labour meant that new, and very productive, opportunities for the investment of the capital were rather easily found. It is rather easy to see that in such conditions, growth could be very rapid indeed.

Very little of this opportunity was open to Britain, in our period, since already in the fifties the proportion of labour employed in agriculture was very small. The agricultural improvements occurred, in Britain as elsewhere; and as a result the proportion of the working population occupied in agriculture fell—but only from 6·1 to 4·6 per cent (1956–66). This was as large a *proportional* fall as occurred in many other countries, but it had much less effect. For the consequential rise in the percentage occupied *outside* agriculture was (necessarily) only from 93·9 to 95·4—about 2 per cent of the former figure. The industrial expansion that was possible on that basis was necessarily very slight. In France, by contrast, the corresponding agricultural percentage fell from 26·0 to 17·7

[1] Already mentioned, p. 74 above.

(again from 1956 to 1966), a proportional fall that was only slightly larger. But the consequential rise in the percentage occupied outside agriculture in France comes out (by subtraction from 100) as 74·0 to 82·3, which is a rise of 11 per cent on the former figure. Eleven per cent over ten years is about 1 per cent per year; so that about half of the recorded difference between French and British growth rates is directly accounted for in this simple way.[1]

[1] Even the phenomenal case of Japan (with a *trend* growth-rate of 9–10 per cent) is partially explained by the movement out of agriculture, which has been even greater than elsewhere, and started from a still larger percentage in agriculture. The percentage increase in the non-agricultural percentage (which in France was 11) in Japan was no less than 23 (over the same years).

CHAPTER XVII The Terms of Trade

1. There is another set of influences on the Real Income of a Nation, which can be very important but has not so far been discussed. It was not convenient to deal with them in the preceding chapter, since in the particular case of Britain in the sixties, which we have been using as an illustration, they have not played at all an important part. But they have often been important previously, and they might at any time become important again. There are plenty of other countries, even now, for which they matter extremely.

These are external influences, influences that come in from outside. They are not the same as the Balance of Payments troubles, which we have been considering; though they often give rise to Balance of Payments troubles, they do not always do so, and (as we have in fact been seeing) there can be Balance of Payments troubles without them. So they need a separate discussion.

The principal way in which these influences express themselves is through changes in the *Terms of Trade.* This needs some explaining.

Let us begin by taking a simple case to bring out the principle. Let us consider an imaginary nation, whose exports consist entirely of tea, and whose imports consist entirely of rice.[1] If it exported 50 million lb. of tea a year,

[1] I do have a real case in mind in constructing this example—the case of Ceylon. Ceylon has other exports than tea (but tea is about two-thirds in value of her exports), and other imports than rice; but Ceylon is not so far away from my imaginary example. There are many other 'less developed' countries which are very largely dependent upon a single export, or a small

and the price at which it could sell its tea was 20p a lb., the value of its exports would be £10 million. Assuming that its exports and imports are equal in value, it would then have £10 million to spend on rice. If the price at which it could buy its rice was 2p a lb., the amount of rice it could import would be 500 million lb.

Now if the price of tea remained the same, but the price of rice rose to 2½p, the same amount of tea might be exported, yet the amount of rice that was got in exchange would fall from 500 to 400 million lb. The amount of all goods produced at home might remain the same (including the 50 million lb. of tea produced for export) and yet the real income of the people would have fallen by 100 million lb. of rice. Real income would have fallen, not because of a fall in the domestic product, but because the *terms of trade*—the amount of other countries' products which the nation gets in exchange for a unit of its own products—had moved against it.

The same idea can be readily applied to more complex (and more realistic) cases. International trade is largely (though not wholly, because of foreign investment and foreign borrowing) an *exchange* of exports for imports; a 'barter' of exports for imports of equal value. As far as this holds,

$$\text{quantity of exports} \times \text{price of exports} = \text{quantity of imports} \times \text{price of imports}$$

so that the ratio

$$\text{price of exports} : \text{price of imports}$$

can be used as a measure of the *quantity* of imports which the country is getting in return for its exports *per unit of exports.* There are index-numbers of import prices and of export prices (calculated in the same way as the other index-numbers we have considered) so that the way in which the ratio moves can be readily calculated. If the ratio rises (so that the export-price index rises relatively to the import-price index—or the import-price index falls relatively to the other) we say that the country's terms of trade have moved favourably; they have moved unfavourably when the ratio falls.

number of exports; such countries are very particularly exposed to serious disturbances from movements in their terms of trade.

2. An unfavourable (or adverse) movement in the terms of trade, when it occurs for reasons that are external to the country experiencing it, can be very damaging to that country (as our example has shown). But it should not be concluded that all 'unfavourable' movements are of that kind. It is probable, for instance, that during the first half of the nineteenth century the British terms of trade moved very unfavourably; the quantity of exports which Britain was giving in return for a fixed 'unit' of imports appears to have increased, between 1820 and 1860, by about 50 per cent.[1] But this was not a change that occurred for external reasons; it was a consequence of the enormous increase in productivity which occurred, during those years, within Britain. The cost of producing exports was rapidly diminishing; so a larger volume of exports could be produced with less strain in 1860 than the smaller volume of 1820 had been produced. It is indeed true that Britain would have been richer if she had been able to sell her increased exports on more favourable terms; what was in fact happening was that a part of the gain from the increase in productivity in Britain was not accruing to the people of Britain but was being transferred to others. These were the days when Britain was the 'workshop of the world'. When productivity in one country runs on ahead of what is happening in others, a transfer of this sort is very likely to take place.

Later on, when many other countries became *developed*, there was, for the same reason, a transfer the other way. The 'unfavourable' movement of the British terms of trade appears to have stopped about 1860; from 1860 to 1914 there was a movement (a more modest movement, perhaps 20 per cent) the other way. This may have been due in part to a slower growth in productivity in Britain; but it was mostly an advantage which was coming to Britain from the faster growth that was occurring elsewhere. These were the years when the growth in food supplies from North America (and from Australia and Argentina) had their first important effect on the *real* earnings of British labour; the *improvement* in the terms of trade shows it up.

[1] This is the estimate of Professor Imlah, whose figures are printed in Mitchell and Deane, *British Historical Statistics* (Cambridge 1962), pp. 331–2.

The general movement since 1914 (war-time and post-war shortages being omitted) has been in the same direction. It is not easy to make comparisons over so long (and so disturbed) a period; but the general tendency from 1914 up to the middle fifties has clearly been very favourable. A crude comparison of 1914 with 1960 actually shows a movement of 30 per cent in Britain's favour. But the 'gain' has been far from regular. Thus in the Great Depression of the thirties there was a violent 'favourable' swing—no less than 20 per cent in the two years 1929–31. So violent a movement was naturally a disaster to the countries which 'lost' by it; but to the country which 'gained' it was also very upsetting. We have already seen a way in which an 'unfavourable' movement may be less unfavourable than it looks; here we have an instance of a 'favourable' movement going wrong, because it comes too suddenly.

What happened, in these years, from the British point of view, was this. The prices of both imports and exports fell heavily, in money terms; but the prices of imports fell much more.[1] So it looks as if it would have been possible (in view of what we have been saying) for Britain to have expanded her imports on a great scale, while giving up no more than before in the way of exports; but things did not work out like that. With the depression in trade, there was little demand for more imports; it was therefore inevitable, either that exports should be reduced, or that they should be financed (directly or indirectly) by some form of lending. But this latter, again because of the depression, was very difficult; so the adjustment had to fall on exports. Now this again, from the British point of view, could have been fairly satisfactory; for the goods which were not needed as exports could have been consumed at home—the 'gain' being taken out in that way if not in the other. But this also, in the shock and bewilderment, could not come about rapidly; so the 'favourable' swing in the terms of trade, which could have

[1] All over the world, industry was grinding to a halt; so the demand for the materials of industry fell off, *before* there were corresponding effects on the markets for finished products. So the prices of materials fell sooner, and faster, than the prices of finished products; since materials bulked larger in British imports than in British exports, import prices fell faster, on the average, than export prices.

been of great advantage to the nation, was in fact reflected in unemployment in the export trades.

That, however, was only the beginning; as spirits recovered, the opportunities presented by the swing were in fact, at least to some measure, taken. The people whose labour was no longer needed for the production of exports turned over to produce for the home market (either in their old occupations or in new occupations to which they moved). So it was that in the late thirties (though unemployment remained quite severe) there was a marked rise in real income—a rise which was due, at least in part, to the improvement in the terms of trade. Even by 1939 this adjustment was not completed; but it was well under way.

I pass to the more recent history. For a while, after 1945, the 'favourable' movement was reversed. There was a world-wide shortage of materials (and foodstuffs); this showed itself in an 'unfavourable' movement; at the beginning of the fifties all that had been 'gained' in the thirties appeared to have been lost. Though the war had been over for five years, Britain was still (economically) in a state of siege. But at last the supplies came in—with the restoration of order and the repair of war damage in the supplying countries. The 'gain' in the terms of trade from 1951 to 1957 was almost as great as the 'gain' from 1929 to 1931; but the effect was very different. British industry was hungry for more ample imports; and was ready to make good use of them when they came.[1]

By 1958 that stage was over; since then the British terms of trade have hardly moved at all. They were practically the same in 1969 as in 1958, and the movements in the intervening years have not been more than 1 or 2 per cent, sometimes one way, sometimes the other. The dramatic swings of the past seem (perhaps only temporarily) to be over.

[1] The 'favourable' movement in the British terms of trade, during the fifties, was of course matched—it had to be matched—by an 'unfavourable' movement in the terms of trade of many suppliers. To those few who had been able to profit by the shortages of 1950 this was indeed a disaster; but to many others it was not a disaster. They were better off when they could sell, even at a moderate price, than they had been when the price was high; for the reason why it was so high was that they had had so little to sell.

3. A word may be added here on another *external* factor, income from external assets—strictly speaking, *net* income, the difference between income from past investments and the payment on overseas debts. In spite of war-time losses, and post-war balance of payments troubles, Britain has retained a positive balance of income from abroad; in money terms, it has (broadly) been an increasing balance. But in order to reckon what that income is worth in real terms, we must divide it by an index of prices: but what prices? Either export prices or import prices; if we use export prices, we are measuring it by the value of the exports which do not need to be made, because there is this other income to pay for some (small) part of imports; if we use import prices, we are measuring it by the value of the extra imports it pays for. There is a case for measuring it either way. But (as we have seen) in the British case, during our period, it does not matter which we choose, since the ratio between these price-indexes (the Terms of Trade) has moved so little.

If we go further back, it does matter; but the information is very sketchy. It has been maintained that the 1938 figure for net income from external assets was about £200 million; but that is probably too high. Imports that cost £200 million in 1938 would have cost £750 million in the early sixties and maybe more than £900 million in 1969. The actual figure that is given for 1969 (as we have seen) is £450 million; so it would seem (if we work in import terms) that something like half of the pre-war net income may well have been lost. This is really no more than a guess, but it would make sense. The post-war figures (even when corrected for price-changes)[1] go up and down rather wildly; but it is not easy to detect a clear growth, or a clear decline.

[1] The 1970 Blue Book gives figures for net external income at constant (import) prices in its Table 14.

CHAPTER XVIII Equality and Inequality

1. In our studies of the national income we have divided it up in various ways; into the part which is consumed and the part that is saved, into the part which is taken by the State and the part that is left in private hands, into the part which is paid in wages and the part that is taken as profits. But so far we have said scarcely anything about what most people would regard as the most important sort of division—the division into the incomes of the rich and the incomes of the poor. This is not at all the same division as the division into wages and profits; there are many wealthy people who earn their large incomes by working for them, so that their incomes count as incomes from labour; and there are some quite poor people (for the most part elderly people) who live on incomes derived from their past savings, so that their incomes belong on the profits side. So the division into small incomes and large incomes is a matter that needs to be studied in its own right.

It is by no means the same as the division into social classes. There is a well-established notion that social classes are income classes: that there is an 'upper class' with incomes much above the average, a 'middle class' with incomes less above the average but still above it, and 'working class' with incomes below the average. But the facts, as they now are, no longer fit into this conventional pattern. The class differences that remain have no close correspondence to differences in income. The distinction between working class and middle class is as much a matter of the way income is earned as of the size of the income. Manual workers tend to regard themselves as working class, clerical workers as middle class; but a skilled manual worker will now earn more than most clerks. It is not possible to divide the population into clearly marked classes, each consisting of people with lower incomes than those in the classes above them, and higher incomes than those in the classes below them. If the division is made on any other basis than that of income, the incomes that are characteristic of the classes will be found to overlap. If the division is made on the basis of income, it will be found, however the income-groups are selected, that the distribution is quite smooth. The largest groups are those nearest the average; as one moves away from it (in either direction) the numbers fall away.

Our knowledge of the distribution of British incomes among income-groups is derived, like so much of our knowledge about incomes, from the records of the income tax. The higher incomes (those in excess of a fixed limit)[1] pay *surtax*, an extra income tax which is formally calculated with reference to the size of the taxpayer's income, taken as a whole; the distribution of these incomes is thus known directly, as soon as the tax to be paid on them has been assessed. The distribution of incomes below the limit is known less precisely, even though most of them pay income tax; for though the rate of tax does in fact bear some relation to the size of the income, this is effected indirectly, by a system of allowances, which avoids the necessity of calculating the total income of the taxpayer in each particular case. So we have to rely, for the distribution of the lower incomes (the vast majority of incomes), upon the 'income census'—a special inquiry, conducted by the tax authorities, every now and then, for the purpose of discovering which of the various bits of income assessed in this way belong to the same incomes.[2] There have now been several of these income

[1] The limit was fixed at £2,000 p.a. in the early twenties, and has remained at the same figure for fifty years, in spite of the continuing fall in the value of money. (But see note at end of chapter.)

[2] It should be understood that these inquiries do not proceed by counting up all the bits of income assessed over the whole population, and fitting them all into their places; that would be a herculean task, requiring far more labour than could be spared for it. What is done is to take a sample, as in a Gallup poll.

The income censuses used to be published in the reports of the Inland

censuses; I make use of two of them—those for 1954–5 and for 1967–8—for the tables in this chapter.

One of the difficulties which beset us when we seek to give a simple picture of the distribution of incomes concerns the family unit. A man and wife, with their children, are reckoned to have just one income for the purpose of income tax; but a boy and girl who are just commencing as wage-earners have two separate incomes, though they will only have one income when the time comes for them to get married. If the income of the family was no more than what the boy (or girl) got separately, it would on any reasonable standard be much worse off. The difficulty cannot be overcome by working in terms of persons, dividing the family income by the number of persons it contains; for needs differ at different ages, and juveniles are often not entirely dependent on the income they themselves earn. It may therefore be suggested that we get a fairer idea of income distribution if we refrain from mixing these different sorts of income together, and look just at one kind of income, classified in such a way as to make it a little more homogeneous. The income census makes it possible to do this. Since we want to take a large group, if we are to get anything like a general impression from it, we must be content with one which includes a good deal of variation in family circumstances. Thus the best group to take seems to be that of married persons, when the income is to be enjoyed by husband and wife, with or without family. This excludes from consideration some cases which may be afflicted by severe poverty (such as the widow with children), but it still gives a better picture of the distribution of incomes than we can get in any other simple way.

Table X thus shows the distribution of incomes of married persons in the 'fiscal year' April 1967 to April 1968. Income is before tax, but it is not altogether 'before transfer' as I should like to have made it; for family allowances are included, and social security contributions have been deducted. (If we were able to make adjustments for these items, it would probably make little difference to the general effect.) The total number of incomes included is about half-a-million

Revenue; but the 1967–8 census appears in a new publication called *Inland Revenue Statistics* (first published 1970).

less than the total number of married couples in the country; while it is possible that some of this half-million have 'slipped through the net', most of them will be old-age pensioners, who are being looked after in other ways. Thus, though the table does not include quite all of the incomes of married persons 'before tax and transfer' it must include nearly all. It would be a very difficult matter to improve upon it.

TABLE X

Personal incomes of married couples (before tax) 1967–8

Income class (p.a.)	Number in class (thousands)	Average income in class (£ p.a.)
Under £500	366	410
£500–1,000	3,356	800
£1,000–2,000	7,802	1,390
£2,000–4,000	1,093	2,560
£4,000–10,000	227	5,660
Above £10,000	33	16,000
All incomes (of married couples)	12,877	1,420

It will be seen that in this year much the largest number of these incomes fell into the £1,000–2,000 group. The average income (of a married couple) over the whole population was £1,420, not far from the centre of that group. There are figures by which we can divide this big group more finely; when we do so, we find that there were 8,057,000 of these incomes (in all groups) below £1,400, leaving no less than 4,820,000 above. Quite a number will cross over when we move the dividing line from £1,400 to £1,420 (for near the average the number of incomes will be very *thick*). But it will surely be safe to say that one-third of the total will still be above the average; and that is quite a lot.

It is not to be expected that in a quite classless society, incomes would be arithmetically equal (in Communist countries they are far from equal). The most that could be expected is that there would be no *bias*; the numbers below the average would be just about the same as the numbers above. (This, indeed, is only one of the tests for *equality*; but it is one of the tests.) On that test the British 1967 distribution is not so unequal. It is a long way removed from what used to be thought to be the distribution—'the number of people with incomes above the average is relatively small, but some of these people have incomes very much above the average' (the average being pulled up by these very large incomes). That is how the British situation was described in earlier editions of this book; but such a description is becoming out of date.

2. I did give, in earlier editions, what was supposed to be a similar table for 1938; but it was little more than a guess, too much of a guess to be worth reproducing here. Income censuses do not begin until 1949; but 1949 is too near to the war, too abnormal because of the persistence of war-time economic conditions, to be useful as a basis of comparison. The next census, 1954–5, is better; we can get some idea of the way the spread has been moving if we look at 1967 in comparison with 1954.

There has, of course, been a large rise in prices (and in *money* incomes) since 1954. There has been this rise all along the scale, so that a crude comparison of the money incomes at the two dates tells us little. The average income in 1954 was only £670; by 1967 it had rather more than doubled. (Prices, of course, had much less than doubled; so a part of the rise—as we have seen—was a rise in *real* income.) If we are to compare the distribution of incomes at all properly, money values must be adjusted, so as to make the averages (at least roughly) correspond. The simplest way of doing this is to multiply all the 1954 money values by 2. One does then find that the income-groups, at the two dates, are fairly comparable.

It is in this sense that Table XI has been put into '1967 pounds'. Its 1967 columns just repeat Table X. But its 1954 columns are constructed by putting the people who were in fact in the £250–500 group in 1954 (with an average income in that year of £400) into what is called the £500–1,000 group (with an average income of £800). Similar adjustments are made for the other groups.

TABLE XI

Personal income of married couples (before tax) in '1967 pounds'

Income group	Number (thousands)		Average income in group	
	1954–5	1967–8	1954–5	1967–8
Under £500	365	366	414	410
£500–1,000	3,855	3,356	800	800
£1,000–2,000	6,662	7,802	1,338	1,390
£2,000–4,000	807	1,093	2,660	2,560
£4,000–10,000	208	227	5,860	5,660
Above £10,000	43	33	17,600	16,000
All incomes	11,959	12,877	1,340	1,420

When the figures are arranged in this way it becomes evident, from the numbers in the classes, that it is corresponding groups that are being compared. The numbers in the lowest group are practically the same; but when we notice that the total number of incomes has gone up by a million, we see that this means that the number in the group has proportionately (somewhat) declined. The number in the second group has decidedly diminished, and so has the number in the top group; all of the other groups have expanded. In fact, excepting for the top group, there has been a general movement up the scale. This is really shown, in another way, by the fact that in all of the upper groups the average income, measured in our way, has 'diminished'; in spite of the fact that the average, over the whole population, has 'increased'. It is true that the average income, in the big central group, has 'increased' by £50; but the average, over the whole population, has 'increased' by £80. The difference between these two latter figures is a reflection of the general tendency to *climb* into higher groups.

Whether one considers that these movements make for greater, or for less, equality is a matter of taste. The fall in the numbers of lower incomes clearly makes for equality, and so does the fall in the numbers of the highest incomes; the *climb* in the middle may be looked at either way. But whether or not the *climb* is equalizing, should one wish it away?

3. What are the reasons for these changes in the distribution of income? That is a very hard question; we should have to draw on many branches of economics (and maybe of other social sciences also) before we could attempt to answer it properly. I can do no more here than suggest a few points which might come up.

As soon as we begin to think about the matter systematically, we see that any such question divides into sub-questions. Incomes are derived from work, in the broadest sense, and from the ownership of property; is the explanation to be found on the work side, or on the property side, or (perhaps) in changes that have occurred in the relation between the two? In the present case we have already discovered that the proportion of all personal income which is property income is rather small (about one-eighth we found it to be for the year 1969, in Chapter XIV);[1] so it is hard to believe that changes on that side can have been mainly responsible for the *climb* (since that affects too large a number of people). It certainly looks as if it is on the side of work that the main explanation is to be found.

It is surely clear, in any case, that the reduction in the number of sub-average incomes (the £500–1,000 group in Table XI) can only be explained by something on the side of labour incomes. There cannot, at that level, be sufficient property to make so much difference. There must have been a fall in the number of people who are doing low-grade, unskilled, jobs; there must have been a *climb* in the character of jobs, not only in earnings. This can only be explained as the effect (the long-run effect, as we have seen)[2] of educational improvements. Industry has had to adjust itself to this improvement in the *quality* of labour; and that again is a slow process. But it is here, in these figures, that we see the clearest indication that it is a reality.

Having identified this, we may well be disposed to admit the probability that much of the rest of the *climb*, in the middle and higher income-groups, has a similar cause. Though the number of people who are fitted to do the higher jobs is still small, it is growing, and the increased supply has been fitted in. That is what it looks like; and conceivably, with the increased supply, it has become unnecessary to

[1] See above, pp. 188–9. [2] Above, pp. 227–8.

pay so much for the services of the 'highest' talents—so that (as we see) the numbers in the top group are coming down.

There may be something in that; but, surely, in the case of the upper groups, we cannot neglect the property side. We must look at that, before going further.

It is not to be ruled out that some part of the *climb*, among the upper income-groups, is due to an *increase* in income from property. For between our two dates the share of property incomes in the total of personal incomes has in fact been rising. In 1954 it was 11 per cent, but in 1967 it was 13 per cent; not a large rise, in relation to total income, but quite a large rise, in relation to property income. So it could be the case that a rise in (personal) property income has something to do with the *climb*.

We do not get this increase into focus unless we look at it more widely. Though the pre-war figures are very uncertain, there can be little doubt that the corresponding figure, in the thirties, was much higher—it may well have been over 20 per cent. From pre-war to post-war it fell heavily; so the 1954 percentage, in relation to what went before as well as to what came after, was abnormally low. The reason is well-known; there was a period, lasting from the end of the war until the late fifties, when companies were distributing, to their shareholders, a quite abnormally small proportion of their profits.[1] After 1959 they became more generous; accordingly, throughout the sixties, the property percentage was this bit higher.

[1] Though some of this 'restraint' was due to government pressure, it is clear, by now, that its main cause was different. It had been traditional practice to hold back profits in 'good' years in order to be able to maintain dividends in 'bad' years; to diminish the risk of damage to credit which would follow from a reduction in dividend. When they were looked at from this point of view, the post-war years seemed a long succession of 'good' years; so the regular behaviour, thought proper for 'good' years, was followed. Very slowly it became clear that this was not what was happening; so policies were adapted to the expectation of continuing inflation.

That this is the right explanation is made evident by the very limited success of the extensive measures that were taken by the Wilson government to discourage distribution of profits. It is true that our percentage reached a peak in 1965 (at 13·5) and subsequently fell (to 12·8 in 1969); but even at the latter level it was much higher than the 10–11 per cent which had been usual in the fifties.

The rise then is a fact; but for it to contribute to our *climb*, two conditions are necessary. It is necessary (1) that the larger incomes should have more property in them than the smaller, and (2) that the share of property income in the larger incomes should not be diminishing. The first of these conditions, one would suppose, is satisfied; but is the second satisfied? That is by no means so clear.

Property is acquired in two main ways—by personal saving and by inheritence. The small savings which the ordinary man puts aside for his old age, or as a nest-egg against emergencies, do in the end make him a capitalist, though a very small one; these are hardly relevant. The successful man, who earns a large income from his labour, but spends only a small part of that income, may become a capitalist on a considerable scale before the end of his working life; this used to be the way by which a large part of personal property was accumulated. But since 1940, in view of the stiffening of income taxes, it has become much more difficult. So it is hard to believe that personal saving, of any sort, has much to do with what we have been noticing.

Inheritance, perhaps, is another matter. The acquisition of property by inheritance is usually regarded nowadays[1] as less justifiable than acquisition by personal saving; the State has therefore considered that the passage of property at death is a suitable occasion for special taxation. The British death duties were first imposed in 1894; but the rates of tax long remained at a low level, which is unlikely to have had any appreciable effect on the inequality of property ownership. The system of rates imposed in 1930 was much more onerous; but even in 1938 an estate of £200,000 paid no more than 25 per cent, and it was only on giant estates of more than £2 million that the already formidable figure of 50 per cent was reached. There were further increases between 1939 and 1949; an estate of £200,000 subsequently paid 60 per cent, and one of £1 million paid 80 per cent. Then the inflation of prices came to add to the burden of

[1] In earlier times it would not have been regarded in that light; one may indeed question whether this modern attitude towards *inheritance* of property does not have some connection with a more general tendency to exalt the individual as against the family—a form of individualism to which socialists are even more prone than conservatives.

death duties; an estate of £400,000 now has a real value which is no more than £100,000 in pre-war pounds. If we make that comparison (as for our present purpose is clearly appropriate) we find that the rate of tax on such an estate has risen from 20 per cent to more than 60 per cent since 1939.

Death duties, at this level, have a confiscatory effect on large properties, and so on the incomes from large properties. The effect is certainly slow; it does not operate until an estate changes hands; and, as we have seen, it is only since 1940 that the rates of tax have become so formidable. Nevertheless, between 1940 and 1967, most estates will have changed hands; so the effect of the high death duties should have worked through, if not completely, then nearly completely.

Accordingly, for this reason alone, we should not be surprised to find that the number of incomes in the top group (of Table XI) has been declining. It can hardly be doubted that the fall in the number of large properties, which is the result of death duties, is one of the causes of the decline. It is certainly the most obvious cause; but it cannot be the only cause. For it is not the case that the bulk of the income in the top group (as given in our table) is income from property. More than half of it is described as 'earned income'. (This is not quite the same as what an economist would think of as 'income from work', but it is roughly the same.) It is hard to make sense of this information without supposing that the largest *incomes from work* have also been (relatively) declining.

We have seen one reason why that might have happened; but it was not a particularly convincing reason. One does not train people for the top jobs; for there is no one to train them. They learn by example, by following on from others; but to a large extent they have to teach themselves. Why should it have got any easier for them to teach themselves? There must, it would seem, be something else.

4. The incomes we have so far been considering are incomes before tax. They are the incomes on which income taxes are paid, not those that remain after the payment of these taxes; but it is only incomes in the latter sense that are *disposable* for the satisfaction of personal wants. The rates of tax on high incomes are much higher than the rates of tax on low incomes; so the incomes which are disposable for personal expenditure are less unequal than the incomes we have been discussing. It is high time for us to turn our attention to the distribution of disposable incomes.

Here, unfortunately, we lose the help of the income census. We cannot take the groups of married couples (of Table X or of Table XI) and show the tax paid in each group, thus calculating the average disposable income; for we do not have the figures. (It would be possible to calculate the tax which is payable on the average income in each group, but that is not the same thing.) So we have to use figures which run all sorts of income together, without reference to family circumstances. Such figures are somewhat misleading, since they exaggerate the numbers of incomes in the lower ranges, by including a large number of juveniles, and others who are not fully independent. Here, however, they are the best we have.

The result is shown in Table XII. As compared with Table X, the numbers of incomes in all groups are, of course,

TABLE XII

Personal income (before and after tax) 1967–8

Income class	Number in class (thousands)	Average income before tax (£)	Average income after tax (£)	Average rate of tax (per cent)
Under £500	3,110	391	377	3·4
£500–1,000	7,800	750	682	10·4
£1,000–2,000	9,316	1,373	1,189	13·4
£2,000–10,000	1,547	3,200	2,410	24·7
Above £10,000	40	15,970	6,370	60·1
All incomes	21,800	1,160	986	15·0

increased; but the increase is much greater, as we should expect, in the lower groups than in the higher. The average income (before tax) in all groups is diminished, but in the highest group the diminution is not appreciable. In all groups, even the lowest, an appreciable percentage of income is paid in tax; on all except the lowest the tax is at least 10 per cent. (It should be remembered, further, that in the tax shown in this table social insurance contributions are *not* included. They are bound to be a higher proportion of income in the case of the lower incomes.) It is, however, on the incomes above £2,000 (the surtax limit) that the rate of tax rises really steeply. In the highest group there is little resemblance between the income before tax and the income that is left.

It will be seen, if one looks at incomes before tax, that the average income in the highest group is 13½ times the average income of the whole population; but if one looks at incomes after tax, this ratio is reduced to about 6½. The latter, surely is a better measure of the inequality of incomes (at the upper end).

It is generally accepted that this measure of equalization (at least this measure of equalization) is desirable. But the method which is used for bringing it about has its snags. A 60 per cent rate of tax (as appears by our table to be paid by the highest group of incomes) does not look unreasonable; after all, these people have a good deal left. But it is not possible to tax the top group at 60 per cent *and the lower groups at much lower rates*, without taxing the extra income, got by moving up the scale, at much higher rates than 60 per cent. In fact, at our date, a man and wife with an income of exactly £10,000 (all of it earned, and a part of it earned by each of them) could have paid a little less than £4,200 in tax, so that 58 per cent of their income would remain to them; but it would still be true that if either of them earned an extra pound, beyond the £10,000, nearly 84 per cent of that extra pound would be taken in tax. (At an income of £15,000 the *marginal* tax would be even higher.)

Just what is the trouble with these high rates of *marginal* tax? They have often been criticized for their effect on incentive; why bother to earn an extra pound when so little is left? In order to get the working man to work overtime, he has to be offered, for the extra effort, something more than his basic rate; if he was only paid for overtime at less than his basic rate, little overtime would be worked. It is hard to believe that something corresponding to this does not happen, sometimes, with the higher incomes; but it is probable that this is not the main thing that goes wrong. There are other ways out. It becomes exceedingly advantageous to take one's earnings in a form which does not 'attract' such heavy taxation—in some non-financial advantage, or in a financial advantage that does not reckon as taxable *income*. From the point of view of the tax authorities these are loopholes, and they bestir themselves to close the loopholes, one after another; but new devices are continually discovered, and there are some that cannot be closed without reactions, on the efficiency of business, and even on common fairness, that cannot easily be faced.[1] Thus what in fact happens, as a consequence of this high *marginal* taxation, is that the nominal income 'before tax', and even the disposable income 'after tax', become less reliable as an indicator of the true income, in the higher income-groups, than they would otherwise be. (Not that something of the same kind does not happen in other income-groups; for it is not only the wealthy who pay heavy taxes on marginal income.) Too great reliance on income taxation to equalize incomes weakens the power of the income taxation itself to do what it is supposed to do.

One is bound to suspect that in this (as well as in the effect of death duties) we have a part of the explanation of the fall in the number of higher incomes. To the extent that this is so, the fall is only apparent.

5. This is as much as can easily be said about the effect of income taxes on the spread of incomes; but what about the other taxes, the indirect taxes, the taxes on commodities? These, we have already discovered, are a large part of the total taxation that is paid by persons; should they not also be taken into account?

One's first reaction is to say that of course they must be allowed for; but that is not quite so clear as it looks. For the incomes, the disposable incomes which we have already

[1] To take two leading examples. (1) There is a difficulty, at every level of income, in distinguishing between expenditure, which is to be regarded as consumption expenditure out of income, and expenditure which is incurred as a means of earning the income; there cannot, in practice, be a firm line between the two. There is a strong incentive, at high rates of tax, to arrange one's life in such a way as to make as much as possible claimable as expenses; it is worth while to accept some inconvenience in order to do so. (2) When tax rates are low, a man will be ready to provide for his old age by saving—saving out of an income that is taxed; but when tax rates are high, the gain he can get from having the provision made for him, in the form of a pension from his firm, becomes overwhelming. This too, strictly speaking, is a form of tax avoidance; but it is a form which cannot easily be stopped.

considered, are the incomes which people can spend in the shops. The fact that some of the things they buy are taxed, while some are not taxed (or are subsidized) does not prevent the incomes that are spendable in this way being a fair measure of relative wealth or poverty. That one man has a disposable income four times that of another does measure their relative position; we do not need to bother about indirect taxes before we measure it.

That is quite true; but it does not settle the matter. For when we are *comparing* the spread of incomes, at one time against another, we should make a check to see if it has been affected by what has been happening to these taxes. Otherwise we shall get caught. For suppose that as between two dates the distribution of disposable incomes (as we have been reckoning them) was exactly the same, but that in the meanwhile the rates of tax on some commodities had been greatly increased. If the proportions of income that were spent on these commodities were much the same in all income-groups, the increase in taxation (in itself) would make everyone poorer, but everyone would be poorer to much the same extent—the distribution of income would be much the same. But if the poorer people spent relatively more than the richer upon the taxed commodities, there would clearly be a sense in which incomes had become *really* more unequal, in spite of the fact that (nominal) disposable incomes had remained the same.[1] There ought to be a check-up.

A satisfactory check-up, for the period with which we have been concerned, does not seem to have been made. One would however guess, from the available evidence, that the point can hardly, *for that period*, have been of much importance. For though there was a slight increase in the proportion of personal incomes (taken as a whole) which was paid in indirect taxes (net of subsidies) it was a very slight increase—from 12·3 per cent in 1955 to 12·7 per cent. in 1967. Since it is probable that this proportion is higher for

[1] It should be noticed that the same kind of thing may happen because there is a change in relative prices for other reasons than taxation. If food becomes dearer, relatively to other things, that may fairly be regarded as increasing the inequality of *real* incomes.

the lower incomes than it is for the higher (they spend, *on the average*, a higher percentage of their incomes on highly taxed commodities), the increase in the proportion, over all incomes, would have been somewhat disequalizing—if it had been just the same indirect taxes that had been imposed and they had all changed proportionately. This, however, was not the case. The Selective Employment Tax (SET) introduced in 1966 must clearly have affected different income-groups in a different way from other indirect taxes; it is possible that it may have offset the other effect. All of these effects, however, will have been small.

There has been a much more marked rise in indirect taxation since 1967. The (general) percentage which was 12·7 in 1967 had risen to 14·9 in 1969. The effects of this more substantial rise would clearly deserve examination.[1]

[1] The income-tax system described in this chapter is that which was in force in 1969, and which will continue in force up to 1972. After that, according to the plans set out in the budget of 1971, it is due for considerable change. But even then it will be some years before it can be possible to re-write the present chapter with figures derived from the working of the new system. Here, in this edition, I am throughout using 1969 figures for illustration; it is the 'old' income-tax system which belongs to those figures.

CHAPTER XIX Further Horizons

There have been several occasions in this book (most frequently in the later chapters) when we have encountered questions, questions of great interest and importance, which we have been obliged to leave unanswered, or to answer in what was obviously a makeshift manner. There was a reason for this. Although the reader who has mastered what has been set before him will have learned a good deal of economics, the economics he has learned will be all on one side of the subject. A question such as that which has often arisen in these later chapters—why the national income is divided between wages and profits in the proportions that it is—such a question cannot be answered along the lines we have been following. The same applies to the reasons for the differences in the earnings of different kinds of labour, and to the reasons for changes in the terms of trade. We had to be very sketchy in our discussion of these matters, although they embody economic problems of the first importance. There are branches of economics which do deal with them in detail, but they are different branches of economics from that which we have been studying.

The relation between our branch (which might be called Social Accounting) and the rest of economics can be made clear by an analogy from another science. The study of the human body is divided into two main parts—anatomy and physiology. Anatomy deals with the structure of the body, the various organs and their relations, the plan of the organism as it is discovered by dissection after death. Physiology is concerned with the working of the organism—the living body as a going concern. What we have been studying in this book is economic anatomy, the structure of the body economic, as it can be discovered by statisticians working on figures collected *after the event*. Only very casually have we learned anything about economic physiology—the way the economic system works. Yet economic science cannot get on without its physiological branch;[1] there are indeed many books on elementary economics which deal with little else. It is only as a result of the great advances made in social accounting during the last thirty years that it has been possible to write a book like this which concentrates on the 'anatomical' side; the 'physiological' side was developed earlier, and many elementary books still follow that earlier tradition.

I hope the reader will have found that our 'anatomical' method has told him the answers to a good many of the questions he wanted to ask about the economic system when he began his studies; I do not think that so many important questions could have been answered so speedily in any other way. Yet in spite of that it must be insisted that the field we have been covering is only one side of economics; to treat it as more than that would lead to serious error—error of a sort that has been only too common in recent years.

It is easy to look at the social accounts, and to say that the country is getting into trouble because it is not producing enough, not saving enough, not exporting enough, or importing too much. Speeches are then made exhorting people to produce more, save more, export more, or import less. We have had plenty of such speeches, and we have learned by experience that they are very ineffective. Even if, for instance, they are successful in persuading people to work harder, it rarely happens that it is possible for people to work harder without the extra effort having other effects than those

[1] Since economic physiology cannot be based upon statistics collected after the event, and since it cannot perform experiments, it is inevitably rather more speculative than a science ideally should be; more of it is *theory*, and less of it is *applied economics*, than one could wish. But this seems to be in the nature of the case, and cannot altogether be helped. Although statistical methods (called *econometric* methods) for use on this side of economics have been, and are being, devised, the results obtained by their use are still rather limited.

intended. At the very least, more production is likely to mean more imports of raw materials; and it is not necessary that there should be more exports to balance. More often, the speeches have little effect of any kind; in order to have an effect, they would need to be backed by positive action, as, for instance, a change in some tax or subsidy, a change in prices, or the imposition or removal of some 'control'. All such action is liable to have effects which go beyond the immediate purpose which was in mind. It is rarely possible to bring about an important change in one of the magnitudes which enter into the social accounts without changing several other magnitudes at the same time; it is not possible, until we have followed through these various effects to the best of our ability, to say whether the original decision will in fact have the effect on production or saving, on imports or exports, which was intended.

Many of the most important questions people want to ask about the economic system are questions of the type—*if such and such a thing were done, what would be the probable consequences?* Now hardly any of these questions can be properly answered from a knowledge of social accounting alone. Just as it is impossible to forecast the effect of performing an operation merely from a knowledge of the anatomy of the human body, so it is impossible to forecast the probable effects of an economic reform without having a knowledge of how the economic system works. Therefore, once the student has mastered the groundwork of social accounting, he must go on to the 'physiological' side of economics, whose centre is the theory of value. The mechanism by which the economic system works is the system of prices; the fundamental principles of price are what the theory of value studies.

Although the theory of value incorporates so important a body of knowledge, it is perhaps at first sight a less attractive study than social accounting is. The theory of value does reach important conclusions on great questions, but it has to spend a good deal of time on small and apparently trivial questions in order to get there. This is of course a common experience in science; the elementary stages of most sciences are trivial enough. One reason why I have written this book is because I think that a preliminary grasp of social accounting may make the elementary stages of the theory of value easier to bear.

I hope that the reader of this introductory book will finish it with a number of general questions in his mind—questions which were probably not there when he started, questions which have not been answered here, but which he would now like to have answered. Some of these questions may be of the type we have just been discussing—questions of the probable consequences of economic changes. Some may be of other kinds. There are questions concerned with the organization of the economic system; we have seen that more goods and services were produced in some years than others, but could not still more have been produced in any year if things had been organized differently? Then there are questions about definitions: is it really necessary to classify things in the particular compartments we have chosen? could not the classifications be improved? (A very fundamental question of this last sort is the question whether the money measure of the national income can be justified; if a loaf of bread costs 3p, and a box of cough lozenges 12p, we have taken it that the cough lozenges represent the same 'product' as four loaves of bread.) Along some or all of these lines, the intelligent reader will want to criticize; but he has not been given much help towards criticizing. He will find that help if he pursues his studies in the theory of value.

At this point I take leave of the elementary reader, for whom this book has been primarily written. For the reason just stated, he will get a biased view of economics if he sticks any longer to the social accounting approach, without broadening out in other directions. But at some stage in his further study he will have to come back to social accounting; he will then want to approach it from a less elementary angle. He may still find it useful to look again at this book, when he will notice things he missed at a first reading. But at that stage he will want to go further. The supplementary chapters, which I have put into Part V, may then provide something of what he needs.

PART V

Supplementary Chapters on Social Accounting

8281730 S

CHAPTER XX

The Social Accounting System

1. Although this book is not intended to be more than an introduction to economics, it has gone a good deal further in one direction, that of the study of the National Income, than is usual in an elementary book. Having got so far, it is likely that some readers will want to go further. They will want to get to the point where they can take the current National Income Blue Book and make some sense out of it. Not enough has yet been said to enable them to do that. Some further help will still be needed, and this is probably the place where it can best be given.

As was explained in Chapter XIV, the function of a modern Blue Book is to provide a set of accounts—accounts of the whole nation as a going concern. That this is so was only realized gradually; since there was no experience of the correct form in which a set of national accounts should be presented, it is not surprising that successive Blue Books (or rather the White Papers which preceded them) should have exhibited a great deal of tiresome rearrangement (very inconvenient to students).[1] Much of this rearrangement was

[1] Most of the differences in form between successive White Papers were due to this cause. But in addition to these differences in form, there are also differences in figures, due to the fact that information about the past only comes to hand gradually as time goes on. Thus the first figures for the year 1949, which appeared in the White Paper of April 1950, could be no more than provisional figures; by April 1951 extra information about 1949 was forthcoming and the 1949 figures were accordingly revised. Revision of this

nothing else but a process of discovery, whereby the correct form was gradually established. This process may, by now, be taken to be complete; there is therefore no reason why we should not try to set down, in simple terms, the main principles of social accounting, as they have developed. With these principles in our minds, we shall be able to study the official figures with more advantage.

2. The best way of looking at the national accounts is to regard them as a consolidation (or combination) of the individual accounts of all the persons, businesses, and other concerns which compose the national economy. It is true that this is not the way in which the national accounts are actually drawn up; for since many of the individual accounts have never been put down on paper, it is impossible to proceed by combining what is not there to combine. What is done is to construct the combined account itself by indirect methods. But what the statisticians are trying to reach in this way are the accounts which would theoretically be reached by combination of individual accounts, if the individual accounts were available. Thus if we want to understand the national accounts, it is best to think of them as if they were constructed from individual accounts, in the theoretical way. The actual method of construction (though we have given, and shall be giving, some indication of it as we go on) is for the most part a matter of economic statistics rather than of economics proper, so that it falls outside the scope of this book.

The first thing which has to be done is to prepare the bricks out of which the structure is to be built, by constructing a standard form of accounts for the individual units out of which the national economy is composed. Much of this task has already been performed by professional accountants, and we can draw heavily upon their work at this stage of the argument. But though we can keep quite close to the standard accounting practice, we cannot follow it exactly in all

sort is always likely to go on to some extent for several years. The 1969 figures, given in this book, are those shown in the 1970 Blue Book; it is not likely that those shown in later Blue Books will be exactly the same.

respects. For the main job of the practising accountant is the preparation of the accounts of businesses (especially of businesses which are organized in the form of companies); our standard form has to cover the case of businesses, but it has also to cover other cases as well. Thus what we need is something a little more general than the standard form of the professional accountant.

The standard form of company accounts does, however, give us a good start. It consists of (1) a balance sheet, showing the assets and liabilities of the company at a moment of time—or rather at two moments, the beginning and end of the year, (2) a set of running accounts, in which all the payments which the firm makes and receives during the year are duly classified. In the days before modern company legislation, an old-fashioned firm might content itself, under this last heading, with a mere cash-book, in which receipts and payments were set down without classification; but it is impossible to tell from such a cash-book, without examining each item separately, how the firm is really getting on. The modern firm accordingly splits up the cash-book items into a minimum of three separate accounts. These are (*a*) the trading account, which shows how profits have been earned—profits being shown as the difference between the value of sales and the expenses which have to be put against them; (*b*) the appropriation account, showing the distribution of profits and other income among shareholders and other claimants; (*c*) the 'capital account', which might be better described as a change-in-capital account, for it shows the differences in the balance-sheet items between the beginning and end of the year. The part which has been played by these three accounts in the argument of Chapter XI above will be readily recognized by the reader.

All receipts and payments of money have to find their places in one or other of these three accounts, but there are items in the accounts (taken separately) which do not represent payments of money within the year. These 'artificial' items are introduced in order to give the 'change-in-capital' account its proper meaning. When the three accounts are taken together, we must revert to the cash-book, so that when an artificial item is introduced on one side in one account, it must also appear on the other side of another account. Since the artificial items do not correspond to actual receipts or payments, they are less 'solid' than the other items. There is some room for judgement about the precise sum to be put down, though accountants are generally guided by conventional rules about them.

The most important of the artificial items is Depreciation. Fixed capital declines in value by use, quite apart from any purchases or sales of capital goods. An entry for this requires to be made in the 'capital' account; the corresponding entry goes into the trading account. This is the artificial item of which the correct value is most uncertain. Another source of artificial items is the delivery of goods which have not been paid for at the end of the year; the value of these goods is entered in the trading account, and a corresponding entry made in the capital account.

These are the principles on which the accounts of a company are constructed. There is not much point in writing out these accounts in a formal manner at the moment, since we shall require to write them out very shortly, when we have submitted them to a little generalization.

3. The first thing which has to be done, in the way of generalization, is to ask: how can the accounts of the private person (or family) be fitted into a system of this kind? We can recognize, in the case of the family, something which can be regarded as a rudimentary balance-sheet; it may conceivably show nothing in the way of assets, save such things as furniture, and no liabilities to outside parties, but it could be put into balance-sheet form all the same. If there can be a balance-sheet, it follows that there can be a 'change-in-capital' account. This may show no more than some small savings, and the purchase of more furniture out of those savings; but even if it goes no further than that, it is in principle analogous to the firm's 'change-in-capital' account, so that an account of this sort is also quite recognizable. The other two accounts cause rather more trouble.

For much the most important account, in relation to the private family, is its income-and-expenditure account, which shows the family income on one side, and the allocation of that income between consumption and saving (and payment of taxes) on the other. At first sight the firm seems to have no account corresponding to this. But closer examination shows that the income-and-expenditure account of the firm is its appropriation account. The appropriation account does in fact contain items exactly corresponding to those which figure in the income-and-expenditure account of the private family. It is true that the firm, not being a human person with wants, cannot consume; but it can pay taxes and it can save. The appropriation account shows it paying taxes, and saving, out of its income.

If the income-and-expenditure account is (at least in principle) 'fuller' in the case of the family than in that of the firm, the family account which corresponds to the firm's trading account is relatively quite rudimentary. When the members of a family are regarded as producing units,[1] the only form of production, which has to be attributed to them and which has not already been covered in the accounts of firms, is the direct supply of their own labour. Thus the 'earning account', as it had better be called, shows nothing in the way of sales but the supply of labour, and nothing in the way of expenses against these sales,[2] so that the wage received appears alone on the other side equalling the value of labour supplied. Such an account seems hardly worth writing down. Nevertheless, we require to write it down, for (as we shall see) it has a vital part to play in the system of social accounting.

Thus the system of accounts which accountants apply to the firm is in principle applicable to the family as well. The system can be transferred from the one use to the other without any substantial change. But what does seem

[1] When the family contains more than one wage-earner, it will require a corresponding number of separate earning accounts. This is analogous with what may happen with a firm, which carries on two or more distinct kinds of business, and may conveniently be given a separate trading account for each of its sections.

[2] It would be very reasonable to take into account the expenses for tools, travelling, etc., which are incurred by workers in order to earn their wages, and some of which are allowed as expenses for income-tax purposes. But the information available on this matter is so incomplete and inadequate that it is at present customary to leave it out.

awkward, in the application to the family, is the names of the accounts, which are natural enough in the case of the firm, but become very unnatural in the wider application we want to give them. It may therefore be suggested that for social-accounting purposes we should use a set of names suitable for the wider application. The names proposed in the following table seem to fit in well with modern usage.

In drawing up our table we need not worry about the balance-sheet, which does not relate to the year (or accounting period); it is the running accounts which are our concern. That leaves us with three accounts, each of which requires (*a*) an accountant's name, suitable when it is applied to the firm; (*b*) a name suitable when it is applied to the private family; (*c*) a general name suitable for either application. These would seem to come out as follows:

Standard system of accounts

	Applied to firm	*Applied to family*	*General name*
I.	Trading a/c.	Earning a/c.	Production a/c.
II.	Appropriation a/c.	Income-and-expenditure a/c.	Income-and-expenditure a/c.
III.	Capital a/c.	Saving–investment a/c.	Saving–investment a/c.

The general names will be used when we wish to refer both to the firm and to the private family, or to pass easily from one to the other; but they can also be used when we are concerned with the accounts of economic entities which fall into neither category. Such are (1) private 'non-profit-making' bodies, such as churches, universities, and charities; (2) the various organs of the State. These, like firms and families, can in principle have their three accounts of the above types.

4. Just as the set of accounts can be put into a standard form applicable to any entity, so the items entering into the accounts can be classified in a standard manner. These standard classifications have in fact been used in our discussion of the social income and output in Chapter XI above,

so that a more formal arrangement will contain little that is new to the reader. The chief thing which is new concerns the financial relations between private entities and the State (taxes and such like)—a matter which was left out in Chapter XI, and was not fully discussed in Chapter XIII. Something can usefully be said about the places of taxes in these accounts before going further.

Although (as has been explained in Chapter XII) the taxes paid to the State are used to finance the production of useful things, many of them things which are directly or indirectly useful to the taxpayer himself, it is the distinctive feature of a tax (as against a purchase) that there is no clearly discernible relation between the payment by the taxpayer and the services received in exchange. Thus, from the accounting point of view (though in this case that may not be a very profound point of view), it is impossible to regard a tax as a payment for goods and services rendered; it is much easier to regard it as something analogous to a gift from the taxpayer to the State. We cannot exactly reckon it as a gift, for the nature of a gift is that it is voluntary, while a tax is compulsory; but gifts and taxes can both be regarded as instances of a wider class of transactions. Though the word has not always been strictly employed in this sense, the natural word for this class of transaction is *Transfers*; we shall therefore say that a gift is a voluntary transfer from one private entity to another, a tax is a compulsory transfer from a private entity to the State.

The State uses the transfers made to it, as we have seen, partly to finance the performance of services of general public usefulness, which can be reckoned as a form of public 'consumption', partly (as any entity may have to do) to pay interest on its debts, and partly to make transfers in the other direction. For if we are reckoning taxes as a transfer (or as a kind of 'gift' made to the State) then we must certainly also reckon the subsidies and grants which the State pays out as transfers from the State to other bodies. From the accounting point of view, they are clearly the same kind of thing.

Where do transfers fit into the system of accounts? This is a very awkward point, which gives us a great deal of trouble.

It would evidently be convenient if we could get all the transfers into one of the three accounts, so that the others would be untroubled by them; and if this could be done, it is in the income-and-expenditure account that we should like to put them. But in fact it is very awkward to put all transfers into the income-and-expenditure account. Take the case of a rich man, who makes a benefaction, say, for the purpose of founding a college. He does this by transferring to the college, not a part of his income during the current year, but a part of his capital assets; the sum transferred may be much larger than his income in the year when the benefaction is made, so that if we deducted it from his income, we should have to say that his saving during that year was an enormous negative quantity, which would be highly inconvenient, and does not accord with common usage. It is therefore necessary to distinguish between income transfers, which do figure in the income–expenditure account, and capital transfers, which do not appear there, but must be allowed for when we come to the saving–investment account. Unless we make such a distinction, we get nonsensical results. But unfortunately it is very difficult to give a firm test for distinguishing between income and capital transfers—the line between them is not at all easy to draw.

And this is not all. There are some transfers which get involved with the production account. When the government lays a tax upon the import of tobacco, the firms which import raw tobacco have to pay the tax when they import their raw material, so that the tax appears to them as an expense of production, an additional cost which they have to meet before arriving at their profits. Taxes which enter into the production account in this way are *indirect taxes*. Further, the transfers which enter into the production account do not all go one way. Nowadays, while the government taxes some sorts of production, it subsidizes others; subsidies, which are paid in proportion to the outputs of particular articles produced by particular firms, also enter into the production accounts of those firms. Thus, both indirect taxes and subsidies may be called indirect transfers, as contrasted with the direct transfers (direct taxes and grants) which enter into income-and-expenditure accounts, and the capital transfers which only appear in saving–investment accounts.

5. We are now at last in a position to write the three accounts in their standard forms. When setting out these standard forms, we shall again find it convenient to make a slight modification in the usual accounting procedure. In order to make the structure of each account as clear as possible, we shall divide it into stages, each stage showing the construction of some significant item, which is then carried down to the next stage for further adjustment, or to be divided up. When the accounts are written in this way, they can be applied to any economic entity whatever (firm, family, charitable trust, or government department); though, of course, we shall find that in some special cases a good many of the entries will be blank. The same form of accounts can be applied to the nation as a whole. Incomings are shown on the right, outgoings on the left, in the traditional book-keeping manner; the totals of the columns are not significant, but the two columns need to be added for each stage to ensure that the left-hand and right-hand sides are equal in value.

On this plan, the production account is divided into three stages:

Production account for any entity

Stage I	
Cost of materials and services used in production.	Gross output of goods and services.
Indirect transfers payable.	Indirect transfers receivable.
Residue.	
Stage II	
Depreciation.	Net output (or gross product) of entity (residue of preceding stage).
Residue.	
Stage III	
Earnings of entity (profits or wages).	Net product of entity (residue of preceding stage).

In this case the division does no more than mark the central importance of the items which are carried down between the stages—gross product and net product.

The income–expenditure account is likewise divided into three stages:

Income–expenditure account for any entity

Stage I	
	Earnings.
Interest and dividends payable.	Interest and dividends receivable.
Residue.	
Stage II	
	Net income of entity (residue of previous stage).
Direct transfers payable.	Direct transfers receivable.
Residue.	
Stage III	
Consumption.	Disposable income (residue of previous stage).
Saving.	

In this case the first stage shows the adjustment of earnings through the receipt and payment of interest and dividends to get the net income attributable to the entity; the second shows the effect of transfers. Net income after transfers we call disposable income; and disposable income equals consumption plus saving.

The saving–investment account is divided into two stages:

Saving–investment account for any entity

Stage I	
	Saving.
Capital transfers payable.	Capital transfers receivable.
Residue.	
Stage II	
	Net investable surplus (residue of previous stage).
Gross investment.	Depreciation.
Net lending to other entities.	Net borrowing from other entities.
Accumulation of cash.	

In this case the first stage shows the adjustment of saving through capital transfers (if any) to get what we may call the net investable surplus. The second stage shows this net investable surplus being transmuted into net investment and net lending. I have here shown net investment as the difference between gross investment and depreciation (which thus appear explicitly on the two sides of the account); with net lending and borrowing[1] shown separately.

6. The three accounts just written are the bricks from which the system of social accounts is constructed; we come now to the process of construction. This is always a matter of consolidation; that is to say, we take a group of entities and put their accounts together, producing a set of accounts (still the same three basic accounts) for the group as a whole. The putting together is largely a matter of addition, but since what we want is a set of combined accounts for the group as a whole, transactions internal to the group must be cancelled out.

The process is exactly the same as that which occurs when a consolidated account for a group of companies is constructed from the individual accounts of the separate companies. Sales from one company in the group to another, loans from one company to another, interest or dividends paid from one to another, all become internal transactions once the group is taken as a whole. These transactions would appear on both sides (or as corresponding positive and negative items) if the accounts were simply added; but since it is identically the same transaction which appears on each side, the two entries are cancelled out in the consolidated account. This is precisely the process by which the social accounts are (in principle) constructed from the individual accounts.

The ultimate consolidation takes the form of a set of accounts for the nation as a whole, still consisting of the same three basic accounts. All the production accounts of individual entities are consolidated into a production account for the nation as a whole; all the income-and-expenditure accounts are consolidated into a national income-and-expenditure account, all the individual saving–investment accounts into a national saving–investment account. These final national accounts are the central part of the structure. But when consolidation has been carried as far as this, many

[1] In the account as written, net lending (on the outgoing side) means new lending less repayment of old loans made by entity; net borrowing means new borrowing less repayment of old loans made to entity.

things, which are of interest in themselves, and which can be measured to a sufficient degree of accuracy from the statistical information available, will have been cancelled out in the process of consolidation. A set of social accounts, as published, will therefore generally contain something more than the three accounts finally consolidated. The multitudinous individual accounts will be divided into groups (preferably quite a small number of separate groups); and consolidated accounts will be constructed for each group (or *sector* of the economy) separately. The social accounts will then take the form of a set of accounts for each sector, together with a combined account for the nation as a whole, all the sectors together.

The sectors can in principle be chosen in many ways, but there is one division into sectors which arises naturally in practice, and which is therefore particularly important. It more or less corresponds to our division of accounts into the accounts of firms, of families, and of public bodies. In technical language these become the Business Sector, the Personal Sector, and the Public Sector. The boundaries between these sectors are not always very easy to draw. For instance, do one-man businesses come into the business sector or the personal sector? Do nationalized industries come into the business sector or the public sector? These questions cannot be settled upon any principle; they have to be settled on grounds of convenience, mainly (it must be confessed) statistical convenience.

If we accept the three-way division into sectors as being sufficient, the social accounts will consist of twelve (3×4) tables, a table of each sort for each of the three sectors, and a table of each sort for the economy as a whole. This is in fact more or less the system at which the Blue Book on National Income, in its modern form, is aiming. The information available is not sufficient to enable all twelve accounts to be put down fully; there are still a few blanks. Nevertheless, for a country like Britain, the greater part of this standard system can be provided.

7. Enough has now been said to explain the essential structure of the accounts which we shall be examining in the following chapter. But before we pass on to study the figures, there are two further points which it will be useful to discuss here, so as to prevent them from giving us too much trouble when we come upon them in practice. One of these points is concerned with transfers; the other with the Balance of Payments.

In the standard system of accounts, which we have been describing, individual production accounts are combined in various ways, income-and-expenditure accounts in various ways, saving–investment accounts in various ways; but an account is never consolidated with an account of another kind. This is good accounting practice. For it is the accountant's job to classify business transactions into such compartments as will make the effects of the transactions understandable; once they have been classified, it is thoroughly muddling, and most destructive to the accountant's work, if they are mixed together again. In constructing social accounts, we should like to follow the same rule, and on the whole we do so; but there are a few cases where it becomes difficult to apply the rule, so that special (and perhaps rather peculiar) measures have to be taken in order to enable us to keep to it.

Take first of all the case of capital transfers. A transfer which is regarded as a capital transfer by the donor and as a capital transfer by the recipient, gives no trouble; when the accounts of the two parties are consolidated, it cancels out, as it should. But suppose that the transfer is regarded as an income transfer by the donor, and as a capital transfer by the recipient; it will then be left standing in the consolidated accounts, as a transfer out of income on the income-and-expenditure account, and as a capital transfer received on the saving–investment account. But in fact it is an internal transaction which ought to cancel out. We can only make it cancel out if we doctor the accounts of one party or the other (it does not matter which). If we doctor the accounts of the recipient, we shall put the transfer, as an income transfer, into his income–expenditure account, and shall then reckon what he has called a capital transfer to be an addition to his saving.

In the light of this, consider the case of property passing at death. From the estate of the deceased, it reckons as a capital transfer; to the estate of the inheritor, it reckons as a capital transfer; there is no trouble here. But what about the part of the estate which is paid in death duties? If the government reckons this as part of its ordinary tax revenue, it will be treating it as an income transfer. But then, on the same principles, we shall only get a proper cancelling-out if we doctor one of the accounts; and in this case it is a matter of some importance which account is doctored, since the transfer is from one sector to another, so that what is done will show. It is generally agreed, nowadays, that it is the government account which ought to be doctored; the transfer will then appear as a capital transfer on both sides. That is what the Blue Book does.[1]

A worse trouble, which is basically similar, arises with indirect taxes (and other indirect transfers). An indirect tax is a tax which is paid, in the first instance, out of a firm's production account. But it is not transferred to a public production account; it is treated like other taxes, going into the income-and-expenditure account of the government. Thus when the accounts of firms and government are consolidated together to form the unified accounts of the whole economy, we shall find (if we take no special precautions) that the indirect taxes are left as an outgoing from the national production account, and as an incoming into the national income-and-expenditure account, without being cancelled out, as they should be if the unified accounts are to make sense.

[1] A more contentious case is that of the investment grants, which complicated the Social Accounts in the later years of Mr. Wilson's government (including the year 1969, to which our illustrative accounts refer). These were intended to be regarded as capital transfers, entering into the saving–investment accounts of the firms that received them, but not into their appropriation accounts. This is the reason why the Blue Book shows them, in the account of the Public Sector, as capital transfers *from* government. But though there may well have been cases in which firms received investment grants, in respect of new invest-that they were undertaking, although they were not making any profits, this must have been unusual. In a more normal case the grants would simply have been taken as replacements of the *investment allowances* previously given (they did in fact replace them). These investment allowances were deductions from the direct tax due to be paid, so they were unquestionably income transfers. One of the first acts of the new Conservative Chancellor (autumn 1970) has been to revert to the old system. I have therefore felt that it makes more sense, in this case, to doctor the accounts that are given in the Blue Book. I shall therefore be treating the investment grants (like the investment allowances) as income transfers throughout.

The anomaly arises, it should be emphasized, for no reason of principle, but simply because the indirect taxes have been classified in a different way in the accounts of the taxpayers and of the government. (The same difficulty arises, of course, in the case of subsidies, which are indirect transfers in the other direction.) The right way to deal with it must therefore be by some device analogous to that used in the case of capital transfers; we must doctor one account or the other so as to bring them into line.

The alternatives which now confront us have already been described in Chapter XIV. If we adopt one solution, we come to the national income at market prices; if we adopt the other, we come to the national income at factor cost. From the accounting standpoint, what we do if we adopt the first method is to regard the government as an 'invisible shareholder' of the tax-paying firm. The production account of the firm is then left undoctored, so that the value of the firm's output is shown at the prices paid by the people to whom the products are sold. It is the income-and-expenditure account of the firm which has to be doctored. The indirect taxes ought to be shown as being transferred, along with profits, from the production account to the income-and-expenditure account; they should be shown as being paid over to government along with the direct taxes.[1] This is the easiest way out of the indirect taxation tangle; it involves the statistician in fewer guesses than its alternative, so that it is being increasingly adopted. The trouble about it is that it does not make much sense. It makes the indirect taxes appear to be paid by the firms which are the immediate taxpayers; but these taxes are not meant to be borne by such firms. They are intended to be passed on to the consumers of the taxed article, who are the real taxpayers the government has in mind. If the accounts of the nation are to show the indirect taxes as being paid by these consumers, the other alternative has to be adopted.

On this alternative it is the production account of the firm which is doctored. The indirect taxes (and subsidies) are

[1] I have never seen this formally done in an actual set of social accounts; but something like it requires to be done if accounts 'at Market Price' are to square up properly.

taken right out of the production accounts. Since the tax is to be shown as being paid by consumers, the value of the firm's output must be shown *net of tax*—at the price which the consumer pays to the firm itself, excluding what he merely pays to the firm as an agent of the government. If all prices (including those paid for materials by one firm to another) are doctored in this way, the national product still contains the same real goods as before, but they are valued at prices which correspond to the prices paid for the services of factors of production (including the profits of capital). The national product is then said to be valued at *factor cost.*

If production accounts are shown at factor cost, no indirect transfers will appear in production accounts. But the sums paid by consumers for consumption goods (which figure in their income-and-expenditure accounts) will be shown divided into the part that corresponds to the factor cost of the goods, and the part which represents indirect transfers. Thus the indirect transfers will appear in the income-and-expenditure account alongside of the direct transfers, and will cancel out with the corresponding items in the government's budget when all income-and-expenditure accounts are taken together. The accounts have been made to square, and they do make sense; but in order to achieve these desirable objects, it has been necessary to engage upon a process of doctoring that is rather extensive.[1]

8. The last question which we have to consider is that of the balance of payments. The balance of payments account, which we examined in Chapter XII, does not figure among the twelve tables. What is its relation to them?

The answer is that we have here the only case when it is justifiable to infringe the principle of strict separation of the three sorts of accounts. For this one purpose we do find it

[1] Since some of the products whose prices have to be doctored will be purchased by firms who are making additions to their equipment (investment), the doctoring cannot in strictness be confined to the production and income–expenditure accounts; it will affect the saving–investment account as well. Indirect taxes paid on new investment will appear, after doctoring, as capital transfers; in a Factor cost account that is undoubtedly the right way to show them. But the Blue Book is able to avoid so unconventional a classification, since all that part of its accounts is only exhibited at Market Price.

useful, after the three accounts of the nation as a whole have been completed, to forget the principle of separation, and to put the three accounts together in a general mishmash. Suppose that the three accounts for the nation as a whole have been completed. Then take all incomings, whether on production account, income-and-expenditure account, or saving–investment account, and put them together; take all outgoings together in a similar fashion; cancel out all transactions which are made between entities reckoned as internal to the economy; what have we left? In a closed economy we should have nothing left, so that the procedure we are following would be completely futile. But in an open economy we do have something left; we are left with all the *foreign* transactions, transactions with entities not included in the *nation*, with the 'rest of the world'. The account which consists solely of these transactions must balance, because it has been constructed from accounts which were already balanced, merely by a process of cancellation. It is this account which is the balance of payments.

A full system of national accounts will thus include a table of the balance of payments, in addition to the twelve tables previously enumerated.

CHAPTER XXI The Social Accounts of the United Kingdom

1. Let us now return to the figures which we examined in a preliminary manner in Chapter XIV; and let us re-examine them in the light of what we have been learning about social accounting. The National Income Blue Book, in its modern form,[1] contains a quantity of detail which is becoming rather frightening in its complexity. But if we look at it in the light of what we have now learned, we shall find that the core of the document consists in a system of tables, very much as described. Much of the apparent complexity is due to the fact that, in addition to the tables for main sectors such as we have distinguished, tables (of one type or another, but usually not a complete set of tables) for many sub-sectors are given. A word about sectoral division is therefore needed before going further.

The basic sectors into which the economy is divided, for the purposes of the accounting system adopted, are similar to the sectors (business, personal, and public) that were described in the last chapter. But we should notice the particular way in which the boundaries of the sectors are defined. What corresponds to the business sector is a 'Corporate' Sector (as it is called in the Blue Book); this does not include all businesses, but only those businesses which are organized in the company form. Thus it does not include small businesses,

[1] All references are to the 1970 Blue Book, as before. The arrangement of the tables has in fact remained very largely unaltered for a number of years.

such as shops and farms, which are not companies; these are left in the personal sector, which also includes 'non-profit-making bodies', such as churches and universities ('charities', to use the taxman's brief but perhaps surprising description). The Blue Book's Corporate Sector does, however, include the nationalized industries, or Public Corporations, since they are organized as companies, publishing their accounts in the company form, though the State is the only shareholder. We are, however, at liberty to re-classify. The accounts of the Public Corporations, taken together, are presented (very fully) as one of the sub-sectors, so we can move it across. That is what I shall do. We are therefore left with (i) a Company Sector—in the narrow sense, excluding nationalized industries; (ii) a Personal Sector, including small businesses and 'charities'; (iii) a Public Sector, including nationalized industries.[1] We can then refer to (i) and (ii), taken together, as 'private' sectors.

Looking at the Blue Book, in the light of this explanation, what do we find? Its first table (1) is in effect an income–expenditure account for the whole economy. This is indeed the most important of all the tables—so that, though it is hardly the logical table with which to start, it is understandable why it is put in that place. Next (2–5) come separate income–expenditure accounts for the separate sectors (nationalized industries combined with other industries, while central and local government are shown separately). Then (6) comes a saving–investment (or 'capital') account for the whole economy, and (7) what is in effect a balance-of-payments account. What are lacking, at this round, are the production accounts, and the separate saving–investment accounts for the sectors. Can we find them?

The separate saving–investment accounts for the sectors are easy to find; they occur, among much more detailed information about the sectors, in later parts of the Blue Book. They are all there. The production account for the whole economy (or most of it) appears in a table (12) entitled 'Gross National Product by category of expenditure'—not, perhaps,

[1] The Blue Book provides much information about the other sub-sectors of the Public Sector, Central Government and Local Government. But I shall not be using that information here.

where one would quite have expected to find it. But where are the production accounts for the separate sectors? This is a gap which it has not been possible to fill.[1] A production (or 'operating') account for the nationalized industries will be found in the section which deals specially with them; but there is no production account for the rest of the public sector. And there is no division between 'personal' and 'business'. If the personal sector did in fact consist (as we should like it to have consisted) of workers and house-owners only, it could have had a production account that would be easily put together; but when we remember that it also includes the smaller businesses, we can see why it is that a division between its production and that of the companies would be difficult to make, and would not mean very much if it could be made.

Thus what we get is a complete set of income–expenditure accounts, and a complete set of saving–investment accounts; but on the side of production we have to content ourselves with a production account for the whole economy.

2. I shall later be showing how these accounts will appear, when written in our standard form; but before we can do the translation, there are some special points which need attention.

1. *Gross and Net.* As the tables are printed in the Blue Book, profits (of every kind—public as well as private) are shown gross—of depreciation; rents are also shown gross; and capital investment is similarly shown gross, to correspond. The reason is evident. There is a great deal of doubt about the proper depreciation figure to use,[2] so that the gross figures are much *firmer* (they can be more accurately ascertained) than any net figure can be. There can nevertheless be no question that if business is to be carried on—if it is to go on being carried on—it must provide for depreciation; so that the habit of thinking in gross terms, though it is natural (for this reason) to the statistician, is to the economist exceedingly dangerous. It is better to have a poor figure for depreciation than no figure at all. The Blue Book does in fact provide depreciation figures (it calls them *Capital Consumption*) tucked

[1] Some of the items which would appear in the separate production accounts can be picked up from other tables.

[2] See Appendix, Note C.

away near the end;[1] they are provided for each sector and for each sub-sector of the Public Sector. They are given this lowly place as a sign that they are not reliable; still, they are better than nothing. I shall freely use them (but I shall indicate the places where I am doing so); I shall apply them to all profits and rents, and to capital investment, so as to reduce gross to net.

2. *Stock Appreciation.* This is another adjustment to the profit figures, which is generally made in the Blue Book when it is dealing with the whole of the national economy, but is generally not made in the sectoral tables. It is a question of changes in prices that occur *during* the year. Changes in the price-level, from one year to another, can be dealt with—as far as one can deal with them—by the index-number technique that was described in Chapter XV. What this in fact amounts to is recalculating the Social Product as if prices were constant. That does enable us to compare the Real Product of one year with that of another; but it has the awkward consequence that there are some profits which (apparently) accrue when prices are rising, but which disappear altogether in the *constant price* calculation. A firm which had exactly the same real stock of materials (and work in progress), at the end of the year as it held at the beginning, would show no profit on that stock in a constant price calculation; but in fact, when prices are rising, the stock is worth more at the end of the year than at the beginning, and the difference is treated as a profit. This is why the Blue Book makes a deduction for *Stock Appreciation* in its national tables, but does not show it as a deduction in its sectoral tables. But the result is, of course, that the national tables and the sectoral tables do not square. Economically, they ought to square; even in the sectoral tables the stock appreciation is only an apparent gain; it does not correspond to any *real* saving, or accumulation of capital. So even the sectoral tables make better sense if the adjustment is made. I have therefore carried it right through, in accordance with the information which the Blue Book (again) provides.[2] In view

[1] Table 58 (in the 1970 Blue Book).

[2] Table 67 (in the 1970 Blue Book). It will be understood that these Stock Adjustment figures (like the Depreciation figures) can be no more than estimates.

of the inflation that was proceeding, the adjustment for 1969 is quite large—no less than £815 million (for the whole economy).

3. *Factor cost.* As the tables are printed in the Blue Book, the general table (income–expenditure account of the whole economy) is at factor cost; but the sectoral tables are at market price (though the receipts from indirect taxes—and the subsidies—are shown in the account of the Public Sector). Quite a bit of adjustment is needed if the tables so given are to be made to square. I have endeavoured to show my tables at factor cost throughout; the adjustment to factor cost being, however, marked out, as 'net indirect tax'—n.i.t. Most of the material for this is given in the Blue Book; but in order to carry this arrangement through to the saving–investment accounts I have had to make some guesses of my own.

4. *Tax payment and tax liability.* This is a question of discrepancy in accounting practice between taxpayer and government. The sum which the taxpayer allots (or ought to allot) for payment of taxes is the sum which he is due to pay on his income (or profit) in the current year. But the sum which the government enters as revenue is what it actually collects during the current year, and this often depends upon the taxpayer's income in preceding years, not the current year. (Since the introduction of PAYE, there is no lag of this sort in the case of wage incomes, but in the case of profit incomes it is quite important.) For the proper understanding of the economic position of the country, it would be more important to consider the taxes due than the taxes paid; but on the taxes due we get no direct information. What we do get is an estimate of 'additions to tax reserves'. 'Tax reserves' are the amount which the taxpayer would still have to pay if his payment of taxes were to be brought fully up to date. Some of these will be taxes due on the current year, but some will be taxes due on previous years. Yet since the taxes due on previous years were already due at the beginning of this year, they should not greatly affect the 'addition to tax reserves'. Thus if we add this addition to the tax actually paid, we get what should be a fair estimate of tax due. I shall therefore regard the 'tax reserve' item that is shown in the Blue Book as *unpaid tax*; I shall treat it as if it were actually

paid over to the government, and then lent back to the taxpayer. It is in fact notorious that British business has been relying quite largely, for the financing of its working capital, upon a 'loan' of this type.

5. *External taxes.* It is of vital importance, when setting out the Social Accounts of the British economy, to distinguish between payments to the British government and payments to other sectors; but the distinction between the public and private sectors of foreign countries is, from the point of view of the British accounts, of no importance. They are all in the 'Rest of the World'. Thus the taxes which are paid to foreign governments, out of the proceeds of British investments in their countries (though they are shown separately in the Blue Book) do not logically require any separate treatment. What matters, to the British economy, is the net income from these investments (after deduction of the foreign taxes); that is what I shall show.

3. With these explanations, we are ready for our main task, to put the main Blue Book tables (for 1969) into our standard form. In the tables that follow, I shall set out the 1969 figures in £millions, not the hundreds of millions which I used in the summarised tables of Chapter XIV. There I wanted the reader (at least to some extent) to remember the figures; here it is not important to remember them, but it is important to be able to see at a glance what figures correspond. I begin with the *Combined Production Account* (Table A).

This should be thought of (as was explained in the last chapter) as being put together from the *trading* accounts of firms and public authorities, together with the *earning* accounts of the personal sector (workers, houseowners, and landowners). In the consolidation of these accounts all sales of goods *and services* from firm to firm, and from worker to firm, *within the national economy*, cancel out. The only purchases which do not cancel out are those made from abroad—imports (of goods *and* services). Since we are distinguishing imports on the left-hand side of the account, it is obviously useful to distinguish exports (in the same sense) on the other. Thus we show the gross output, on the right-hand side, divided into 'gross retained output'[1] and exports. The 'residue' of the first stage in the Production Account is net domestic output, or *Gross Domestic Product.*[2]

TABLE A

Combined Production Account for all sectors (1969)
(£ million—at factor cost)

I.			
Imports	9,505	Gross retained output	38,599
Residue	38,492	Exports	9,398
Total	47,997	'Gross domestic output'	47,997
II.			
Depreciation	3,694	Gross domestic product—	
Residue	34,798	residue of stage I	38,492
	38,492		38,492
III.			
Earnings of		Net domestic product—	
(*a*) Personal Sector:		residue of stage II	34,798
Wages and salaries	27,174		
Self-employed	2,547		
Rents	1,051		
Total, personal	30,772		
(*b*) Company Sector			
Profits	2,836		
Rents	212		
Total, company	3,048		
(*c*) Public Sector			
Profits	129		
Rents	849		
Total, public	978		
Total earnings	34,798	Net domestic product	34,798

Source. Tables 1, 12, and 13 of Blue Book; with Table 58 for allocation of depreciation (capital consumption).

[1] See above, p. 160.

[2] My figure differs from the Blue Book figure, since I have added back the 'Residual error' (see above, p. 186, and below, p. 292). Stock Appreciation, it will be noticed, has already been deducted.

The second stage in the production account shows the adjustment for Depreciation (as given in Table 1 in the Blue Book). Net domestic product is then carried down to the third stage, where it is shown as the source from which the factors of production are paid. Here we can begin to classify by sectors. Company profits (accruing to the company sector) appear as one item; the profits of government and local authority trading, including those of the nationalized industries (all accruing to the public sector) appear as another; while in the personal sector the mixed incomes ('income from self-employment') are shown distinct from wages and salaries.[1] Rents are shown divided between the sectors. Both profits and rents are shown *net* of depreciation.

4. We now turn to the sectoral accounts (IE and SI accounts, as we may now allow ourselves to call them, for each sector). We begin with the company accounts, since they are naturally the most straightforward (Table B).

On the right-hand side of Stage I of the IE account of the company sector, we have (1) the profits and rents, net of depreciation, taken over from the production account; (2) interest and dividends received from other sources; (3) net property income from abroad. The interest includes interest paid by the private sector (on such things as house mortgages and bank advances), a substantial amount of interest on public debt (paid, for instance, to the banks), as well as interest and dividends received from abroad. Some of these last will have paid taxes to foreign governments; but for lack of information I have deducted the whole of the tax paid to foreign governments from the property income (which is mostly the profits of overseas branches of British companies). Thus this property income from abroad is shown net of overseas taxes (and also net of whatever branch profits are paid out abroad).

Against these, on the left-hand side of Stage I, we have the interest and dividends paid out to other sectors of the British economy (mainly the personal sector). The residue, after these outgoings have been allowed for, is the share of 'net income before transfers' attributable to the company sector.

[1] Wages and salaries include pay of the armed forces; they also include payments in kind; and they also include employers' contributions to social insurance (see Appendix, Note F).

TABLE B

Accounts of Company Sector
(£ million—at factor cost)

Income–Expenditure Account

I.			
Interest and dividends paid	3,427	Earnings	
		(from production account):	
		Profits	2,836
		Rents	212
		Interest and divs. recd.	1,675
Residue	2,178	Other income from abroad	882
	5,605		5,605
Net direct taxes due	1,168	Net income before	
Transfers to charities	35	transfers (residue of	
Residue	975	stage I)	2,178
	2,178		2,178
III.			
Saving	975	Net disposable income	975

Saving–Investment Account

I.			
Net indirect taxes			
on investment	350	Saving	975
Residue	625		
II.			
Net investment within sector		Net investable surplus	625
(at factor cost):		Unpaid taxes	591
in fixed capital	1,420	Net borrowing	445
in working capital	241		
	1,661		1,661

Source. Table 26 of Blue Book (with tables 58 and 67 for depreciation and stock appreciation).

This is taken down to Stage II, where it is adjusted for transfers. These are mainly the direct taxes that are *due to be paid* to the Public Sector,[1] but also include a (relatively) small

[1] Being chiefly the tax (corporation tax) which is due to be paid *by* companies out of profits; not taxes on dividends, which are 'deducted at the source', but reckon as income tax paid by shareholders, so that they appear in the

amount that is contributed as gifts to charities. The latter, of course, is transferred to the Personal Sector.

The residue of Stage II (the undistributed profits of the companies) is the *disposable income* of the company sector. Since the company sector cannot, as such, consume, its disposable income equals its saving (its contribution to the national saving).

To see what is done with this saving, we pass to the (company) SI account. The main things that are to appear on the left-hand side of this account are the real investment, in fixed capital, and in working capital and stocks. Each of these gives us some trouble. The investment in working capital is shown in the company table of the Blue Book with stock appreciation included, but it must be taken out (the company share in it must be taken out) if we are to show the value of the *real* increase in working capital, which is all that belongs in an account such as the present. On the side of fixed capital, we must similarly deduct depreciation (the company share of depreciation); but that is not all. We are trying to write the accounts at factor cost, and must do so systematically, if the accounts are to square. The value of fixed capital investment that is given in the Blue Book is, however, at market price; so it must be adjusted for n.i.t. to get the factor cost measure. The n.i.t. deduction is a genuine tax, paid over to government; but it is here a tax on investment, which belongs in the SI account, not in the IE account. I therefore (rather awkwardly) put it in Stage I of the SI account, as a capital transfer.[1]

As a result of these deductions, the net investment of the company sector is brought out at a much smaller figure than the gross figure shown in the Blue Book. But even so, the net investable surplus is quite insufficient to finance it. A

account of the personal sector. I have, however, included some other taxes (such as capital gains tax) which the Blue Book reckons as capital taxes. I have also included the 'additions to tax reserves', since we are concerned with tax liability (see p. 280 above). I have, on the other hand, deducted the investment grants, which the Blue Book treats as a capital item (see p. 272 above).

[1] The Blue Book gives a figure for n.i.t. on the total investment expenditure of all sectors, but does not allocate it between sectors (nor between fixed and working capital). I have made an arbitrary allocation (putting it all to fixed capital, and dividing it between sectors in proportion to *gross* fixed capital investment).

considerable part of it is financed by unpaid taxes; the rest is borrowed (from other sectors).

5. The Company Sector having been dealt with in this way, the Personal Sector gives little (extra) trouble (Table C). The Blue Book does not here give a figure for interest paid out—only a figure for 'Rent, dividends, and *net* interest'. The rents can be taken out;[1] when we have also deducted taxes paid abroad (which are shown separately), we get the *net interest* figure that is shown in our table. Adding this to the net earnings (from the Production account), we get the *net income before transfers* of the Personal Sector.

TABLE C

Accounts of Personal Sector
(£ million—at factor cost)

Income–Expenditure account

I.			
		Earnings (from production account):	
		from employment	27,174
		self-employment	2,547
		rents	1,051
		Interest and dividends received (net)	3,038
			33,810
II.			
Direct taxes due	5,300	Net income before transfers	33,810
National insurance contributions	2,243	National insurance benefits and other grants	3,930
Net indirect taxes on consumption	5,482		
Voluntary transfers abroad	77	Company transfers to charities	35
Residue	24,673		
	37,775		37,775
III.			
Consumption (at factor cost)	23,136	Net income after transfer	24,673
Saving	1,537		

[1] It is the figure for *gross* rents which must be deducted.

As appears from Stage II of the Personal IE account, this is knocked about, very heavily, by transfers. There are the direct taxes due, the national insurance contributions paid, and the small amount of personal gifts going abroad; on the other side is the large sum for social benefits and other grants from government. But that is not all; since we are concerned with a factor cost calculation, we must also deduct the n.i.t. on consumption. As a result of all these transfers the personal income after transfer is less than three-quarters of what it was before.

Saving–Investment Account

I.

		Saving	1,537
Taxes on capital (net)	571	Capital transfers from government	184
Indirect taxes on investment	76		
Residue	1,074		
	1,721		1,721

II.

Net investment within sector (at factor cost):		Net investable surplus	1,074
in fixed capital	314	Unpaid taxes	94
in working capital	43		
Net lending outside sector	811		
	1,168		1,168

Source. Table 19 of Blue Book, with 58 and 67 as before, and 46 for n.i.t.

The Personal SI account needs little comment. The capital transfers from government are mostly to charities; the taxes on capital mainly death duties. The net investment within the sector is mostly the net increase in (private) housing; but it also includes the expenditure (for instance by universities) out of the capital transfers, and some business investment by the self-employed.

6. Most of the hard points in the account of the Public Sector (Table D) have already been covered, since they are simply the reverse side of transfers which we have already met. The net interest paid by the Public Sector is greater than its earnings; so its income before transfers is negative (as we know). Items which have not yet occurred are *external* items, such as grants or subsidies to overseas governments, and the net indirect taxes which fall on exports. Though the whole of the indirect taxes are reckoned as revenue by government (local government as well as central government, since indirect taxes include local rates), it is only that part of n.i.t. which falls on private consumption and on exports which we bring into the IE account of the Public Sector. The part which falls on private investment is brought into the SI account as a capital transfer (so as to have it in a place which corresponds to that which it occupies in the other accounts).

TABLE D

Accounts of Public Sector
(£ million—factor cost)

Income–Expenditure account

I.

		Earnings (from production account):	
Interest on public debt	2,016	Profits	129
Residue	−745	Rents	849
		Interest and dividends received	293
	1,271		1,271

II.

		Net income before transfers	−745
		Direct taxes due:	
		from personal sector	5,300
		from company sector	1,168
		from abroad	6
National insurance benefits, etc.	3,930	National insurance contributions	2,243
Grants made abroad	175		
Residue	9,673	N.i.t. paid to public sector (on consumption and exports)	5,806
	13,778		13,778

III.

Consumption (at factor cost)	7,526	Net income after transfers	9,673
Saving	2,147		

Saving–Investment account

I.			
		Saving	2,147
Capital transfers to personal sector	184	N.i.t. on private investment	426
Residue	2,960	Other taxes on capital	571
	3,144		3,144

II.			
		Net investable surplus	2,960
Net investment within sector (at factor cost):			
in fixed capital	1,873		
in working capital	10		
Unpaid taxes	685		
Balance (net lending or debt repayment)	392		
	2,960		2,960

Source. Table 48 of Blue Book (with checks against tables used previously).

There remains the part that falls on the expenditure of the Public Sector; this is internal to the Public Sector, so it does *not* appear. It is deducted from the consumption of the Public Sector, and from the net investment of the Public Sector, in order that these should be shown at *factor cost*. The unpaid taxes are shown in the SI account (as we arranged to show them) as a loan from the Public to the private sectors; but it is a peculiar sort of loan, so it is distinguished (as it clearly should be) from other sorts of lending (or debt repayment).

It will be remembered that the distinction between consumption and investment, in the Public Sector, is often very arbitrary.

7. The sectoral accounts having been written in this form, the Combined Accounts for All Sectors can be put together by consolidation (Table E)—striking out all those items which appear as a receipt in one sectoral account and as a payment in another. One of the advantages of our arrangement is that each stage in each account can be consolidated separately. Thus the national income before transfers is the sum of the sectoral incomes before transfers; the national disposable income is the sum of the sectoral disposable incomes (or

incomes after transfer); the saving that is shown in the combined account is the sum of the sectoral savings; and the net investment (in fixed and in working capital) should similarly add up. It will be seen that in all cases but one (of which more below)[1] these additions come out right.

TABLE E

Combined Accounts of All Sectors
(£ million—factor cost)

Income–Expenditure account

I.			
		Net domestic product (earnings of all sectors)	34,798
		Net income from abroad	451
II.			
		National income before transfers	35,249
Transfers to abroad:		Transfers from abroad:	
Personal transfers	77	indirect taxes falling	
Government transfers	175	on exports	324
Residue	35,321		
	35,573		35,573
III.			
Consumption (personal and public)	30,662	National disposable income	35,321
Saving	4,659		

Saving–Investment account

Net investment (at factor cost)		Saving	4,659
in fixed capital	3,607		
in working capital	294		
Foreign balance *should be*	758		

Source. Table 1 of Blue Book, and those used in previous tables.

We distinguish, it will be observed, even in the Combined Account, between *national income before transfers* and *national disposable income.* The difference, as it appears in our table, is a

[1] See note 2 opposite.

small one; nevertheless it exists. All of the big transfers between sectors, which figured so largely in the sectoral accounts, have cancelled out; but there are still some transfers that remain—external transfers. Some of these are voluntary transfers (remittances and grants); but there is also the item of the share of n.i.t. that falls on exports, which belongs in this place when we are valuing at factor cost. It is logical to regard this as a tax on foreigners,[1] so it comes in at this place as a transfer from abroad. Thus, in a factor cost calculation at least, we cannot avoid the distinction between the two senses of *national income*.[2]

Finally, it will be noticed that I have not shown the combined SI account divided into stages. This is because the capital transfers, which figured in the sectoral accounts, are all internal to the nation; in the combined account they all cancel out.[3] Net lending and borrowing between sectors should also cancel out; so that all that remains, as the difference between total saving and total net capital investment, is the *foreign balance*, net foreign lending in the widest sense, which includes all net accumulation of external assets. And that should square up with what we find in the account of the balance of payments.

[1] This proves, in the end, to be an inescapable result of the decision to value at factor cost. For though we could say (quite arbitrarily) that the factor cost valuation did not apply to exports, we should not avoid the difficulty in that way; we should still have to decide what was to be done with the proceeds of the taxes that fell on exports. To reckon them, as the old White Papers sometimes did, among the profits of the public sector, is confusing; to put them among the profits of the business sector is worse. There is really no clear alternative to the treatment here recommended.

[2] It does seem to be avoided in the Blue Book; but it must be remembered that at the critical point the Blue Book is mainly working in market price terms. So it does not have to allow for n.i.t. on exports; that has already been dealt with by valuing the exports at market price. The remittances and grants are (presumably) regarded as forms of consumption. One can see that this simplifies things; but it does not deal with the whole of the issue. For there are still some direct taxes paid by non-residents; in the Blue Book they are all lumped in with net income from foreign assets, in order to keep National Income *before* and *after* transfer the same. I have used the Blue Book figure for net income from foreign assets, since that plays so key a part in the central table (Table 1 of the Blue Book) that it seemed unwise to doctor it. But it must in fact contain some transfers; this is presumably the reason why my 'net incomes before transfer' do not quite add up.

[3] There were some important international capital transfers just after the war, when there had to be some elaborate international compensations and settlements. Now they have effectively disappeared.

8. This, however, in the case of the United Kingdom in 1969, is extremely tricky. When the social accounts are written out in the form described, the combined accounts (in which the external items have been clearly distinguished), should already tell us a good deal about the balance of payments. If we take the three combined accounts (production account, IE account, and SI account) and add them together, striking out all the *internal* items which appear on one side of one account and on the other side of another, we should get an account of the Balance of Payments.[1] But what do we find?

Balance of Payments
(*£ million*)

Imports		Exports	
(goods and services)	9,505	(goods and services including indirect taxes)	9,722
Transfers to abroad	252	Net income from external assets	451
Residue	416		
	10,173		10,173

These are all the external items which are left from our tables after the general consolidation; but the residue which remains from them, which should equal the foreign balance (and is shown as the foreign balance in the Blue Book) is £416 million, not the £758 million which emerged from our combined SI account. The difference is exactly equal to the £342 million of *Residual Error*.[2] There is no doubt that the figures ought to be the same; they can only fail to be the same because some of the figures are not right. In fact we know that most of the figures are estimates; some are mere guesses; it is not surprising that separate estimates of a lot of separate figures fail to add up properly.[3] This is the point at which the imperfect reliability of the statistics forces itself on our attention.

An error of £342 million is not large, relatively to many of

[1] See above, pp. 274–5. [2] See above, p. 186.

[3] I have, however, not changed the view (which I expressed in a former edition) that in presenting their accounts in this way, the national income statisticians have not properly done their job. It is not their job to make best estimates of each of the figures separately, but to make a best estimate of the whole system of figures. When the figures are looked at as a system, it is *certain* that they must add up; that certainty should override the uncertainties of detail.

the figures we have been using; it is, for instance, not more than 1 per cent of the National Income. It should not shake our confidence in the general impression that is given by the accounts. We could adjust every one of the figures by a little —1 or 2 per cent—which would easily be enough to make the account come out right; and the result, in terms of the general picture, would be hardly noticeable. Yet it is not really likely that the error is so evenly distributed; some of the figures (one can see straight off) are much *firmer* than others. It is much more likely that the errors are concentrated in some particular parts of the table. But we are not given much help in discovering what those particular parts are likely to be.

These general considerations, applied to the accounts of 1969, give us no special reason to suppose that it is the Balance of Payments account which is at fault. There must be a fault somewhere; but it need not be in the particular place where we have happened to show it. There is, however, a reason why the Balance of Payments account may be particularly suspect. For if we try to track down the 'net accumulation of external assets', which should correspond to the foreign balance in question, we find[1] that there was a repayment of no less than £699 million to overseas banks (and to the International Monetary Fund); there was an increase of £44 million in the Bank of England's reserves of international money; so that *net* external assets were increased by far more than the £416 million in these (perfectly well authenticated) ways alone. All of the other odds and ends of international capital transactions which the Bank has been able to track go practically no way towards making up the difference. There does accordingly remain a very considerable doubt about the Balance of Payments figures.

The reader will probably be shocked; and I think he ought to be shocked. This is in fact the impression I want to leave with him. The Social Accounts are exceedingly useful as a means of getting an impression of what the economy is like, and what it is doing; but they will not bear the weight which over-enthusiastic people have been putting on them. They are really not certain enough to be usable for 'fine tuning'.

[1] These figures are not given in the Blue Book; I take them from the *Quarterly Bulletin of the Bank of England.*

Appendix

NOTE A *On the Definition of Production*

I have kept fairly strictly in this book to the definition of *productive work* as *work done to satisfy the wants of other people through exchange.* This definition corresponds to the definition of *income* used in calculations of the British National Income, and it has the great advantage of being unambiguous. But it is not by any means wholly satisfactory. There are at least three kinds of socially useful work which are excluded from productive work on this definition: (1) domestic work, done within the family, by housewives and others; (2) direct production for use of the family, mainly of foodstuffs, on gardens, allotments, and small-holdings; (3) 'voluntary' work, done for its own sake or from a sense of duty to the community or social group to which one belongs. These kinds of work are only distinguished from the kinds which we do count as productive on the one ground that they are not paid: there is no payment in the ordinary sense, that is, though of course there are other compensations. Exactly similar work can often be found which is paid for; domestic work may be done by a paid housekeeper, the allotment-holder may sell his produce, the club may employ a paid secretary. It would therefore be possible for *production* (in our sense) to go up, merely because some work, which had previously been unpaid, was transferred to the paid class; yet the wants of the community as a whole need not be any better satisfied as a result.

Transferences of this sort do not often occur nowadays on a large scale; but when they do, we must allow for them in some way, if we are not to be led into serious error. It is a serious error, for example, in the economics of war, if we neglect the fact that by drawing women into munition making and other war services the supply of labour for necessary domestic work is diminished. Again, when rapid improvements in transport take place in a hitherto undeveloped country, farmers will change over from producing mainly for their own wants to producing mainly for sale. On our definition of *production* this would cause agricultural production to shoot up from almost nothing to a considerable height; but though the farmers would almost certainly be better off for the change, they would not be as much better off as such figures would indicate. In cases such as this last, there is a great deal to be said for using a wider definition of production, including all agricultural production, whether produced for sale or not; this is in fact what is usually done when estimating the national income of such a country as India. The object of any such calculation is to get the most useful figure possible; in a case where the habit of selling agricultural products is spreading, a figure which includes all such products will be more useful than one which includes only those products which are produced for sale.

It is tempting to seek for a way round the difficulty by widening our definition, including some of the things we have left out; but the trouble then is to know where we should stop. The most promising suggestion for widening is that made (but ultimately rejected for this purpose) by Pigou:[1] that we should include all those kinds of work which can somehow be brought into relation with the 'measuring-rod of money'—not merely those which *are* paid, but those which *might* be paid. Unfortunately it is impossible to interpret this wider definition in a way which would command general agreement. A man might employ a secretary to write his letters; if he writes his own letters, are we to say that the time he spends in doing so is spent in productive work? A man may employ a gardener; if he works in his own garden, how are we to separate out the work which he does to satisfy his own wants for vegetables and flowers, from the work which is an end in itself, which no one could do for him since no one else could give him the pleasure he gets from watching the growth of a shrub, raised from his own cutting and planted by his own hands? The wider definition gets us into inextricable knots; and no other wide definition has been suggested which would not do so. We are therefore driven to adopt the limited definition here used, though we must be prepared to modify it by including some particular things not produced for sale, in cases where it would be seriously misleading not to do so.

[1] *Economics of Welfare*, Part I, chs. 1 and 3.

It is also interesting to observe that an issue exactly parallel to that which we have discussed in this note arises in another connection.[1] If we decide to reckon as productive only those services of labour which are paid for, we ought to do the same with the services of capital. The durable-use consumers' goods, which are in existence at the beginning of a year, render valuable services to their users during the year; but if user and owner are one and the same person, no payment is made for these services. People derive advantages from the durable-use consumers' goods in their possession, just as they derive advantages from the work which they do to satisfy their own wants; but as we are excluding the one because no payment passes, so it would appear that we must exclude the other. On the same principle, we must include the services of those durable-use consumers' goods for which a rent is paid, since these are analogous to the work which is paid for.

This is the principle; but in this case we meet a difficulty just like that of agricultural production for the farmer's own use. Houses are the most important class of durable-use consumers' goods; but some houses are rented, some are owner-occupied. If we reckoned the services of the rented houses as a part of production, but not the services of the owner-occupied houses (which would be the logical thing to do), we should get into a difficulty just like that which arose over agriculture. An increased tendency for people to own their own houses would appear as a fall in the social income, but it would be absurd to regard it in that light. Since a change of that sort may well occur (and has in fact occurred in Britain) it is much safer to include the services of *all* houses.

NOTE B — *On the Idea of an Optimum Population*

When discussing the economics of Population in Chapter V, I have carefully avoided making any use of the idea of an Optimum Population, an idea which has sometimes been used in discussions of the subject. It is easy to see how the idea arises. If the population of a particular area may be too small for full efficiency of production, and if it may also be too large, then there must be some level in-between at which it would be *just right*. The same thing

[1] See above, p. 40.

can be put in more technical language by defining the optimum population as that level of population which would make output per head a maximum. A country will then be under-populated if its population is less than the optimum, over-populated if its population is more than the optimum.

We have seen that it is possible to give definite and important meanings to the terms under-population and over-population; but this does not suffice to show that an optimum population between the two can be precisely defined. No one has ever been able to say what the optimum population of any particular area is in fact; for this inability there are several very good reasons.

In the first place, what do we mean by saying that *net output per head* is a maximum? The output of society consists, not of one good, but of an immense variety of goods and services. In consequence, in order to say that net output per head is greater in one set of circumstances than in another, we have to find a means of reducing the variety of goods to a common measure. Methods of doing this are discussed in Chapter XV; but the methods discussed in that chapter are none of them perfect ways of making the reduction; they are all of them makeshifts. It is indeed extremely unlikely that a perfectly suitable method of making the reduction can possibly be found. It is thus extremely probable that a *range* of possible sizes of population would exist, each of which would have a good claim to be regarded as *the* optimum population, if a suitable method of reduction were taken. If population increases, some kinds of goods become harder to get, some become easier; we have got to decide whether the shift from the one sort to the other is advantageous or not, and on that opinions may differ. Sometimes it may be very clear that the advantage exceeds the disadvantage, or vice versa; then we need have no hesitation in saying that the country is under-populated or over-populated as the case may be. But between these extremes there is likely to be a range (conceivably quite a wide range) where the advantageousness of a change is largely a matter of opinion. Within this range it would be venturesome to claim that any particular size of population is optimum; it is far more important to notice that it is only when the actual size of population falls outside this range that the size of the population becomes an urgent economic issue.

This is one of the difficulties which has to be borne in mind; but there are others of greater importance. It is impossible to define the optimum population of an area unless something is taken for granted about the other conditions of economic welfare apart from population. These other conditions include the state of industrial technique, the amount and the character of capital equipment, and the opportunities for external trade. Changes in these other conditions may change the optimum size of population very markedly. England would be grossly over-populated today if her capital equipment were no greater than it was a century ago; she would be grossly over-populated today if her opportunities for foreign trade were no greater than they were a century ago. The way in which a problem of over-population in England can most easily arise in the future is by a failure of sufficient expansion in the opportunities for foreign trade.

This being so, an optimum population, defined with reference to the conditions of technique, capital, and foreign trade *as they are at present* is a notion of extremely little practical interest. For in the time which it would inevitably take (by any other route but that of catastrophe) to adjust the actual population to the optimum, we may be sure that the optimum itself would have shifted, and would probably have shifted to an important extent. Further, it is very probable that the optimum size of a population will depend on the age-distribution of that population; but in the process of adjusting the size of population age-distribution must change. An area could not be said to have reached a fully optimum state of population until its age-distribution was such as to keep the population optimum; but such a condition could hardly be reached from any actual population within a foreseeable future.

These difficulties are not of importance when a country is decidedly under-populated (or over-populated); for we should then be safe in maintaining that an increase (or diminution) of population would still be advantageous, even if the other conditions of production changed in any way that seemed at all probable. But a statement of this sort is not made any clearer by using the phrase 'optimum population'.

NOTE C *On the Depreciation of Capital*

The using-up of capital equipment as the result of productive activity takes two forms: (1) the gradual wearing-out of fixed capital—this is what the business man calls depreciation; (2) the using-up of single-use producers' goods—working capital and stocks. Each of these kinds of depreciation raises awkward problems of measurement, perhaps the most awkward of all the problems connected with the national income. Here we can do no more than indicate the general nature of the difficulties.

We have already seen (p. 127 above) that the valuation of a durable-use good, at a time when there is no question of selling it, is always a very delicate matter; different values may be put upon it by different people, and by the same person for different purposes. Naturally the same trouble persists when it is a question of estimating the reduction in the value of a particular piece of equipment, which has resulted from the year's operations: different people might estimate the reduction in different ways. In practice there are two estimates for the depreciation of a firm's fixed capital which need to be carefully distinguished.

In the first place, there is the estimate made by the firm for its own purposes—for example the purpose of deciding the amount which is available for distribution in dividends. In a well-managed firm care will usually be taken when framing this estimate to be well on the safe side; when there is any doubt on the matter (as there usually will be) a high figure for depreciation will be chosen rather than a low one. (The systematic choice of high figures for depreciation is the easiest way of setting aside 'hidden reserves'.)

The other practically important estimate is that made for purposes of taxation. Since there is this arbitrary element in a firm's own reckoning of its own depreciation allowances, and hence of its own profits, taxes on profits cannot be assessed on what firms themselves declare their profits to be; this would give far too much opportunity for evasion. It is therefore necessary for the government to lay down rules for the determination of depreciation allowances (or, as these statutory allowances are called, wear-and-tear allowances); the profits on which taxes are paid are calculated by deducting, not the firm's own depreciation allowances, but the wear-and-tear allowances laid down by law. Now it is these profits, calculated for purposes of taxation, which are recorded in the statistics used for calculating the national income on the income method; accordingly, unless some special precaution is taken, the figures given for the national income will be dependent on the particular rules for the calculation of wear-and-tear allowances that have been laid down by Parliament.

During the early years of national income calculations, this is in fact what happened; but it was quite wrong that it should happen—that wear-and-tear allowances, given for the purpose of securing fairness in taxation, should affect the figure which we get for the national income. It may be quite proper for the

Chancellor to decide that circumstances call for a rise in the share of profits that is taken in tax; it may be quite proper for him to carry this out by a change in the definition of profits that are taken as taxable; but it is clearly not right that we should reckon this as an increase in the amount of profits, and hence in the national income itself. If we are to avoid such arbitrariness, there are only two alternatives: one is to dispense with a measure of depreciation altogether, reckoning everything 'gross'; the other is to establish an independent measure. There is a sense in which both of these alternatives are present in a modern Blue Book. The figures are in fact generally given 'gross'; but since 1956 an independent figure for depreciation (on a method devised by Mr. Philip Redfern) has also been given, so that we can 'net' the figures if we choose. For the purposes of this book I have thought it best to use the 'net' figures.

It is not possible in this place to go far into the economic theory of depreciation, not all of which is well agreed among economists; two points which are well established nevertheless deserve to be mentioned. One is the distinction between depreciation and capital losses. When calculating the income or output of a year we have to deduct as depreciation the capital equipment used up in the process of production; but we should not deduct any accidental destruction of capital equipment which occurred otherwise than as a consequence of production. In the year 1941 a considerable amount of capital equipment was destroyed in air raids; a loss of this sort must not be deducted before arriving at the net output of the year, if only because the figure got after deducting that loss would be less significant than the figure for output without such deduction. It would be absurd to regard 1941 as having no output at all until it had produced enough to offset the air-raid damage! But it will be noticed that if we regard such losses as *capital losses*, not included in depreciation, then it is not necessarily true to say that the capital of the community at the end of the year equals the capital at the beginning *plus* net investment. The capital at the end of the year may be reduced below this level to the extent of such capital losses.

The official rules for calculating wear-and-tear allowances make no mistake on this point; they proceed by allowing a certain percentage of the original purchase price of each piece of fixed capital equipment still in use during the year, and are thus under no temptation to include capital losses. But although it is necessary, in the interests of fairness, to go back to the original purchase price (for that is firm ground, not somebody's guess), to do this is *not* economically satisfactory. For the original purchase price of a piece of equipment is not one of the prices of this year; it belongs to an earlier year, sometimes a much earlier year; thus when prices are changing, the practice of reckoning wear-and-tear allowances on this basis introduces a new complication into the problem of expressing the national income in real terms. When prices are rising, the fact that wear-and-tear allowances are based on conditions as they were when prices were lower means that they may underestimate the real economic depreciation; the national income is therefore made a little higher than it should be. Conversely, when prices are falling, the national income may be made a little lower than it should be.

Redfern's method of calculating depreciation (which I shall not attempt to explain in detail),[1] is largely a matter of correcting for these price-changes. The capital equipment of the economy is divided into various types, and each type is given a fixed period of 'write-off'. But the sum which is 'written off' is not the original cost of construction, but the original cost adjusted for the change in the price, which has since taken place, of that particular type of capital good. While such a computation is inevitably open to plenty of criticism in detail, it seems clear that something of this sort is the best that can be done. And I think it does appear that we get a sensible impression of what has happened if we use these official (Redfern) figures.

NOTE D *On the National Balance-sheet*

The sketch of a national balance-sheet which appears on p. 133 above is a very different affair from those which appeared in the first editions of this book. They were really just guesses, put together in a few hours from odd bits of information; this is a professional estimate, into which a great deal of work has been put.

The figures which I gave in the first edition 'for some date in the nineteen-thirties' were based on the work of Sir Harry Campion (*Public and Private Property*, 1939). That was a solid foundation, as far as it went; but Campion was chiefly interested in distri-

[1] It was originally set out in a paper 'Net Investment in Fixed Assets in the United Kingdom 1938–53' which appeared in the *Journal of the Royal Statistical Society*, 1955. A briefer description is given in the official handbook *National Accounts Statistics; Sources and Methods* (1968).

bution, in the distribution of property among classes; one could not put his work in the form of a balance-sheet without doing considerable violence to it. The table that succeeded in the second edition (1952) was, admittedly, a 'very poor thing', for there was then no similar inquiry on which I could draw for the basic information. The balance-sheet of the national capital, as it was given in both of these editions, had little more than illustrative value.

Subsequently I have been much better off. I was already able, in my third edition, to draw upon the work of Professor E. V. Morgan (*The Structure of Property ownership in Great Britain*, 1960), from which I got a considered estimate of the balance-sheet for 1953–5. But this, as it turned out, was only a beginning. A further advance was marked by the work of Professor J. R. S. Revell (*The Wealth of the Nation*, Cambridge 1967), whose estimates for 1957–61 do not merely carry forward Morgan's work but in some important respects supersede it. These were the latest available to me when I began to prepare the present edition; I found, however, from consultation with Professor Revell, that an estimate for 1966, on the same lines as his previous estimates, was in preparation by Mr. A. Roe, of the Department of Applied Economics at Cambridge. They have kindly given me permission to quote from this later work, though it will not be appearing in full until about the time when the present edition is likely to appear. The table that appears on p. 133 above is accordingly based on Mr. Roe's calculations as is there explained.

This is no place to go into statistical detail; some of the basic issues that are involved may nevertheless be usefully discussed. As is explained in the text (p. 128 above), the chief difficulty of principle, which arises in any construction of a national balance-sheet, is that the same item, which appears as an asset in the account of one unit, and as a liability in that of another, may be valued differently by the one and by the other. (This is a difficulty which does not arise, to anything like the same extent, in the account of the national income; for the things which there appear on opposite sides of two accounts are for the most part actual current transactions, which buyer and seller, payer and receiver, may be expected to value in the same manner.) It is therefore in principle impossible to put together a national balance-sheet by combining actual accounts; for the items which appear in a single balance-sheet must be valued consistently, and in the actual balance-sheets of different entities they are not valued consistently.

We should nevertheless not allow ourselves to be unduly

frightened by this multiplicity of valuations. It is perfectly true that if the actual balance-sheets of British companies (to take only the sector where such balance-sheets unquestionably exist) were put together and consolidated, we should not get the cancelling-out we ought to get, since we should find that the same obligation was frequently set at different values in the books of creditor and debtor. But though we have to think of the national balance-sheet as being put together theoretically by such consolidation, this is not the way in which the statistician will actually go to work; any more than the corresponding process in the field of national income calculation is the one that the statistician actually carries through. The combined balance-sheet of all companies will not be put together by consolidation of actual accounts—it will have to be *estimated* by indirect methods. Now in the process of estimation we can transcend the difficulty. We can decide that *for our purposes* valuation is to be done in a particular way; we can keep to that system of valuation consistently. If we do so, our national balance-sheet will hang together; even though the individual accounts which (in principle) compose it will not be identically the same as those which would be put forward in practice for their own purposes by the constituent units.

We can, in this manner, achieve consistency; but there is not just one system of valuation which will do this for us—there are several. Whichever we use, provided we use it consistently, we shall get a coherent balance-sheet; but the balance-sheets that are constructed, on the different systems, will look very different.

It is possible, in the first place, to say that the basic system should be that which is appropriate for the property of persons. What matters to the private person is the market value of his property, the price at which he can sell it. This applies to all forms of private property, including that which is represented by the shares of companies. These must therefore be entered at their stock exchange values. The balance-sheets of companies and of government will then have to be adjusted so as to maintain consistency with the personal sector. The shares and bonds, as they appear in the balance-sheets of the companies sector, must be entered at the values which have been given them in the balance-sheet of the personal sector, not at the values which have been given them by the companies. In spite of this, we must hold to the principle that the *net assets* of companies are nil. This means that we must not attempt to value the *real assets* of companies directly. We must accept the 'shareholders' value' of those real assets; not the value which is set upon them by the company, but the value that is implied in the market value of the shares.

This, I think one should insist, is a perfectly defensible way of proceeding. If our chief interest is in personal property and in the distribution of such property, it is the right way to proceed. (A balance-sheet which was based on such figures as those of Campion—used in my first edition—would have to be of this type.) It must nevertheless be recognized that the 'adjustment' that has to be performed on the companies and on the government account on these lines is very drastic, so drastic (especially in the case of the companies) that very little of the information which is in fact available about their situation will survive. Thus although the 'national capital' which emerges from a balance-sheet of this character is the total of *property*, the total which has to be divided when we are considering the distribution of property, it is no measure of *real capital*, of capital as Factor of Production.

The later investigators (Morgan and Revell) have therefore proceeded in another way. They begin from the real goods (owned by companies, by persons, and by government); they set values on those real goods, and value the paper claims from the values of the real goods, so as (again) to keep the *net assets* of the companies zero. By this means they get an intelligible balance-sheet for the whole economy, though it does not very easily divide into separate balance-sheets for the sectors. (It shows the shareholders, for instance, as apparently owning property over which they do not in fact have disposal.)

And this is not all. There is still a question of the values that should be put on the real goods. They 'stand' at certain values in the 'books' of the companies, but these are based on the prices at which the goods were originally acquired, and (especially in times of inflation) these may have little relation to current values. One may say that the book value is the value the companies set upon them, so that is the value which ought to be used. That is (effectively) what Morgan did. But it is at least equally possible to argue that the values that are to be used should be further adjusted, so as to bring them into line with current costs of replacement. This is the method of valuation which has been used in the table that appears on p. 133 of this edition.

It will be appreciated that in the inflationary conditions which have persisted since 1950, this last adjustment involves a very considerable writing-up of the book values. Since the national income (in money terms) had rather more than doubled between 1954 and 1966, we should not be surprised to find that the national capital (if valued in the same way at both dates) had increased in something like the same proportion. Mr. Roe's 1966 figure is, however, no less than five times the figure that was given in my third edition for 1953–5 (taken from Morgan). The explanation is mainly a matter of the difference in method of valuation.

NOTE E *On Comparisons between the Real National Incomes of Different Countries*

In principle, the same methods as those used in Chapter XVI, for comparing the economic welfare of the same country in two different years, may be used for comparing the economic welfare of two different countries. But the difficulties in the way of getting a result that means anything are far greater. The circumstances existing at the same time in two different countries may easily differ far more drastically than those which are likely to exist in the same country in successive years; for the purposes of such comparisons, even France in 1941 was more like France in 1938 than England is like the United States. These great differences in national circumstances make it necessary to pay particular attention, when making international comparisons, to all those defects of the national income as a measure of economic welfare which we discussed in Note A. National habits about the sorts of useful work which are paid for differ widely; the amount of effort needed for similar sorts of work varies with climate and national temperament; the proportion of the national income used for defence varies greatly within a nation as political circumstances change, but it varies between one nation and another for simple reasons of geography. Then the comparison of prices between different nations is a particularly intricate matter. It often happens that there are wide differences between the sorts of commodities which different peoples principally consume; this means that the basket of commodities consumed by a representative (say) Italian will nearly always cost more in England than it would in Italy, but at the same time the basket of commodities consumed by an Englishman would cost more in Italy than it would in England. Are we then to say that prices are higher in Italy than in England, or vice versa? We can probably arrive at a moderately satisfactory answer by some device for splitting the difference; the result thus reached may have some meaning, but we should be unwise to place more than a limited amount of confidence in it.

Even if all these difficulties can be overcome—and with care (which is not always taken) they can be overcome more or less—there is still the fundamental difficulty that people who live in favourable geographical circumstances acquire freely all sorts of things which others have to earn by the sweat of the brow. Those who live in cold climates need more fuel, more clothing, and probably even more food, than those whose allowance of free sunshine is more generous. This is not at all to deny that there are poor nations and rich nations, just as there are poor and rich people within a nation. Their existence is obvious; international inequalities create social problems as grave, or graver, than the inequalities of class. The warning is concerned with a limitation of economics; what economics has to say about the comparison between the economic welfare attained by the same person (or similar persons) in different economic circumstances is extensive; but comparisons between people who differ in other important respects are a much more slippery matter.

NOTE F *On Factor Cost*

The reader has been given a lot of trouble, in the later chapters of this book, by the distinction between the factor cost and market price measures of the national income. When we first met the distinction (in Chapter XIV) it was explained that valuation at factor cost was necessary in order to show the burden of indirect taxes falling where the government meant it to fall—on the consumers of the finished product. That sounds sensible; but I imagine that there will have been readers of this book who will have wondered, even then, whether the refinement was worth the trouble. Why not mark up 'profits before tax' by the amount of the indirect tax, and then show it being taken away by the government, like the direct tax on profits? These doubts will have been enhanced by the discovery (in Chapter XX) that valuation at factor cost involves a good deal more calculation (and a great many more guesses) than valuation the other way. Why do we want to concern ourselves with factor cost at all?

There is in fact a good reason for doing so. Whenever we want to study the division of the national income between one use and another—the division between capital and labour, between rich and poor, between public and private purposes, between consumption and investment—it is the proportion of the nation's resources which is devoted to the one purpose or the other which is what matters; and that is what is shown by the valuation in terms of factor cost. A simple example will make this clear. Suppose that it were to be the case that rich people spent all their extra incomes on whisky. Their total expenditure might be very large; but if they were deprived of the means of making this expenditure, only a very limited quantity of resources would be set free to satisfy the wants of more abstemious people. The principal result would be a considerable loss of revenue to the government from the duty on spirits; this loss would have to be made up in some way before anything much was available to be used for other purposes.

This, of course, is a strong case; and I would not maintain that the factor cost measure, as commonly calculated, is anything like a perfect measure of resources employed, in the sense required. There are a good many ways in which it falls far short of being a perfect measure.[1] If we were dealing with a country where indirect taxes were fairly low, or fairly uniform, the gain which we should get by making the correction would be so doubtful that it would hardly be worth making. But when we consider the large divergences between factor cost and market price which are created by some of the indirect taxes (on drinks and smokes, and the higher ranges of purchase tax) and by some of the subsidies (especially on housing) that are now in force in Great Britain, we can see that we must do something about them, or our impression of the allocation of resources will be badly wrong. That, I think, is the justification for the procedure which we have adopted.

The factor-cost measure is the appropriate measure when we are considering the distribution of resources between uses; but there is another purpose for which the market-price valuation is actually better. This is for the purpose of comparing the average level of real income (or consumption) over time—the purpose with which we were concerned in Chapter XVI. For the safest way in which we can be sure that there has been a rise in *real* consumption between two dates (between which there have been all sorts of changes in prices, and all sorts of changes in the quantities of particular commodities consumed) is to inquire whether the representative consumer could or could not have bought, at the latter date, the same quantities of goods which he bought at

[1] A good illustration of its inadequacy is to be found in the case of employers' contributions to social insurance: are they, or are they not, a part of factor cost? There is no sure answer to such questions; we can do no more than establish conventions about them.

the earlier date; if he could, but does not, he cannot be worse off; it is his own look-out if he has made a change. This is the basis on which index-number comparisons of real income are made; but it obviously requires that the comparisons should be made at market prices—the prices the consumer pays.

NOTE G *1957 and 1969*

It seemed quite enough, when setting out the national accounts of the United Kingdom (in an elementary manner in Chapter XIV, and in a more sophisticated manner in Chapter XX) to illustrate with figures for a single year—1969. Anything more would have been distracting. But of course, when setting out the 1969 figures, I had the 1957 figures (used in the previous edition) in front of me. The comparison between them is very interesting; there will be some readers, no doubt, who will wish it to be made.

It so chances that (in one way at least) it can be made rather easily. We have already discovered (in Chapter XVIII) that the distribution of personal incomes between 1955 and 1967 could be compared, rather conveniently, if we multiplied 1955 incomes by a factor of 2. The same conversion works, for the national accounts as a whole, between 1957 and 1969. In 1957 the Gross Domestic Product was £19,220 million; in 1969 (reckoned in the way we have reckoned it) it was £38,492 million—almost exactly double. The National Income in 1957 was £17,672 million, in 1969 £35,249 million; the doubling is even more exact. So we need not take the trouble to calculate percentages. We can take the 1957 figures, multiplied by 2, and set them against the 1969 figures. The change that is then shown between the two dates will indicate the way in which the item has changed, relatively to GDP, or to national income, whichever we prefer.

It is sufficient to round into hundreds of millions (£H) as we did in Chapter XIV. So all of the following tables are expressed in £H (1969); the 1957 figure (adjusted) being put in the first column, the 1969 figure in the second.

For the division of the net domestic product into earnings of labour and capital we get:

Wages and salaries	259	272
Self-employment	31	25
Profits and rents (private)	58	41
Profits and rents (public)	1	10

Here we notice (1) a fall in income from self-employment—but this, for reasons previously discussed,[1] may well be exaggerated; (2) a rise in public profits—partly due to additional nationalizations, but chiefly to a reduction in losses in some of the industries previously nationalized; (3) a notable swing, even when these other points are allowed for, from private profits to wages. But in considering this swing, we should remember that 1957 was a 'good' year, with rather low unemployment, while 1969 was a relatively 'bad' year, with unemployment a good deal higher. It is common experience that in 'bad' years, profits are low, so that the ratio of wages to profits is high.

When we pass from this to the division of income before tax (allocating dividends and interest, including interest on government debt, among their recipients), the first two items (income from wages and self-employment) simply reappear. The others are redistributed:

Personal income from property	36	41
Undistributed profits	42	22
Net public income	−15	−7

The change in public income is already accounted for; so the only new things which emerge are the heavy fall in undistributed profits (partly, but not wholly, accounted for by 1969 being a 'bad' year) and the actual rise in personal property incomes. This, as previously suggested,[2] is probably to be associated with a change in dividend policy, between the fifties as a whole and the sixties as a whole.

Next comes the effect of direct taxes and 'direct' transfers. It will be best, in this case, if self-employment income and property income are taken together. Using the formula 'income before tax − tax (or + transfer) = disposable income' the change may be set out as follows:

Wages and salaries	259−31 = 228	272−60 = 212
Personal income from property and self-employment	68−15 = 53	66−14 = 52
Transfer incomes	0+25 = 25	0+38 = 38
Undistributed profits	42−22 = 20	21−11 = 10
Public income	−15+43 = 28	−7+47 = 40

The remarkable things at this stage are (1) the increase in the share of transfer incomes, matched by a nearly corresponding fall in disposable income out of wages and salaries—so that if the two are taken together the labour share is a little diminished,

[1] See above, p. 73. [2] Above, p. 244.

instead of being increased, as it appeared to be when taken before tax (2) the hardly distinguishable fall in personal disposable income from other sources.[1] The average rate of tax on undistributed profits (as we have reckoned it) is unchanged; so they fall, after tax, just as they did before tax. The increase in public disposable income has little significance, except as the counter-item to the direct taxes otherwise shown.

We have yet to include the indirect taxes. When these are allowed for, the expenditure of personal incomes appears as follows:

Personal income before tax		327			338	
Transfer incomes		25			38	
			352			376
Direct taxes		46			74	
Indirect taxes (net of subsidies)		42			55	
Disposable income (at factor cost)		264			247	
Consumption (at factor cost)	242			232		
Saving	22			15		

Thus (on our way of reckoning) there is a substantial fall in consumption, and also in personal saving. We are here unable to distinguish between consumption (and saving) out of labour incomes and out of other incomes. But it is evident that the 'fall' in consumption could not come about without a 'fall' in consumption out of labour incomes; and the shift to transfer incomes (which are unlikely to be saved) is sufficient, in combination with what is shown in the rest of the table, to account for the 'fall' in personal saving.

Looking at the *national* expenditure account in factor cost terms, it appears as follows:

Personal consumption	242	232
Public 'consumption'	70	77
Saving: personal	22	15
company	20	10
government	1	19

The total of saving only increases from 43 to 44; the enormous increase in government saving just over-balances the fall in personal and company saving.

When we pass to consider the corresponding investment, we are in trouble (as has been explained)[2] with the Foreign Balance

[1] This is explained on pp. 191–2 and p. 244 above.

[2] Above, pp. 292–3.

and the Residual Error. To square the accounts, we need a Foreign Balance of 5 in 1957 and 5 in 1969. For home investment we have (writing 'net investment in fixed capital+net investment in working capital = total net investment').[1]

Company sector	10+7 = 18	14+2 = 16
Personal sector	4+1 = 5	3+0 = 4
Public sector	14+1 = 15	19+0 = 19

The fixed capital investment in 1969 (even in the private sector) is remarkably high, for a 'bad' year; but the working capital investment, as befits a 'bad' year, can only be called deplorable.

I will try to sum up. A considerable part of the changes between the two years here compared are changes of a kind that we should expect, between a 'good' year and a 'bad'. It is intelligible, for this reason alone, that there should be a swing from profits to wages, that there should be a fall in undistributed profits (company saving) and a rise in transfer incomes (unemployment benefit). But the effects which we find, in all of these directions, are greater than what can readily be attributed to this cause alone. Even if the additional unemployed were given income fully equal to what they would have earned in employment, no more than 2 out of the additional 13 of transfer incomes could possibly be accounted for. There must be something else, and of course there is.

The principal thing which is revealed in the tables set out in this note is a massive redistribution of income from earners to non-earners. This already appears in the division of disposable income, at market prices; a factor cost division, if it could be made, would evidently show the same redistribution, even more sharply. For suppose, as a rough approximation (which certainly does not exaggerate) that net indirect taxes are paid by each class in proportion in consumption (and that there is no saving out of transfer incomes). We would then find that consumption out of transfer incomes (at factor cost) would have been 22 in 1957 and 31 in 1969; leaving consumption out of other incomes (also at factor cost) 220 and 201. Since the proportion between disposable income out of wages, and disposable incomes from other sources (not transfer incomes) has not changed appreciably, it is safe to conclude that consumption out of wages and salaries, as a proportion of national income, must have changed in a corresponding manner.

[1] The reader will not expect these 'sums' to add up in every case, because of rounding to the nearest hundred million.

Though the share of wages and salaries, in income *before tax and transfer* has risen by 13 points (as appeared in the first table of this note), this is as misleading a figure as one gets from taking the pre-tax figure for payers of surtax. For if one turns to what is left to the wage-earner, *after tax and transfer*, one finds that his share has fallen by at least a corresponding amount.

The reason, of course, is not simply transfer—from the personal disposable income of one class (or age-group) to the personal disposable income of another. Much of the difference is the counterpart to the rise in 'public consumption'—from 70 to 77. Not all 'public consumption', nowadays, confers *indivisible benefit*; much of it accrues, without much doubt, to particular people. But even if the people who benefited were the people who paid for it, it would still be a substitution, for income from work, of income that is received in another manner.

As this accounting makes plain, it is upon the wage-earner that there falls—as indeed there must fall—the greater part of the costs of the Welfare State. He cannot avoid that cost by pushing up his money wage, nor even his real wage before tax. He may try to do so; but all that happens as a consequence of the wage-inflation which then occurs, is that the economy has to be kept, as it was in 1969 and in 1970, in a state of 'bad trade'.

Index

PRINTED IN GREAT BRITAIN
AT THE UNIVERSITY PRESS, OXFORD
BY VIVIAN RIDLER
PRINTER TO THE UNIVERSITY